Megamergers in a Global Economy

Megamergers in a Global Economy

Causes and Consequences

Edited by BENTON E. GUP

QUORUM BOOKS
Westport, Connecticut • London

Library of Congress Cataloging-in-Publication Data

Megamergers in a global economy : causes and consequences / edited by Benton E. Gup.
   p. cm.
   "Earlier versions of several of the [12] papers were presented at the annual meeting of the
Financial Management Association in Seattle, in October 2000, and at other venues"—Pref.
Includes bibliographical references and index.
   ISBN 1–56720–402–3 (alk. paper)
   1. Industrial concentration—United States.   2. Industrial concentration.   3. Consolidation
and merger of corporations—United States.   4. Consolidation and merger of corporations.
5. International economic relations.   I. Gup, Benton E.
HD2785.M44   2002
658.8'3'0973—dc21   2001019184

British Library Cataloguing in Publication Data is available.

Library of Congress Catalog Card Number: 2001019184
ISBN: 1–56720–402–3

First published in 2002

Quorum Books, 88 Post Road West, Westport, CT 06881
An imprint of Greenwood Publishing Group, Inc.
www.quorumbooks.com

Printed in the United States of America

The paper used in this book complies with the
Permanent Paper Standard issued by the National
Information Standards Organization (Z39.48–1984).

10 9 8 7 6 5 4 3 2 1

To Jean, Lincoln, Andrew and Carol, and Jeremy

Contents

Preface   ix

1. Industry Consolidation: The Natural Thing to Do   1
   Benton E. Gup

2. A Century of Mergers and Acquisitions   19
   Carolyn A. Carroll

3. Large Mergers during the 1990s   45
   Jonathan M. Karpoff and David Wessels

4. Big Bank Mergers in the United States: Motivations, Effects,
   and Likely Competitive Consequences   65
   Bernard Shull and Gerald A. Hanweck

5. Megamergers: Causes and Effects—A European (Swiss)
   Perspective   85
   Rudolf Volkart

6. Mergers "Down Under": An Australian Perspective on Mergers
   in Financial Services   103
   Ian R. Harper

7. Bank Consolidation in Japan: What Can We Learn from It?   111
   Benton E. Gup

8. Bank Mergers in Spain: Are They Unique?   135
   Benton E. Gup

9. Risk Management Systems for Merging Banking and Casualty/
   Property Insurance   149
   D. Johannes Jüttner

10. Risks Associated with Mega Financial Institutions   171
    Steven A. Seelig and Peter J. Elmer

11. Addressing the Too-Big-to-Fail Problem   187
    Ron Feldman and Gary H. Stern

12. How Some Mergers Go Wrong   207
    Benton E. Gup

Selected Bibliography   213

Index   215

About the Contributors   219

Preface

One cannot read the business sections of major newspapers or financial websites without seeing some articles about completed and pending mergers. What is striking about the articles is that merger activity is on a global scale involving a wide variety of industries. By way of illustration, several of the mergers in the headlines in late November 2000 included a bank merger in the United States, "Fifth Third Bancorp to Buy Old Kent,"[1] and one between a Spanish bank and one of the largest banks in Brazil, "Santander Pays $3B for Banesta."[2] The pending mergers included international telecommunications and food deals: "Deutsche Telecom May Try to Buy Sprint"[3] and "Danone Eyes Quaker Oats."[4] Deutsche Telecom is a German firm and Danone is a French firm. Both targets are U.S. firms. Danone, however, decided not to acquire Quaker Oats.[5]

As reflected in the mix of companies mentioned here, a merger snapshot from the *Wall Street Journal's WSJ Interactive Edition* reveals that cross-border merger activity has increased dramatically in recent years. Moreover, European purchases of non-European companies far exceed U.S. purchases of non-U.S. companies.[6]

This book is about *megamergers*, a term that we use to refer to the very large mergers and consolidations.[7] The Vodaphone–AirTouch (U.K.) merger with Mannesmann (Germany) for about $181 billion, the America Online and Time Warner merger (also for about $181 billion), and the Citicorp and Travelers Group merger (about $73 billion) are examples of megamergers. The lower dollar limit of what one considers "large mergers" is arbitrary. The issue here is not their size, but the causes and consequences of these mergers.

This book attempts to address this issue by providing chapters from a variety of authors, each of whom has a different perspective on the matter. The authors come from universities in the United States, Australia, and Switzerland, a Federal Reserve Bank, the Federal Deposit Insurance Corporation, and the International Monetary Fund. Earlier versions of several of the chapters were presented at the annual meeting of the Financial Management Association in Seattle in October 2000 and at other venues.

More of the chapters are about mergers in banks than about mergers in other industries. This is not to say, however, that bank mergers are unique, for many of the lessons learned from them do apply to other industries. Equally important, a substantial portion of the book is devoted to international and cross-border mergers, reflecting the globalization of financial markets.

NOTES

1. "Fifth Third Bancorp to Buy Old Kent," *Washington Post Online* (www.washingtonpost.com), November 20, 2000 (visited 11/23/00).

2. Tony Smith, "Santander Pays $3B for Banesta," *Washington Post Online* (www.washingtonpost.com), November 20, 2000 (visited 11/23/00).

3. Peter S. Goodman, "Deutsche Telekom May Try to Buy Sprint," *Washington Post Online* (www.washingtonpost.com), June 24, 2000 (visited 11/23/00).

4. "Danone Eyes Quaker Oats," CNNfn (http://cnnfn.com), November 22, 2000 (visited 11/23/00).

5. James Mackintosh, "Quaker Oats Proves to Be a One Day Wonder for Danone," *Financial Times* (www.ft.com), November 23, 2000 (visited 11/24/00). Quaker Oats was subsequently acquired by Pepsi.

6. "Merger Snapshot/Cross-Border Deals," *WSJ Interactive Edition* (www.wsj.com), November 13, 2000 (visited 11/24/00).

7. In general terms, a merger is the combination of two or more companies with only one company surviving. A consolidation is the combination of two or more firms to form a new company, to the point that the original companies cease to exist.

Chapter 1

Industry Consolidation: The Natural Thing to Do

Benton E. Gup

In the age of the modern corporation, mergers contribute to consolidation and economic concentration in particular industries, but concentration of economic power existed before the modern corporation. Henry George wrote the following in *Progress and Poverty*, which was first published in 1886 (George, 1946):

When James I granted to his minion the exclusive privilege of making gold and silver thread, and prohibited, under severe penalties, every one else from making such thread, the income which Buckingham enjoyed in consequence did not arise from the interest upon the capital invested in the manufacture, nor from the skill etc., of those who really conducted the operations, but from what he got from the king—viz., the exclusive privilege—in reality the power to levy a tax for his own purposes upon all of the users of such thread. From a similar source comes a large part of the profits which are commonly confounded with the earnings of capital. Receipts from patents granted for a limited term of years for the purpose of encouraging invention are clearly attributable to this source, as are the returns derived from monopolies created by protective tariffs under the pretense of encouraging home industry.

Corporations control industry today, and one way a corporation grows is through mergers. What makes megamergers different from other mergers is their size. U.S. Steel, Du Pont Inc., Standard Oil, General Electric, and so on were considered billion-dollar megamergers of their day at the turn of the twentieth century (Gaughan, 1991). They would be considered small today in current dollar terms.

The size of megamergers today should not be surprising. The size mirrors the growing level of the population and economic activity and the existence of well-developed capital markets. The U.S. population increased from 75.7 million in

1900 to about 260 million in 2000. Globally, the United Nations designated October 12, 1999 as the "Day of Six Billion," referring to the six billionth person being born. The 1999 gross domestic product (GDP) in the United States was about $8.8 trillion! In contrast, the next two largest economies, Japan and Germany, had GDPs of $3.1 trillion and $2.4 trillion respectively (*The World in 1999*, 1999). In June 2000, the United States observed the longest peacetime expansion in its history.

Equally important, stock prices were at record levels in the United States. This reflects expectations of continued growth in the economy. It also reflects well-developed capital markets where corporations can raise billions of dollars for internal and external growth, and where companies can be acquired by friendly or hostile takeovers. Notice, however, that most of the megamergers involve old economy (brick and mortar) firms. This is not to say that new economy companies are sitting on the sidelines. Cisco, Microsoft, and other large "new economy" companies have active acquisition programs, but they are acquiring smaller firms.

Although mergers today are larger than those in the past, the result may not necessarily be increased concentration. First, vertical mergers may reduce concentration rather than increase it. Second, as Ravenscraft and Scherer (1987) found, many mergers do not pay off in the long run; rather, they may result in spin-offs because of their poor performance. Wall and Gup (1989) found that bank merger announcements adversely affected the stock returns of the acquiring banks and that the acquiring banks may have overestimated the historic earnings of the acquired firms and underrated their growth potential. It follows that not all mergers are winners.

Against this background, we will try to understand more about mergers, their causes and consequences.

WHAT'S BEHIND THE MEGAMERGERS?

Are mergers part of a natural process of economic growth, or do they reflect the desires of management and shareholders to maximize their wealth? In this section we examine both notions, as well as the motives for mergers and the catalysts that trigger them.

A Natural Process

The notion that corporate growth is stochastically determined can be traced back to Charles Darwin's *Origin of the Species* (1859), where he advanced the biological principles of evolution and natural selection. These principles were thought to involve evolutionary and quasi-random changes, and economists incorporated them in growth analysis. Alfred Marshall (1907, p. 240) discussed the link between biology and economics. He explained that "biologists and economists have studied the influence which the struggle for survival exerts on organizations." Marshall went on to discuss the "survival of the fittest." Marris (1979, p. 97) gave an example of trees growing in a forest as a sociobiological analogy of the growth of firms. He stated that, by observing trees, one will find many more small saplings than mature trees. But those trees that do survive to maturity reach a maximum height.

How do these observations relate to corporate growth? Adelman (1958) and Alchain (1950) provide the background for understanding some of the issues involved in the process of stochastic growth and persistent profits. Both authors postulate that firms use adaptive, imitative, and trial-and-error behavior in pursuit of positive profits. In this process, the opinions of decision makers within firms will differ. Although they do not make their decisions by tossing coins, Alchain (1950, p. 216) argues that "the aggregate set of actions of the entire group of participants may be indistinguishable from the set of individual actions each selected at random."

Accordingly, corporate growth and persistent profits may be considered as part of a stochastic process. This is consistent with Gibrat's (1931) law of proportionate growth, which generates the lognormal size distribution of firms readily observable in the automobile, banking, pharmaceutical, and software industries, to name a few. A few large firms dominate in each of these industries. That is the same pattern that was discussed previously—there are a lot of small saplings and a few big trees in the forest. The lognormal pattern is examined further in connection with the life cycle that is discussed later in this chapter.

Gibrat's law of proportionate growth has been replicated by simulation techniques, leading some observers to conclude that market structure may be determined stochastically and that the financial characteristics of firms change as firms mature (Gup, 1980; Scherer, 1980). This theme also appears in the title of several books, *Random Processes and the Growth of Firms* (Steindl, 1965), *An Evolutionary Theory of Economic Change* (Nelson and Winter, 1982), and *Profits in the Long Run* (Mueller, 1986b).[1]

Corporate Control

Although most of the discussion here is about mergers, they are only one form of corporate control. Marks and Mervis (1998) have identified five types of corporate alliances that have different impacts on controlling investments, integration, and the cost of separation if they don't work.

At the low end of the scale is a *license* to use a firm's products, services, or trademark. Next is an *alliance or a partnership* that represents cooperation between two or more firms for business purposes. Third, a *joint venture* represents a separate organization formed for business purposes. Fourth, *mergers* involve the combination of two or more previously separate organizations. Finally, an *acquisition* is the purchase of a firm that is integrated into the acquiring firm or a new entity. Marks and Mervis make the point that alliances are more likely to fall short of expectations than mergers and acquisitions.

Michael Jensen (1990) wrote about corporate restructuring in the United States in the 1980s. He stated that corporate restructuring takes the form of hostile takeovers, voluntary mergers, leveraged buyouts, spin-offs, split-ups, divestitures, asset sales, and liquidations. He went on to explain that the takeover market serves as a court of last resort in the market for corporate control. Takeovers play an important role in (1) generating changes in organizations, (2) motivating the efficient use of scarce resources, and (3) protecting the shareholders when internal controls and the board of directors' control mechanisms are not working properly.

Kane (2000) identified another aspect of corporate control—the political power of mega-size banks. He points out that very large banks have political clout, and that if and when they become insolvent, government regulators may delay failing them beyond their "socially optimal takeover point." One reason for this is that opportunistic regulators may benefit privately from decisions on insolvency resolution (Kane, 1989).

Free Cash Flow

It was during the 1980s that the agency problems and conflicts between managers and shareholders eventually led to an informal incentive-based approach to capital structure that is called the *free cash-flow theory* (Jensen, 1986, 1987, 1988). Free cash flow (FCF) is the excess of the cash required to fund all projects that have positive net present values. The theory predicts that firms with excess FCF will expand the size of their firms beyond the size that maximizes shareholder wealth, even when it is not profitable to do so. The corporate expansion is financed, in part, by increasing debt. The debt may be used to repurchase shares and/or to acquire new assets. The interest payments on the debt serves to discipline managers and to further reduce FCFs. Moreover, managers have an incentive to hold on to their FCF rather than paying it out in the form of cash dividends. The payment of cash dividends reduces managers' resources and power.

Jensen (1998) found support for the FCF theory in the fact that managers in the oil industry, when faced with excess capacity and excess cash flows, made bad investment decisions outside their industry. These investments included Mobil's (oil) acquisition of Marcor (a retail chain), Exxon's acquisition of Vydec (office equipment), Sohio's (oil) acquisition of Kennecott (copper mining), and Atlantic Richfield's (oil) acquisition of Anaconda (mining). According to Bernanke (1989), "Companies in industries that no longer have much potential for expansion—the U.S. oil industry, for example, have a lot of free cash flow."

Even if FCF plays a role in some mergers, it fails to explain why shareholders of the acquiring firms do not generally benefit from them and why they do not lead to greater profitability or efficiency. Nor does it explain why mergers occur in waves. The first wave of mergers in the United States occurred during the 1897–1904 period, resulting in monopolies and finally the passage of the Sherman Antitrust Act of 1890 (Nelson, 1959). Under the terms of this law, federal government approval is required for large mergers affecting interstate commerce, in order to prevent restraints on trade or commerce, and reducing competition. The antitrust legislation was expanded to cover the acquisition of assets as well as stocks. The Justice Department is charged with enforcing the antitrust laws.

The second wave of mergers (1916–1929) was characterized by horizontal and vertical integration during the roaring 1920s. The third wave (1965–1969) was characterized by conglomerate mergers (Gaughan, 1991).[2] Consider the large number of conglomerate mergers, including those made by the oil companies. In the 1960s and beyond, large horizontal or vertical mergers were less likely to be approved than conglomerate mergers. Thus, government antitrust polices helped to shape the conglomerate merger movement, but they do not explain the increase in merger activity. The number of mergers increased during the 1980s and 1990s. In 1980 there were 1,558 mergers; in 1990, there were 4,239; and by 1996 they totaled 5,639.[3] These figures are for firms of all sizes. It's clear that other factors other than FCF must also be considered in any discussion of mergers.

The number of leveraged buyouts (LBOs)—acquisitions financed by borrowed funds—increased from 11 in 1980 to a peak of 621 in 1993. Subsequently, the number of LBOs declined to 169 in 1996. LBOs are one form of corporate restructuring that follows takeover activity financed by debt. They also may be a defensive strategy to avoid takeovers. What is not generally recognized is that financing mergers with debt can produce tremendous tax savings. Most of those savings come from the deductibility of interest payments that in some cases may reduce taxable income to zero (Samson and Gup, 1989). Other tax benefits come from reacquiring stock that paid cash dividends and from issuing zero-coupon bonds where the interest deduction is amortized over time and the actual cash outlay for interest expense can be deferred for 10 years or longer.

The "pooling of interest" method of accounting for mergers allows companies to generate paper profits by acquiring undervalued companies. The assets of the two firms are combined at book value, and no charges are made for good will. Using this method, companies with high price/earnings ratios could buy firms with lower P/E ratios and add to their earnings. The pooling of interest method of accounting for mergers was phased out in the early twenty-first century, but it did have a positive effect on the number of mergers when it was applied.

The need for government approval for large mergers affecting interstate commerce, as well as tax and accounting issues, suggests that the FCF does not provide a complete explanation for why firms merge. FCF may be the loaded gun in some cases, but the motives and catalysts described in the next section are the triggers that make them happen.

Motives

Ravenscraft (1987) reviewed the industrial organization literature on the motivations for mergers. Although he found no consensus on the primary motives, he did discern agreement on the following potential motives:

1. Replacement of inefficient management
2. Synergies, including economies of scale and scope
3. Sharing of complementary resources
4. Free cash flow
5. Monopoly power
6. Tax savings
7. Undervalued assets
8. Hubris
9. Stock market inefficiencies, including accounting adjustments
10. Empire building
11. Pecuniary gains, such as breaking long-run unfavorable labor contracts
12. Divergent expectations due to economic disturbances
13. Diversification
14. Speculative motives
15. Retirement of senior management

Catalysts

Different catalysts affect different industries. In the U.S. banking industry, bank failures and deregulation are two important catalysts. During the 1980s, there were large numbers of bank failures and acquisitions of failed banks. The Federal Deposit Insurance Corporation's primary means of dealing with failed banks is to pay off the depositors of failed banks or to arrange for the failed bank to be acquired by another bank (called a purchase and assumption, or P&A). The total number of banks declined from 14,434 in 1980 to 12,353 in 1990. In the 1990s, state laws and the Riegle-Neal Interstate Banking and Branching Efficiency Act of 1994 opened the door for further consolidation, and the number of banks declined to 8,675 in June 1999. As the number of banks declined, the asset holdings of a handful of very large banks increased. In 1990, 49 banks with assets of $10 billion or more accounted for 39.24% of the total assets held by all banks. By 1999, the number of banks in this category increased to 77 and accounted for 65.5% of the total assets held by all banks (*FDIC Quarterly Banking Profile*, 1990, 1999)![14]

Passage of the Financial Services Modernization Act of 1999 (Gramm-Leach-Bliley Act),[5] which eliminated the 1933 Glass-Steagall Act prohibitions concerning acquisitions among banks, investment banks, and insurance firms, is another catalyst for the U.S. banking industry. This act sanctified the combination of Travelers Insurance Company with Citicorp. It also opened the door for Charles Schwab & Co., a securities broker, to acquire U.S. Trust to help serve high-net-worth customers with estate and tax planning, and other services.[6] Merrill Lynch, the nation's largest brokerage firm has been in the trust business since the 1980s. Other brokers (e.g., Morgan Keegan, Inc., Legg Mason, Inc., and A. G. Edwards) and mutual funds (Fidelity Investment, T. Rowe Price, and Putnam) also have set up trust units (McReynolds, 2000). Finally, UBS AG (Switzerland) acquired the U.S.-based PaineWebber Group Inc. brokerage firm (Gasparino, 2000). Other bank and brokerage deals in 1999 and 2000 include Chase Manhattan and Hambrecht & Quest, Chase Manhattan and Robert Flemming, Salomon Smith Barney and Schorders-Worldwide.

Different catalysts can affect the same industry in different locations. As previously noted, bank failures and deregulation represent the catalyst for bank mergers in the United States. In Japan, slow economic growth during the 1990s, very low interest rates, and the government's unwillingness to fail banks were the principal catalysts for bank mergers and consolidation. Deregulation followed. Dai-Ichi Kangyo, Fuji Bank, and the Industrial Bank of Japan joined together to form the Mizuho Financial Group. Other mergers included Sumitomo and Sakura banks, and Sanwa and Tokai banks. Collectively, these banks control about 75% of banking assets in Japan.

The creation of the European Union, which removed trade barriers, has been the catalyst for bank mergers in Europe. Deutsche Bank and Dresdner banks planned to merge to form the biggest bank in the world, but the merger was called off when a disagreement arose over the disposition of an investment banking affiliate. Currently, Germany's HypoVereinsbank and Bank Austria are planing to merge.

The opening of global markets is the catalyst for cross-border mergers. Deutsche Bank acquired Bankers Trust (U.S.), and Spain's Banco Bilboa Vizcaya Argentaria (BBVA) SA is acquiring Grupo Financiero Bancomer SA, Mexico's second largest bank. BBVA also announced a merger between its online banking business, Uno-E, and First-E, a Dublin-based online bank. HSBC Holdings Plc. (formerly Hong Kong Shanghi Bank Corp.) and Merrill Lynch have joined together to create a global online banking and investment banking services company (Harris, 2000). And HSBC announced plans to acquire Credit Commercial de France SA. In the 1980s, HSBC acquired Marine Midland Bank (New York), which was the tenth-largest bank in the United States in 1999. It also acquired Republic New York Corp. in 1999.

In the pharmaceutical industry the catalysts in recent years have been slowing sales, expiring patents on blockbuster drugs, and rising drug development costs. The alleged benefits of the mergers would come from "research synergies" and large sales forces that would generate double-digit growth. These factors, together with globalization, contributed to megamergers, some friendly and some not so friendly: SmithKline Beecham and Glaxo Wellcome, Pfizer and Warner Lambert, Bristol-Myers and Squibb, Glaxo Wellcome, Novartis and Astra-Zeneca, Pharmacia and Upjohn, Pharmacia & Upjohn & Monsanto, Smithkine Beecham, and Rhone-Poulenc and Hoescht.

In the oil industry, low commodity prices and excess capacity have been the catalysts. Crude oil prices declined from about $20/barrel to $10/barrel in 1999 and then rebounded. Mergers in this industry included Exxon and Mobile, BP and Amoco, and Total Fina and Elf Aquitaine.

In the communications industry, new technologies and the growth of information technologies contributed to the mergers of America Online and Time Warner, Vodaphone and AirTouch, ATT and MediaOne, Lucent and Ascend, Quest and U.S. West, and WorldCom and MCI. However the WorldCom and Sprint merger was not consummated because of antitrust considerations by the Department of Justice and the European Commission. A related issue is Deutsche Telekom AG acquiring a U.S. communications company. The German government owns 59% of Deutsche Telekom's stock. U.S. law prohibits the Federal Communications Commission from giving a telecommunications license to any company in which a foreign government owns 25% or more of the stock, unless it is in the public interest to do so (Goodman, 2000).

Globalization requires that firms be of sufficient scale to operate in international markets. To some extent, this was behind the merger of Chrysler and Daimler-Benz ("How Mergers Go Wrong," 2000).

Notice that most megamergers are in industries where there are high costs to entry (e.g., banking, oil, telecommunications) and where barriers to trade have been reduced or eliminated. Not all barriers to trade are economic or legal in nature. Black and Rose (1993) found that foreign direct investment in Europe was associated with the countries' quality of labor force, cultural diversity, international trade balance, and infrastructure. Similarly, it seems reasonable to assume that dictatorships, religious extremism,[7] and wars act as barriers to foreign direct investments and cross-border mergers. Conversely, liberalization of financial markets and other sectors of the economy contributes both to economic growth and consolidation (Ariff and Khalid, 2000).

This listing of industry catalysts, though not exhaustive, is sufficient to demonstrate their importance in the evolution of mergers.

Pooling of Interest

Equally important to an understanding of megamergers are the accounting rules that facilitate mergers and high stock prices that are the currency of many mergers. The *pooling of interest* method of accounting for mergers has a number of advantages over the *purchase accounting* method. Pooling hides certain operating problems that are more difficult to hide in cash earnings, and there is no goodwill to be amortized in mergers of equals. In the Disney purchase of Capital Cities/ABC, use of the purchase accounting would have reduced Disney's annual earnings $480 million, but there was no reduction in earnings (Coy, 1998). The Financial Accounting Standards Board (FASB) plans to eliminate the pooling of interest method of accounting for mergers for reasons that are beyond the scope of this book. The elimination of this method may have a negative impact on the willingness of firms to merge in the future.

High P/E Ratios

Rising stock prices resulted in the price-earnings (P/E) ratio of the Standard & Poor's stock index increased from about 17 times earnings in 1994 to about 29 times earnings in 1999.[8] Stocks with high P/E ratios were the "currency" of mergers. The appendix at the end of this chapter illustrates the effects of acquiring a firm with higher, the same, or lower P/E ratios. If the buyer's P/E is greater than that of the sellers, the buyer's combined earnings will increase. If the buyer's P/E is lower than the sellers' P/E, the combined earnings will decrease. If they are the same, there is no change in earnings. Some mergers involving Internet firms that have losses indicate that other methods of valuation are being employed.

LIFE CYCLE

A number of analytical frameworks can be used to examine corporate strategies and growth. Many of these frameworks are neatly summarized in Weston, Chung, and Hoag (1990, ch. 3). The first in their list of analytical frameworks is the product life cycle. Gup and Agrawal (1996) state that firms go through life cycles as they mature. Over time, a large number of unsuccessful firms fail, resulting in a relatively small number of large survivors. Stated otherwise, there is a tendency toward industry concentration and toward the lognormal distribution suggested by Gibrat (1931) and others.

Gup (1980) and Gup and Agrawal (1996) consider the life cycle from a financial point of view and observe that the financial characteristics of firms change as they mature. Small firms tend to have the highest returns and the greatest variability of returns. From 1926 to 1998, the arithmetic return on small company stocks was 17.4%, and the standard deviation was 33.8% (*Stocks, Bonds*, 1999). In contrast, the arithmetic return for large company stocks was 13.2% with a standard deviation of 20.3%.

Hal Varian (2000), dean of the School of Information Management Systems at the University of California at Berkeley, considers a life cycle in the context of past technological revolutions, and he arrives at the same conclusions. The five stages in his version of the life cycle are experimentation where entrepreneurs introduce new products; capitalization where capital funds are attracted to the new industry; injections of capital, which allow the product to be mass marketed, a stage culminating in hypercompetition, where some firms fail or are absorbed; and consolidation, which results in a few large survivors.

As the firms mature over time and as the growth rate of their sales slows, they tend to increase their cash dividend payments and to acquire debt. To enhance their growth, the cash-laden firms frequently turn to mergers and acquire firms that are growing more rapidly. According to Jensen's (1996, 1998) FCF theory, they are putting their FCF to work by making acquisitions triggered by catalysts, by management's desires to maximize shareholder value, or as part of the process of corporate control. Whatever the reason, the results are the same: a tendency toward increased industry concentration. Consider the automobile industry. Over the life cycle of the automobile industry there have been about 1,500 automobile companies (Kremmerer and Jones, 1959). In 1999 Daimler-Benz acquired Chrysler to form DaimlerChrysler and contribute to further consolidation. Daimler-Benz was the largest industrial group in Germany.[9] Today only a few large automobile companies survive there.

The consolidation tends to occur in industries with high barriers to entry, such as capital requirements (automotive, steel, telecommunications), regulatory requirements (banking), and high research and development costs (pharmaceuticals). The economic structure of these industries tends toward imperfect competition and oligopolies. Consolidation is less likely to occur in markets where markets are more competitive, such as the restaurant industry.

Consolidation takes time. Consider the growth and consolidation in the railroad industry. In 1850, there were 173 railroad companies in the United States (Pfeiffer, 2000). The number expanded and peaked at 1,380 firms in the early 1900s. By 2000, however, only 30 remained. There were 100 automobile companies in the United States in the late 1920s; today there are only 20.

The length of time of waves or long cycles of innovation is shrinking with changes in technology. Joseph Schumpeter (1863–1950) of Vienna, a Harvard economist who described the process of "creative destruction" associated with industrial cycles that were 50 to 60 years long, wrote about business cycles in 1939 and formulated his theory of economic development in 1942 (Schumpeter, 1939, 1942). In his view, it was normal for the economy to be disrupted by innovation. However, he did not foresee the pace of innovation. Indeed, few could visualize the pace of innovation. One of these few was Alvin Toffler, whose *Future Shock* (1970) maintained that innovation is increasing at an increasing rate. As shown in Table 1.1, these industrial cycles were associated with capital goods. With changes in computer and communications technology, the length of the long waves is shrinking to 30 to 40 years ("Catch the Wave," 1999).

Those firms that survive in the consolidated industries tend to have sufficient *capital* to finance expansion and continued operations, sufficient *technology* to provide a continuous stream of new products, and sufficient *scale* so that products can be mass-produced at the lowest possible cost. Technology is changing how this is done.

TECHNOLOGY

Changes in technology may well change the way firms consolidate in the future. Consolidation in the industrial age corporations resulted in vertical and horizontal mergers. However, the growth of the Internet is resulting in increased use of alliances and distributive networks. According to Tapscott, Ticoll, and Lowy (2000), production alliances generate money in exchange for tangible

Table 1.1
Waves of Innovation

Waves of Innovation	Sources	Years	Approximate Length
First wave	Water power Textiles Iron	1785–1845	60 years
Second wave	Steam Rail Steel	1845–1900	55 years
Third wave	Electricity Chemicals Internal combustion engine	1900–1950	50 years
Fourth wave	Petrochemicals Electronics Aviation	1950–1990	40 years
Fifth wave	Digital networks Software New media	1990–2020?	30 years

Source: "Catch the Wave," 1999.

value. The participants in the alliance connect with each other to provide users an integrated solution to their needs. America Online is an example of such an alliance; Linux is another. Banks are one type of distributive network—they accumulate funds from depositors and then invest those funds in loans and securities. Wells Fargo, Bank of America, Bank One Corp., Citibank, and First Union are the top five online banks in terms of numbers of customers (Furst, Lang, and Nolle, 2000). Similarly, Charles Schwab & Company distributes retail investors' funds in various securities markets and provides the investors with investment research from Standard & Poor's, Dow Jones, Reuters, and others.

CONSEQUENCES

Megamergers are not new; the current ones are just bigger than the previous ones. The megamergers in recent years have been in the banking, communications, oil, pharmaceutical, and other industries. Equally important, some of these mergers cross national boundaries, reflecting the globalization of markets. There has also been an increase in concentration in some of the affected industries.

Consider the concentration of banks in the United States. During the 1990–1999 period, the total number of banks declined by 30%. Concentration, meas-

Table 1.2
Banking Structure in the United States

Year	Number of Banks	Total Assets ($ billions)	Number of Banks with Assets Greater than $10 Billion	Percentage of Total Assets Held by Large Banks
1999 3rd qtr.	8,621	$5,507	77	66%
1990	12,338	$3,389	49	39%
1980	14,769	$1,856	18	34%

Sources: *FDIC Quarterly Financial Profile*, 4th Quarter 1990, 3rd Quarter 1999; *FDIC Historical Statistics on Banking, 1934–1992*, p. 221; Brewer, Jackson, Jagtiani, and Nguyen, 2000.

ured by the percentage of assets held by banks with assets greater than $10 billion, almost doubled (see Table 1.2). Stated otherwise, 77 large banks out of a total of 8,621 banks accounted for almost 66% of total assets! However, concentration measured by the Hirschman-Herfindahl Index (HHI) for banks in metropolitan statistical areas (MSAs) has not changed significantly since the mid-1980s. The HHI, a widely used measure of market structure, equals 10,000 for monopoly markets, and lower values suggest less concentrated markets. The Department of Justice guidelines consider an HHI of 1,800 or higher to be highly concentrated (Brewer, Jackson, Jagtiani, and Nguyen, 2000). The average HHI for commercial banks in MSAs during 1985–1998 was about 2000 (DeYoung, 1999). The ratio has not changed primarily because many of the mergers were *market extension* mergers in which banks in different geographic markets, such as Wells Fargo and Norwest, and NationsBank and Bank of America combined. In addition, bank regulators would not approve some *horizontal* mergers unless the banks involved sold some of their branches or deposit accounts. Finally, some new banks have been organized in the MSA, but they are very small. If other types of financial institutions, such as thrifts and credit unions, were included, the HHI would be lower.

Are megamergers a natural consequence of corporate growth? Do they reflect the desire of management to maximize the shareholder's wealth, or does it reflect management's attempt to maximize its own wealth? In truth, there is no single, simple answer. Some elements of truth may be found in all of these explanations.

Regardless of why they occurred, what are the consequences of these mergers? Here, too, there is no single, satisfactory answer. First, we know from past experience that many mergers do not add value. Consider the following financial conglomerates that have not worked as well as expected:

American Express–Shearson (1981)
Betchel–Dillon Read (1981)

Sears–Dean Witter (1981)

Sears–Coldwell Banker (1981)

BankAmerica–Charles Schwab (1983)

American Express–Lehman Brothers (1984)

General Electric–Kidder Peabody (1986)

Travelers–Dillon Read (1986)

American Express–E. F. Hutton (1988)

Deutsche Bank–Morgan Grenfell (London, 1989)

NationsBank Corp.–Montgomery Securities (1997).

The verdict is still out on Travelers–Citibank (1998).

There are many reasons why such combinations did not work, including the following:

1. Too high a price
2. Lack of a compelling strategic reason to merge
3. Unrealistic expectations of synergies
4. Inadequate due diligence
5. Conflicting domestic corporate cultures
6. Different international corporate cultures and lack of effective communications
7. Failure to quickly meld the two (or more) organizations.

Some mergers do work and add to shareholder value. The value can last for a long time for some firms, as is typical in a stochastic process. Over time, however, changes in competition, technology, and other factors will erode monopolistic profits. After all, planes replaced trains; computers replaced typewriters; and today nonbank financial institutions and other firms provide the same services as banks.

As noted earlier, Schumpeter (1939, 1942) described economic downturns as periods of "creative destruction." They were creative in the sense that the worn-out capital of declining industries was being replaced by new firms with growth potential. In a sense, developments in communications technology and the Internet are contributing to the creative destruction of the way businesses operate. It also has to influence the way we think about consolidation of firms and economic concentration. Old measures of concentration have been rendered less useful in a world where strategic alliances and joint ventures between global firms are becoming the norm and the lower cost way to achieve strategic objectives (Walker, 2000). Will social Darwinism and stochastic growth processes apply to the firms operating in these new markets? My guess is that they are subject to the same laws of nature that affected the makers of horse-drawn covered wagons, slide rules, and typewriters.

Table 1.3
P/E Ratios and EPS

	Buyer	Higher P/E	Seller Same P/E	Lower P/E
Earnings	$1,000,000	$600,000	$600,000	$600,000
No. of shares	200,000	300,000	300,000	300,000
EPS	$5	$2	$2	$2
P/E ratio	12	16	12	8
Market value per share	$60	$32	$24	$16
Total equity	$12 million	$9.6 million	$7.2 million	$4.8 million
Addition to buyer's capital shares		$9.6 million $60/share	$7.2 million $60/share	$4.8 million $60/share
		= 160,000 shares	= 120,000 shares	= 80,000 shares
Combined earnings		$1.6 million	$1.6 million	$1.6 million
EPS of combined company		$4.44	$5.00	$5.71

Buyer's P/E		Seller's P/E		EPS after Merger
Buyer	>	Seller		+
Buyer	<	Seller		−
Buyer	=	Seller		=

APPENDIX: PRICE-EARNINGS RATIOS AND EARNINGS

The data presented in Table 1.3 illustrate the effects of acquiring a firm with higher, the same, or lower P/E ratios. If the buyer's P/E is greater than that of the sellers, the buyer's combined earnings will increase. If the buyer's P/E is lower than that of the sellers, the combined earnings will decrease. If they are the same, there is no change in earnings.

NOTES

1. See also Mueller, 1986a.
2. Post, 1994 argues that there were five waves of mergers, and he has somewhat different dates for the merger waves. Neither the number of merger waves nor their exact dates is of particular importance for our purposes.
3. Mergers and acquisitions are reported in the U.S. Department of Commerce, *Statistical Abstract of the United States*, 1992, Table 853; 1998, Table 884.

4. The concentration ratio for banks in 23 emerging economies can be found in "Bank Restructuring in Practice," 1999, Table 1, p. 9.
5. Public Law 106-102.
6. Lee and McNamee, 2000.
7. The religious strife between the Muslims and Christians on the Moluccas (Indonesia) in 2000 is one example (Chandrasekaran, 2000).
8. "Common Stock Prices and Yields," 1999, p. 31. The P/E ratio is the reciprocal of the earnings-price ratio shown in the table.
9. For a discussion of the DaimlerChrysler merger, seek Blaško, Netter, and Sinkey 2000.

REFERENCES

Adelman, Irma G. (December 1958). "A Stochastic Analysis of the Size Distribution of Firms." *American Statistical Association Journal*, pp. 893–904.

Alchain, Armen A. (June 1950). "Uncertainty, Evolution, and Economic Theory." *Journal of Political Economy*, pp. 211–221.

Ariff, Mohamed, and Ahmed M. Khalid. (2000). *Liberalization, Growth and the Asian Financial Crises*. Cheltenham, U.K.: Edward Elgar.

"Bank Restructuring in Practice." (August 1999). Basel, Switzerland: Bank for International Settlements. BIS Policy Paper no. 6.

Bernanke, B. (September/October 1989). "Is There Too Much Corporate Debt?" Federal Reserve Bank of Philadelphia, *Business Review*, pp. 3–13.

Black, Joseph H., and Lawrence C. Rose. (Fall 1993). "An Empirical Examination of Central and Eastern European Diversification Possibilities." *The Journal of International Finance*, 3, no. 1, pp. 29–40.

Blaško, Matej, Jeffry M. Netter, and Joseph F. Sinkey Jr. (2000). "Value Creation and Challenges of an International Transaction: The DaimlerChrysler Merger." Unpublished paper, University of Georgia, Athens, January 24.

Brewer, Elijah, III, William E. Jackson III, Jalapa A. Jagtiani, and Thong Nguyen. (First Quarter 2000). "The Price of Bank Mergers in the 1990s." Federal Reserve Bank of Chicago, *Economic Perspectives*, pp. 2–23.

"Catch the Wave." (1999). *Economist*, Innovation in Industry Survey, February 20, pp. 7–8.

Chandrasekaran, Rajiv. (2000). "Indonesia May Seek Help for Moluccas." *Washington Post Online* (www.washingtonpost.com), July 18, p. A16 (visited 7/18/00).

"Common Stock Prices and Yields." (December 1999). *Economic Indicators*. Washington, DC: U.S. Government Printing Office, p. 31.

Coy, Peter. (1998). "Mergers: Crackdown on Stupid Accounting Tricks." *Business Week*, May 4, p. 41.

DeYoung, Robert. (September 1999). "Mergers and the Changing Landscape of Commercial Banking (Part I)." Federal Reserve Bank of Chicago, *Chicago Fed Letter*, Number 145.

FDIC Historical Statistics on Banking, 1934–1992. (1993). Washington, DC: FDIC, p. 221.

FDIC Quarterly Banking Profile. (1990, 1999). Washington DC: Federal Deposit Insurance Corporation.

Furst, Karen, William W. Lang, and Daniel E. Nolle. (June 2000). "Who Offers Internet Banking?" Office of the Comptroller of the Currency, *Quarterly Journal*, 19, no. 2, pp. 29–48.

Gasparino, Charles. (2000). "PaineWebber's Chief Finally Says 'I Do' after Finding Acceptable Suitor in UBS." *Wall Street Journal*, July 13, pp. C1, C14.

Gaughan, Patrick A. (1991). *Mergers and Acquisitions*, New York: HarperCollins.

George, Henry. (1946). *Progress and Poverty*, 50th Anniversary Edition. New York: Robert Schalkenbach Foundation, pp. 191–192.

Gibrat, Robert. (1931). *Les Inegalites Economiques*. Paris: Sirey.

Goodman, Peter S. (2000). "Telecom Mergers Come Calling on U.S." *Washington Post Online* (www.washingtonpost.com), July 13, p. E01 (visited 7/15/00).

Gup, Benton E. (December 1980). "The Financial Consequences of Corporate Growth." *Journal of Finance*, 35, pp. 1257–1265.

Gup, Benton E., and Pankaj Agrawal. (Fall/Winter 1996). "The Product Life Cycle: A Paradigm for Understanding Financial Management." *Financial Practice and Education*, 6, no. 2, pp. 41–48.

Harris, Clay. (2000). "HSBC and Merrill Lynch in Global Online Joint Venture." *Financial Times* (www.ft.com), April 18 (visited 4/19/00).

"How Mergers Go Wrong." (2000). *The Economist*, July 22, p. 19.

Jensen, Michael C. (1986). "The Agency Costs of Free Cash Flow, Corporate Finance, and Takeovers." *American Economic Review*, 76, pp. 323–329.

Jensen, Michael C. (1987). "The Free Cash Flow Theory of Takeovers: A Financial Perspective on Mergers and Acquisitions and the Economy." In *The Merger Boom*, Lynne E. Browne and Eric S. Rosengren, eds. Boston: Federal Reserve Bank of Boston, pp. 102–143.

Jensen, Michael C. (Winter 1988). "Takeovers: Their Causes and Consequences." *Journal of Economic Perspectives*, 2, pp. 21–48.

Jensen, Michael C. (1990). "The Takeover Controversy: The Restructuring of Corporate America." In *Advances in Business Financial Management: A Collection of Readings*, Philip L. Cooley, ed. Hinsdale, IL: Dryden Press, pp. 567–575.

Kane, Edward J. (September 1989). "Changing Incentives Facing Financial Services Regulators." *Journal of Financial Services Research*, 2, pp. 265–274.

Kane, Edward J. (July 2000). "Dynamic Inconsistency of Too-Big-to Fail Policymaking." Keynote address at the 12th Annual PACAP/FMA Finance Conference, Melbourne, Australia.

Kremmerer, Donald L., and C. Clyde Jones. *American Economic History*. New York: McGraw-Hill.

Lee, Louise, and Mike McNamee. (2000). "Can Schwab Hang on to Its Heavy Hitters?" *Business Week*, January 31, p. 46.

Marks, Mitchell L., and Philip H. Mervis. (1998). *Joining Forces: Making One Plus One Equal Three in Mergers, Acquisitions, and Alliances*. San Francisco: Jossey-Bass.

Marris, Robin. (1979). *The Theory and Future of the Corporate Economy and Society*. Amsterdam, Holland: North-Holland Publishing Co.

Marshall, Alfred. (1907). *Principles of Economics*, Vol. 1, 5th ed. London: Macmillan.

McReynolds, Rebecca. (February 2000). "Brokers Reach for Trust Business." *U.S. Banker*, pp. 44–47.

Mueller, Dennis C. (1986a). *The Modern Corporation: Profits, Power, Growth and Performance.* Sussex, U.K.: Wheatsheaf Books Ltd.

Mueller, Dennis C. (1986b). *Profits in the Long Run.* Cambridge: Cambridge University Press.

Nelson, Ralph. (1959). *Merger Movements in American Industry: 1895–1956.* Princeton, NJ: Princeton University Press.

Nelson, Richard R., and Sindy G. Winter. (1982). *An Evolutionary Theory of Economic Change.* Cambridge, MA: Harvard University Press.

Pfeiffer, Eric W. (2000). "Where We Are in the Revolution." *Forbes ASAP*, February 21, pp. 68–70.

Post, Alexandra M. (1994). *Anatomy of a Merger: The Causes and Effects and Mergers and Acquisitions.* Englewood Cliffs, NJ: Prentice-Hall.

Ravenscraft, David J. (1987). "The 1980s Merger Wave: An Industrial Organization Perspective." In *The Merger Boom*, Lynne E. Browne and Eric S. Rosengren, eds. Boston: Federal Reserve Bank of Boston, pp. 17–37.

Ravenscraft, David J., and F. M. Scherer. (1987). *Mergers, Sell-Offs, and Economic Efficiency.* Washington, DC: The Brookings Institution.

Samson, William D., and Benton E. Gup. (1989). "The Hidden Side of Corporate Restructuring." *Tax Notes*, November 13, pp. 877–884.

Scherer, F. M. (1980). *Industrial Market Structure and Economic Performance*, 2nd ed. Boston: Houghton Mifflin, ch. 4.

Schumpeter, Joseph. (1934). *The Theory of Economic Development.* Cambridge, MA: Harvard University Press.

Schumpeter, Joseph. (1939). *Business Cycles.* 2 vols. New York: McGraw-Hill.

Schumpeter, Joseph. (1942). *Capitalism, Socialism, and Democracy.* New York: Harper and Bros.

Steindl, Josef. (1965). *Random Process and the Growth of Firms: A Study of the Pareto Law.* New York: Hafner Publishing Co.

Stocks, Bonds, Bills, and Inflation 1999 Yearbook. (1999). Chicago: Ibbotson Associates, p. 33.

Tapscott, Don, David Ticoll, and Alex Lowy. (2000). *Digital Capital: Harnessing the Power of Business Webs.* Cambridge, MA: Harvard Business School Press.

Toffler, Alvin. (1970). *Future Shock.* New York: Random House.

U.S. Department of Commerce. (annual). *Statistical Abstract of the United States.* Washington, DC: U.S. Government Printing Office.

Varian, Hal. (2000). "Habits of Highly Effective Revolutions." *Forbes ASAP*, February 21, pp. 73–76.

Walker, M. Mark. (Spring 2000). "Corporate Takeovers, Strategic Objectives, and Acquiring-Firm Shareholder Wealth." *Financial Management*, pp. 53–66.

Wall, Larry D., and Benton E. Gup. (1989). "Market Valuation Effects of Bank Acquisitions." In *Bank Mergers: Current Issues and Perspectives*, Benton E. Gup, ed. Boston: Kluwer Academic Publishers, pp. 107–120.

Weston, J. Fred, Kwang S. Chung, and Susan E. Hoag. (1990). *Mergers, Restructuring, and Corporate Control.* Englewood Cliffs, NJ: Prentice-Hall.

The World in 1999. (1999). London: The Economist Group, p. 79.

Chapter 2

A Century of Mergers and Acquisitions

Carolyn A. Carroll

INTRODUCTION

Over the past century, mergers and acquisitions have tended to form waves, or periods with high activity, followed by relatively inactive periods. The first merger wave occurred from 1897 to 1904 and was primarily a period of horizontal combinations, with two firms operating and competing in the same type of business activity. The second merger wave occurred from 1919 to 1930 and consisted of many vertical combinations, with firms operating at different levels in the same industry. The third merger wave took place in the 1960s and was primarily a period of conglomerate mergers. Conglomerate mergers may be defined as product extension, market extension, or pure conglomerate mergers. The fourth merger wave occurred from 1981 to 1989 and happened amid a period of corporate restructuring. This wave consisted of many horizontal mergers in new industries or deregulated industries. The last merger wave began in 1992 and is still ongoing. The period between the fourth and fifth merger waves was only a brief hiatus and some may refer to the period from 1981 to the present as the fourth merger wave. The last merger wave was primarily a period of vertical mergers in many of the same industries where horizontal mergers were prevalent in the 1980s.

FIRST MERGER WAVE

During the first wave (1897–1904), about 15% of all manufacturing firms disappeared through merger (Markham, 1955). This was generally a period of consolidation in that most business combinations were horizontal in nature. The merger wave was characterized by multifirm consolidations, and some gained considerable market share (Salter and Weinhold, 1979; Scherer, 1980). George W. Stigler (1951) characterized this period as one of "merging for monopoly." Standard Oil Company acquired many small oil companies and emerged with a 90% market share by 1900. In 1901 United States Steel Corporation was formed by the consolidation of 785 companies from ore mining to steel fabrication, controlling 65% of steel-making capacity. Other consolidations took place in the copper, lead, railroad cars, explosives, tin cans, tobacco, electrical equipment, rubber products, paper, farm machinery, brick-making, chemicals, leather, sugar, business machines, photographic equipment, and shoe-making industries. The biggest deal of the first merger wave was the formation of U.S. Steel. Its value was $1.4 billion which, in 1990 dollars, puts this deal as one of the five largest in history (Wasserstein, 1998). However, there was one consolidation that did not take place. Ford was willing to sell to General Motors, but General Motors could not raise the cash so the two auto-makers remain independent to this day.

The merger wave began with the technological and organizational innovations, the Sherman Antitrust Act, and the rise of modern capital markets. New products and new production techniques increased efficiency and encouraged mass production and mass-marketing techniques. Another innovation during this period was the decentralized organizational form (Davidson, 1985). With the decentralized form, the central administration made the major decisions such as planning and financial decisions, and the day-to-day decisions were left to the division managers. This enabled the administration to control more individual locations and thereby encouraged mergers.

Probably the most important business innovation in the late nineteenth century was the advent of railroads. In 1870 the United States was a mass of local markets. The butter-and-egg delivery person had a very small market; the tailor had a somewhat larger market; a bank had a larger market still; and an iron works an even larger market area. But each market area was limited by the ability to transport the product to the customers or the customers to the product. By 1900 railroads connected many markets, making them regional or national in scope. Railroad mileage increased from 53,922 miles in 1870 to 194,262 miles in 1900, a 268% increase (Markham, 1955). Freight rates declined from 18.2 mills per ton-mile to 7.3 mills per ton-mile, a 60% decrease (Markham, 1955). The railroads were carrying 39.3 billion ton-miles of traffic in 1870, but by 1900 were carrying 141.6 billion ton-miles, or a 260% increase. A crude estimate of the increase in market size is 3.24 times (Markham, 1955). Market areas shrunk because transportation, namely railroads, enabled the product to get to the customer much faster and cheaper. This, in turn, encouraged consolidation of businesses through horizontal mergers.

Railroads made a big difference in commerce and growth, but growth was also encouraged by the Sherman Antitrust Act, passed in 1890. Among other things, the law prohibited one company from plotting with another to gain monopoly profits. With collusion prohibited, one company could collaborate with another if it bought the company. In this way, the Sherman Antitrust Act encouraged mergers. This law also banned the accumulation of monopoly power generally, but it was not strictly enforced during the first merger wave. For example, in 1895 the Supreme Court ruled that American Sugar Refining Company did not have monopoly power, even though it controlled most of the market (Wasserstein, 1998). Enforcement finally picked up speed at the turn of the century. The early 1900s found the breakup of the Standard Oil and American Tobacco trusts (Davidson, 1985).

A modern capital market also spurred on the merger wave. The beginning of a modern capital market enabled firms to float large issues of securities to finance a takeover. The period also introduced "producers of mergers" (Markham, 1955). Some of the producers were banks. At this time, banks could engage in all the activities of an investment bank, so some of them actively promoted mergers. With the rapid rise in the stock market, promoters encouraged one company to buy another. To finance the acquisition, the promoters sold more securities against these same assets. With the sky-high demand for securities in a new and rising stock market, this drove the price up even higher, making a valuable profit for the promoter from commissions.

The wave of mergers ended with the stock market crash of 1904 and the Bank Panic of 1907, the high failure rate of many combinations, and the Northern Securities case in 1904. The Northern Securities case ruled that Sherman Antitrust applied to mergers (*Northern Securities Company v. United States*, 193 U.S. 197 [1904]). With buying the stock of another company to increase monopoly power now prohibited, the rationale for many consolidations was restricted. Later in 1911, in the Standard Oil case, the courts stated that the Rule of Reason applied (*Standard Oil v. United States*, 221 U.S. 1 [1911]). The Rule of Reason said that a combination whose main purpose was economies of scale rather than monopoly was permissible.

Many mergers were not successful in that they gobbled up their competitors only to find that new competitors emerged (Steiner, 1975). Trying to gain monopoly power by merging was fruitless. In some industries such as oil, the capital intensity kept competitors to a minimum, but in others such as textiles, new firms arose easily. However, bankers made money whether a merger failed or succeeded. They made money from facilitating the deal and from handling the securities issued to purchase the target. With the "Rich Man's Panic" in stock prices in 1903, companies could no longer finance large mergers by issuing securities at inflated prices. The merger wave ended when merging ceased to become a "fad." With a high failure rate, the investing public, bankers, and industrialists were disappointed and did not buy the securities of merging firms, driving up prices as readily as they had earlier. Out of a sample of 172 firms, Livermore (1935) classifies 78 as failures, 11 as limping successes, 3 as rejuvenations, and only 80 as true successes. About half of the firms in his sample failed. While merging to earn superior profits may have spurred early mergers, the failure of many combinations let the air out of the balloon of the first merger wave.

SECOND MERGER WAVE

The second wave (1919–1930) was larger in absolute size than the first. Of the 11,852 firms that disappeared through mergers, 24% were public utilities and 9% were banks (Markham, 1955). Numerous electric, gas, and water utility holding companies were formed with horizontal mergers. In 1929, 2,750 public utilities or 43% of all utilities disappeared due to merger (Scherer, 1980). Some combinations occurred in the manufacturing and mining sectors, but the impact was smaller than the previous wave. In the manufacturing sector, many mergers were vertical or involved small market-share additions. This period was characterized by the rise of large, number two firms in an industry. For example, Bethlehem Steel and Republic Steel merged to form the second largest steel firm to U.S. Steel. Whereas the first merger wave saw many multifirm consolidations, these consolidations were rare during the second.

Major developments in transportation and communication encouraged mergers—motor vehicles in transportation and radio in communication. Trucks extended market areas. No longer did businesses have to expand along a major rail line, but products could be moved to market by truck. In addition, cars made consumers more mobile, taking consumers to the product. Many horizontal mergers took place consolidating the food, metals, and chemical industries (Markham, 1955). Radio facilitated advertising and the growth of national brands.

As is the case for most periods, target firm shareholders gained value while bidding firm shareholders did not lose value (Leeth and Borg, 2000). During the second merger wave, the target-company gains from one month before the contest to completion was 15.57%. Bidding firms outperformed the market the year before the takeover, experienced no significant gains during the takeover, and lost value in the following year. The combined gains were small.

When horizontal mergers for monopoly power were discouraged by legislation, business turned to vertical combinations. In 1914 the Clayton Antitrust Act was passed outlawing specific actions that could not be undertaken to lessen competition. It forbade the acquisition of the stock of companies that resulted in lessening competition, but it neglected to mention the acquisition of assets. So companies could still combine by purchasing the assets rather than the stock of a rival. The Federal Trade Commission Act was passed in 1914. This law created the Federal Trade Commission whose mendate was to watch big business for actions that lessened competition. So with horizontal acquisitions under close scrutiny by the regulators, business turned to vertical mergers.

Vertical combinations had the advantage of economies of scale in manufacturing and marketing. With the growth of firms in the first merger wave, new firms took over many independent functions that previously had been performed by independent businesses. As a young firm, there were many functions for which there were no inputs (i.e., machinery to make the new product), and so the firm did it by itself. As a firm grew and became larger, however, either by internal growth or by horizontal merger during the first merger wave, it became more profitable for another firm to make the inputs and another to make the end product. So early in the period many companies were making one, specialized product, but by 1919 there were many mergers of companies making successive products or vertical mergers. Some firms chose to grow by acquiring control over their inputs. In 1919, 602 companies out of 4,635, or 13% of companies, had operations for which the end product of one operation was the input of another operation and 34.4% had successive functions (Stigler, 1951). By number or asset value, 53% of the mergers in the 1926–1930 period were horizontal, with the rest primarily vertical or product extension mergers (Scherer, 1980). As a result of vertical mergers, the multiproduct firm arose.

As was the case with the first merger wave, professional promoters, primarily investment bankers, inspired mergers. The security-hungry public and the roaring twenties enabled bankers to make money by promoting mergers. Mergers meant that investment bankers could float new security issues, and that meant more profit for the investment banker.

Although there were bank mergers during the period, most of then occurred after the second wave. During 1919–1920 there were 180 bank mergers, between 1921 and 1925, 330 and between 1926 and 1930, 550. Most mergers increased the bank's size to better serve the bank's business customers. After the market crash of 1929, the number of bank mergers increased, totaling 1,567 in 1930–1931. The major reason for the combinations was to avoid bankruptcy. After 1933, the number of bank mergers averaged 200 per year with 100 per year in the 1941–1945 period.

The wave ended with the 1929 stock market crash and the failure of many firms. Many utility holding companies formed during the second merger wave declared bankruptcy, and many manufacturing firms contracted (Salter and Weinhold, 1979). Legislation during the 1930s sought to prevent a repeat of the 1920s by requiring accurate disclosure of information and by separating the role of commercial banking and investment banking with the Glass Steagall Act of 1933.

THIRD MERGER WAVE

The third merger wave occurred in the 1960s and included primarily mergers of unlike firms to form conglomerates. Firms diversified into unrelated lines of business. For example, RCA acquired Banquet Frozen Foods; LTV acquired GreatAmerica, Braniff Airlines, National Car Rental Company, a bank, and real estate; ITT acquired Sheraton Corporation, Avis Rent-a-Car, Bobbs-Merrill Publishers, and Hartford Fire Insurance. In the 1950–1955 period, most mergers, 70.1%, were horizontal while only 5.3% were pure conglomerate mergers. By

1964–1972, however 38.2% were horizontal while the percentage of pure conglomerate mergers grew to 36.2 (Ravenscraft, 1987). If product extension and market extension mergers are included in the conglomerate merger category, in 1961–1970, the Federal Trade Commission classified 78.5% of all acquisitions with assets exceeding $10 million as conglomerates (Salter and Weinhold, 1979). Companies increased their average number of lines of business 2.85 times from 1950 to 1977 (Ravenscraft, 1987).

The conglomerate merger wave was partially driven by the ferderal regulators' more intense scrutiny of horizontal and vertical mergers. The Department of Justice issued merger guidelines, standards by which the Department would challenge an acquisition under Section 7 of the Clayton Act (Steiner, 1975). With these guidelines, the Justice Department indicated that it would attack any acquisition of a significant size firm by a large diversified firm on the grounds of potential competition, reciprocity, or entrenchment. Under potential competition, the acquisition was attacked because it would reduce *potential* competition in the industry. The acquisition did not have to reduce actual competition, just potentially reduce competition. Reciprocity is an increase in concentration in the overall economy; almost any large combination violates reciprocity. Under entrenchment, the acquisition would discourage entry into the industry, so a company could not be so large as to deter another company from entering the industry. Although the guidelines were formidable, the government lost most of the ensuing court cases. The guidelines acted as a deterrent not so much because businesses were not permitted to combine, but because businesses did not even propose merger in the first place.

Vertical and horizontal acquisitions were also limited by the Celler-Kefauver Amendment of 1950, which closed the loophole so that businesses could acquire neither the stock nor the assets of a prospective target that would lessen competition. In addition, the Celler-Kefauver Amendment to Section 7 of the Clayton Antitrust Act essentially outlawed all vertical and horizontal combinations that created bigness (Davidson, 1985). The Amendment outlawed not only all combinations that reduced competition, but also all combinations that might potentially lessen competition. Two court cases, the Brown Shoe case in 1962 and the Von's Grocery Store case in 1966, convinced business that the government was serious about implementing the potential competition clause of the Celler-Kefauver Amendment. Partly in response to this law and its enforcement, the next merger wave in the latter half of the 1960s was an era of conglomerates. To avoid a challenge on antitrust grounds, businesses acquired targets that were totally unrelated to the acquirer's main line of business. The only type of mergers left to companies that wanted to grow by merging was a conglomerate combination.

The second factor leading to the merger wave of the 1960s was the prevailing philosophy in business schools of colleges and universities that a good manager could manage anything. The theory stated that each division could draw on the expertise of central management and thereby create efficiencies. So, an acquirer could buy any type of company and reap efficiency gains.

A third factor was the rising stock market which created a need for rising earnings to justify the higher prices. Therefore, many CEOs played the earnings game. Acquirers sought out targets with lower price-earnings (P/E) ratios than they had in the past. Instead of equity, many companies issued off-balance sheet securities to fund the takeover deal. Since firms did not have to report fully diluted earnings per share (EPS), the higher relative earnings boosted their with-target earnings per share, justifying higher prices for their stock so as to maintain the same P/E ratio as before the takeover. With the same number of shares as before the takeover because their financing of the takeover was through the off-balance sheet, their EPS appeared to increase, justifying higher prices for their stock. In this way, a firm could have the appearance of a growth firm without ever growing internally.

Fourth, the theory of diversifying to smooth out the ups and downs of the business cycle was widespread. Firms felt they could reduce systematic risk by diversifying into unrelated businesses (Cooke, 1986). This theory of conglomerate mergers was the justification for why many combinations would create value. At first the stock market responded positively to conglomerate mergers and then negatively.

Also important in the third merger wave were institutional investors. Professional money managers managed $9.5 billion of NYSE-listed investments in 1949 and $70 billion by 1960 (Wasserstein, 1998). Competition was fierce between various funds, and the ability to attract new money rested on a manager's reputation for picking high-growth stocks. Professional money managers were therefore in favor of playing the earnings game and sometimes even encouraged takeovers.

During the 1960s the hostile takeover got its start in the world of takeovers. In those years, only medium-sized companies ended up as the target of hostile bidders. Because there were no laws requiring the bidder to share information with the target, a prospective bidder could quietly acquire many shares of the target before the target knew what was happening and before it could marshal a defense (Wasserstein, 1998). All that changed with passage of the Williams Act.

In 1968 Congress enacted the Williams Act requiring that bidders disclose a tender offer. Before then, a company could quietly buy the shares of a potential target, with or without a tender offer, without ever notifying the target firm or the public. The Williams Act made this tactic illegal and also required that the acquiring company notify the SEC, the target company, the exchanges, and the target shareholders of the tender offer. Tender offers must remain open for a minimum of 20 days. This prohibits the bidder from stampeding target shareholders into accepting the offer. The Williams Act also made false and deceptive information to encourage the tendering of shares illegal. Most importantly, the law required any person or group that purchases 5% or more of a company's shares to publicly disclose their intentions. The Williams Act basically set up the rules by which a tender offer could be made.

One loophole in the law applied to two-tier tender offers. Companies could offer two sets of terms, one favorable and a second less favorable. In this way, they could pressure shareholders to tender their shares early to take advantage of the favorable terms. This enabled firms to gain control of the target more easily. In 1982, however, the SEC essentially restricted the use of two-tier offers.

In the combinations of the period, on average, target shareholders gained value, and acquiring shareholders at least did not lose value (Asquith, 1983; Dodd, 1980, 1986; Halpern, 1973; Langetieg, 1978; Mandelker, 1974). In this sense, the mergers were successful, on average, at the time of acquisition. The predominant medium of exchange was stock for some mergers and convertible securities for others, including warrants, options, and convertible and contingent securities. Many of the convertibles were not listed on the balance sheet, so the means of financing the acquisition was not evident. Acquisition premiums averaged 10 to 20% (Salter and Weinhold, 1979). Compared to later premiums, these were not large. The most active acquirers during the period were Gulf and Western, LTV, ITT, Tenneco, and Teledyne (Davidson, 1985). Conglomerate mergers, for the most part, were not pure. There was some potential for reciprocity and supplier-customer relationships within the firm, but the more diversified a company, the less likely it is to engage in reciprocity (Markham, 1973).

One factor that helped end the conglomerate merger wave was the downturn in the stock market in 1969. The earnings game required increasing stock prices to show increasing P/Es, and when this did not happen, investors became disillusioned and stock prices fell. In addition, analysts became aware of the games that corporations had been playing.

Another factor in the decline of mergers was the overleveraging of many companies (Wasserstein, 1998; Weston and Mansingka, 1971). They had issued debt to take over companies or to keep themselves afloat, and, with the economic downturn, many companies found themselves in dire straits.

Yet another factor was the failure of many conglomerates. Conglomerates had a low return on invested capital (Rumelt, 1974), sales and profit instability, and adverse competitive shifts (Weston and Mansingka, 1971). Moreover, they were too diverse to manage efficiently (Ravenscraft, 1986). Conglomerization also failed because, although diversifying into dissimilar lines of business reduced systematic risk somewhat, it did not reduce systematic risk by as much as mutual funds buying shares in a large group of companies (Ravenscraft, 1987).

The Williams Act served as a deterrent to takeovers in general, not just hostile takeovers. While the courts upheld some cases in which target management had sued for inadequate or misleading disclosure, for the most part, the courts sided with the bidder (Steiner, 1975). These laws served as a deterrent in that they prohibited potential takeovers. The Williams Act applies to the accumulation of 5% or more of a potential target's shares, thereby encouraging managerial entrenchment in that management may be alerted to a possible takeover. The act's information disclosure provisions also discourage takeovers. An otherwise sound merger may have a different outcome if the bidder is required to reveal too much information. The more information in the opposition's hands, the more harassing actions they can undertake.

A change in accounting standards also helped deter the third merger wave. Before 1970, pooling accounting was the preferred method of accounting for mergers. With the method, essentially the balance sheet and income statements of the two entities would be added together in the merged company. This had the disadvantage of leaving assets stated as book values rather than market values with the possibility of larger depreciation write-offs. However, it had the advantage of not having to write off goodwill, thereby diluting earnings. In 1970, APB No. 16 and No. 17 limited the use of pooling accounting. To use pooling accounting the firm must purchase at least 90% of the voting stock of the target firm, exchange securities for the voting stock, and keep a substantial portion of the assets for two years. This requirement severely restricted the use of pooling accounting and dampened the merger boom.

The Tax Reform Act of 1969 also helped end the merger wave by eliminating the tax advantage of buying a target with equity instead of cash or debt. Before 1969, the buying company could issue convertible debentures for the target stock. The advantage to the issuing firm is that the interest is tax deductible and the interest rate may be lower than paying dividends might have been. The advantage to the target firm shareholders is that the tax may be postponed for the duration of the holding period. This method of financing taxable mergers gradually gained momentum through 1968. In 1969 the Tax Reform Act of 1969 outlawed the tax deductibility of convertible bonds when used in a merger.

FOURTH MERGER WAVE

The merger wave of 1981–1989 took place amid a period of restructuring (Wasserstein, 1998). It was a period of gaining more efficiency through downsizing, by moving out of one industry into another, by exchanging debt for equity in a leveraged recapitalization, and by merging with another firm. It was a period which undid the conglomerate mergers of the 1960s. The mergers of the 1960s that did not work out, were spun off, carved-out, and sold off in the 1980s. Even those firms that were spun-off or carved out very often became targets of takeovers.

The large size of targets and the large size of acquirers made the 1980s the decade of the megamerger. The large size of targets and the successful hostile takeovers led many firms to believe that it was a world of take over or be taken over. A defensive takeover could dampen a firm's attractiveness as a target in three ways: (1) by increasing the size of the company with a defensive merger, (2) by disgorging cash that might make it an attractive target by paying for the defensive target with cash, and (3) by buying a target that might make antitrust difficulties for a potential suitor.

The merger wave in the 1980s gained strength from a high-flying stock market. A rising stock market implied that many companies were a bargain even at a premium over market. A strong economy added impetus to the movement. Interest rates were relatively low, making the cost of capital relatively low in financing acquisitions.

In the early 1980s, American industry was under fierce competition from foreign businesses. This competition did not actually begin in the 1980s but had been building throughout the 1960s and 1970s. This competition necessitated a belt-tightening for American industry; they had to become "lean, mean, fighting machines" by reducing costs, especially labor costs, and increasing efficiency. In addition, some industries were mature and needed to diversify out of these mature industries and into growth industries. Many companies achieved this goal through acquisition.

At the same time, many new products emerged, and small to mid-sized companies became important. New products included cable television, wireless communications, consumer electronics, computers, and overnight courier services. These products enabled businesses to work faster and better, leading them to sell more and produce more with the same amount of labor input to become more efficient. This development led to consolidation or horizontal and vertical mergers in many industries. The rising stock market, foreign competition, financial innovations, as well as new product innovations, the need to increase efficiency, and dying markets for some mature industries, created an atmosphere that was ripe for mergers.

Leveraged Buyouts

One financial innovation that spurred merger activity was the advent of the junk bond market. Michael Milken of Drexel, Burnham, & Lambert developed the market for junk bonds in the 1980s. In the 1970s he established a junk bond market in trading and sales of "fallen angels," bonds that were investment grade at the time they were issued but had fallen to noninvestment grade bonds. A super-salesman, he convinced his clients that Drexel would keep an active market for the junk bonds (Wasserstein, 1998). In the late 1970s Milken switched into original issue junk bonds—bonds that were rated below investment grade at the time of issue. This market was extremely profitable. By the middle of the 1980s junk bonds totaled $50 billion, with Drexel trading most of it (Wasserstein, 1998).

Financial buyers and leveraged buyouts (LBOs) were very important in this wave. Kohlberg, Kravis, and Roberts (KKR) purchased RJR Nabisco in a leveraged buyout in 1988, the largest transaction up to 1988. In 1980, $2 billion in LBOs were transacted; in 1988, 239 deals were put together, amounting to $81.2 billion (Wasserstein, 1998). Two common types of LBOs were the classic

LBO and the breakup LBO. In the classic LBO, in order to buy the target, the bidders borrowed heavily against the assets and cash flow of the target and took the company private. The debt consisted of several layers, with the senior debt usually purchased by banks and other traditional lenders. The layers of debt between the senior debt and equity was often called "mezzanine financing," often with the last layer financed by junk bonds. Only a relatively few investors owned the equity. The debt was paid off in a relatively short time by selling assets or with the strong cash flow of the target. Then the relatively few equity holders owned the company. Often, the owners would take the company public again for a huge profit.

With a breakup LBO, investors borrowed heavily to buy the target and then took the company private with a relatively few owners just as in a classic LBO. However, the difference was that in a classic LBO the debt is paid off with the cash flow of the target as well as asset sales. In a breakup LBO, divesting parts of the company paid off the debt. The company was literally broken up and the parts were sold off. For this type of LBO, conglomerates were the best targets because they had easily identifiable lines of business that could be sold off. In 1987, tax law severely limited the profitability of breakup LBOs.

The LBO became extremely lucrative. In an LBO of Beatrice Foods, KKR earned over $2.2 billion in the four years it owned Beatrice, or a 50% profit per year (Wasserstein, 1998). Initially, investors in LBOs were institutions, but when the public wanted a piece of the action, KKR and others developed large pools of funds that they could invest in LBOs whenever they saw an opportunity.

The popularity of LBOs was probably due to the salability of junk bonds, the rising stock market, the availability of excellent targets, and the early profitability of the deals. The junk bond market collapsed when Milken and others were indicted for mail fraud, securities fraud, tax evasion, and racketeering and with the enactment of the Financial Institutions Recovery and Enforcement Act in 1989, which essentially forced savings and loan associations to sell their junk bonds. With the ensuing collapse of Drexel and the junk bond market in 1990, the declining economy, too many dollars chasing too few potentially profitable targets, and the declining profitability of later deals, the LBO acquisition all but died out.

Characteristics

Competition became global in the 1980s as many foreign companies bid for and acquired American companies. In the first part of the decade, foreign companies bid for American companies but often did not seem to win the bid. In the latter half of the decade, many foreign companies actually did acquire American companies. British and Canadian companies were among the first to acquire U.S. firms, but in the latter half of the 1980s the Japanese also became prominent buyers. Foreign competitors' purchases were large companies, with British bidders buying Standard Oil, Pillsbury, and SmithKline Beecham. American companies also looked abroad for foreign targets.

Hostile bids were prominent in the 1980s. Their number was small—only 46 hostile deals in 1988—but these were very visible and very large; Time, Inc, Sterling Drug, and RJR Nabisco were all targets of hostile bids (Wasserstein, 1998). Litigation played an important role in hostile merger activity. If the target wanted to fight the bidder or thought the bid was too low, it often filed a suit in federal court stipulating antitrust violations or other grounds. The bidder sometimes countersued in state courts, arguing that the board of directors had violated their fiduciary responsibility. Often, the target was simply buying time to fight the offer, and the bidder was increasing the target's expense in fighting the offer. Hostile bids led to more and stronger defensive measures. Among these measures were greenmail, poison pills, the pac man defense, a white knight or white squire, anti-takeover amendments, and golden parachutes.

Strategic acquisitions were popular. Models such as the McKinsey Formulation, the Boston Consulting Group Model, and Porter's Five Forces were used extensively. These models were designed to assess what a company wanted to accomplish for the future and how an acquisition fit into those goals. In this way, all types of acquisitions were possible, not just those that had stable cash flows or high growth.

Acquisitions were more prominent in some industries than others. The oil industry had many acquisitions that were large by dollar value.

Energy

In the 1980s mergers between the oil companies were commonplace (Davidson, 1985). By that decade, the oil companies had diversified into other energy resources, and some had diversified into other lines of business. Other energy sources included diversifying into coal, oil shale, and nuclear energy. Oil profits were soaring due to high oil prices in the 1970s. In 1979, the Iranian revolution and the subsequent Iran-Iraq War, coupled with OPEC's stranglehold on oil prices, made American oil reserves particularly valuable. Consequently, many oil companies had high free cash flow and valuable resources. Some oil companies wasted free cash flow on the very costly exploration and development of more oil reserves, with the result that oil refining capacity overexpanded. Such oil companies were ripe for takeover by other oil companies to reduce capacity and cut down on the costly exploration (Davidson, 1985). In 1979 Shell Oil bought Belridge; in 1981 Du Pont purchased Conoco, and U.S Steel bought Marathon; in 1982 Occidental Petroleum bought Cities Service; in 1984 Mobil bought Superior Oil, Pennzoil bought Getty Oil, and Chevron purchased Gulf Oil; in 1985 Mesa Petroleum failed to purchase Unocal and Phillips Petroleum (Wasserstein, 1998). In 1985 the bottom fell out of oil prices and oil profits plummeted. In the latter half of the decade and the early 1990s, many oil companies, for example, Exon, Mobil, and ARCO, restructured.

Not only did oil companies consolidate, but so did natural gas producers, primarily as a result of deregulation. In the early 1980s, gas prices were deregulated and price competition ruled. In 1985 the government permitted utilities and industrial customers to buy from the best price supplier. Thus, third-party companies, not just pipeline companies, could sell natural gas. In the process of consolidating, some natural gas companies swallowed others; for example, CSX acquired Texas Gas Resources in 1983, Coastal acquired American Natural Resources in 1985, and Panhandle Eastern acquired Texas Eastern in 1989. This was primarily a time of consolidation.

Telecommunications

In 1982 the courts broke up AT&T because it held too much monopoly power. Therefore, in 1984 it separated into a long-distance carrier and seven regional companies (affectionately know as Baby Bells) offering local phone service. This opened up competition in the long-distance market. MCI, Sprint, and other smaller newcomers began to take market share from AT&T. Access charges increased, and many of the smaller companies could not compete. This led to acquisitions and consolidation. In addition to acquiring smaller long-distance companies, MCI bought RCA Global Communications, a telex company in 1987, and it bought Advanced Transmission Systems with its 700 miles of fiber optic cable in 1990. In 1990 it also purchased Telecom USA with its customer base and 3,000 miles of fiber optic cable. By 1990 there were three major players in the long-distance market—AT&T, Sprint, and MCI.

Under the AT&T umbrella, the Baby Bells were subsidized by long-distance services, but after the breakup the Baby Bells were profitable. Local regulatory agencies permitted ample rate increases to cover costs. This contributed to the profitability of the Baby Bells, as did the explosion in fax machines, online services, discount long distance, paging, and cellular phone usage. Several Baby Bells diversified by acquiring yellow pages publishing companies, and Nynex bought AGS Computers and IBM's computer retailing chain. Perhaps the most important acquisitions were Pacific Telesis's purchase of Communications Industries, a cellular and paging company, in 1985; Bell Atlantic's purchase of A Beeper Corp., also a cellular and paging company, and BellSouth's purchase of Mobile Communications, a cellular operator. The Baby Bells were beginning to enter the cellular market.

The cellular market was new in the 1980s. Bell Labs of AT&T pioneered the cellular innovation, but with the breakup, the cellular licenses went with the Baby Bells. It took two years for the FCC to distribute all of the cellular licenses. Mounds of paperwork were needed in applying for a license. In 1982 Metromedia, a television and radio broadcasting company, became interested in cellular technology, but lacking the time needed to put together an application, it instead acquired several small start-up companies that were well on their way to completing an application. In this way, Metromedia captured several cellular licenses. Metromedia, McCaw Cellular, and the Baby Bells continued to gobble up licenses and small start-up companies. Because developing cellular systems was capital intensive and only large, well-capitalized companies could make profitable investments, the 1980s saw a wave of consolidation in the cellular industry. In 1989 a big battle occurred for LIN Broadcasting, the owner of several potentially lucrative licenses, with BellSouth and McCaw Cellular at each other's throats. McCaw Cellular won the battle. Beginning in 1990, the cellular revolution took off with 3.5 million subscribers in 1989, jumping to more than 10 million subscribers in 1993.

In the 1970s the Federal Communications Commission granted many franchises to start-up companies, giving them the right to enter the cable business. Although some companies lacked the capital to start a cable business, they still owned the license. Other companies entered the cable market in a small way. With only a few large companies and many small ones, the cable market was ripe for consolidation in the 1980s. During the 1980s more than $26 billion in cable assets were acquired (Wasserstein, 1998). The largest purchaser of cable companies was Telecommunications, Inc. (TCI), with Time, Inc., Cox, and Continental Cablevision also gobbling up weaker competitors (Wasserstein, 1998). In 1984 the Cable Act deregulated the cable industry, allowing cable companies to charge higher rates for service and limiting the ability of municipalities to revoke a cable company's right to operate. Television and telephone companies were prohibited from owning cable companies. This legislation raised the value and prices of cable companies, but interest in acquiring them did not wane. By 1991 TCI was the largest cable company with 10 million subscribers, closely followed by Time Warner with 6.6 million subscribers, Continental Cablevision with 2.8 million subscribers, Comcast with 1.7 million subscribers, and Cox with 1.6 million subscribers Wasserstein, 1998). These five large cable companies controlled 44% of the market (Wasserstein, 1998). The consolidation of cable companies virtually ended in 1989 when consumer sentiment against the high cable rates dampened the ability of cable companies to raise rates, limiting their cash flow to purchase other cable companies.

Banks

The commercial banking sector began to consolidate in the later 1980s. Commercial banks had been having problems, one of which was competition from brokerage firms which provided money market funds to compete with banks for savings. In addition, Latin American and some LBO loans soured, and the volatility in oil prices and real estate resulted in lower profits. Moreover, there were too many banks, too much bureaucracy, and too few customers. Many banks had overexpanded by building too many branches. The advent of personal computers and overnight mail service enabled each bank to easily handle many more transactions. There were just too many banks; banks began buying other banks.

The McFadden Act of 1927 prevented banks from building branches across state lines, but some banks circumvented this law by organizing into holding companies. Nonetheless, each subsidiary in each state still had to have its own charter and was subject to the state laws in their state of operation. The Bank Holding Company Act of 1956 prohibited nonbanks from owning banks, so banks were constrained to being small independent entities. The Douglas Amendment, prohibited cross-state line acquisitions unless "specifically authorized by statute laws of the State in which such bank is located, by language to that effect and not merely by implication." In 1972 a few states permitted cross-state-border acquisitions. In 1982, Connecticut and Massachusetts allowed acquisitions crossing state boundaries for New England. This was challenged in court and upheld. When the courts sanctioned cross-border acquisitions, many other states also adopted laws permitting cross-state-lines transactions. In 1982, a federal law was passed authorizing any bank to acquire a failed bank in any region. Thus began the consolidation of the banking sector by acquisition.

Between 1980 and 1994, 6,374 bank mergers occurred, and between 1981 and 1997, banks disappeared through merger at a rate of 1.7 per business day. Thus, bank mergers started during the 1980s but continued through the 1990s. The peak year was 1987, with a secondary peak in the mid- to late 1990s. Some banks simply got larger by gobbling up smaller banks. The 25 largest banks controlled about 70% of the assets in the late 1990s (Dymski, 1999). The 1980s and the 1990s represented an era of bank consolidation.

Media

In 1981 the FCC raised the number of stations a company could own from 7 AM stations and 7 FM stations to 12 each. In addition, the miniaturization of the radio increased the radio audience, making the acquisition of radio stations more appealing. These factors led to a small boom in radio station acquisitions. In 1984, 782 stations were acquired, and in 1985, 1,558 stations were bought, compared to an average of about 100 stations per year in the 1970s (Wasserstein, 1998).

In the 1980s the three major networks changed hands. With the increase in the number of cable stations, the networks' share of the viewing market had declined considerably with the subsequent decline in advertising revenues. The deterioration of the networks' financial positions with their low stock prices put them in play. Capital Cities acquired ABC; Loews Corporation gained control of CBS after attempts by Ted Turner and financier Marvin Davis were overturned; and GE bought out RCA with its NBC subsidiary.

In 1984 the courts ruled that the public could videotape television programs for personal use. Previously, movies had been released to television after their run in the movie theaters, but then they were released to video outlets first to maximize revenues from movies. This led to the proliferation of video rental stores, acquisitions of video rental franchises, and the national chain Blockbuster. Also in the 1980s CDs replaced LPs and tapes.

Movie studios were also becoming the target of takeovers. With the proliferation of cable television and video rental franchises, the producers of movies
and other content became lucrative sources of revenue. Marvin Davis purchased
Fox Studios, Coca-Cola acquired Columbia Pictures, Embassy Communications,
and Merv Griffin Enterprises, and Ted Turner bought MGM/UA. In the latter
half of the 1980s, companies began to put together content and distribution
channels in a vertically integrated model. Cable companies started buying cable
channels and Time and Warner merged to meld interests in cable, movie and
television production, book and magazine publishing, and the record business.
One other trend in the 1980s was foreign ownership of U.S. media companies.

The End

The fourth takeover wave ended with a recession, the Iran–Iraq War, the
advent of strong anti-takeover defensive mechanisms, and a hiatus in the junk
bond market.

FIFTH MERGER WAVE

The fifth merger wave began around 1992 following a recession and is ongoing. Merger activity in the 1990s exceeded acquisition activity in the 1980s.
Whereas acquisition activity in the last wave peaked in 1988 with $287 billion
in 1992 dollars, in the year 2000, the AOL-Time Warner deal alone totaled $165
billion. In 1998, world merger and acquisition activity totaled $2.7 trillion, and
in 1999 the figure rose another 25.9% to $3.4 trillion. By the 1990s, the better
measure of merger and acquisition activity was the value of acquisitions for the
entire world. Acquisitions in the 1990s were truly international in scope, with
all types of cross-border deals taking place. Many of these large deals did not
even involve U.S. companies. Merger and acquisition activity in the U.S. totaled
2,366 in the peak year of 1988 in the 1980s but 9,278 in 1999.

Like other merger waves, the fifth merger wave followed a recession. Rising
stock prices made companies a bargain even at premiums over their current
market price. The heightened economic activity was accompanied by low interest rates, making the cost of financing an acquisition relatively cheap.

Another factor encouraging acquisitions was technological change, especially
the innovations in information systems, computer software, computer hardware,
microwave systems, and fiber optics. Perhaps the most important innovations
were the Internet and e-commerce. Businesses could sell their products over the
Internet, bypassing the middleman or retail outlets. Manufacturers could order
inventory and have it shipped almost immediately, cutting down on inventory
storage costs. The Internet also gave rise to firms that had not existed before
the Internet. For example, one company focuses on linking a company needing
inventory quickly with a company that has inventory available immediately
through the Internet.

With globalization and freer trade, the need for more efficient organizations has acculerated. To take advantage of economies of scale in a world market, many firms have had to become larger, and the fastest way to accomplish that is through horizontal acquisition. In addition, the advent of computers and the Internet enabled companies to do more business with the same amount of resources in order to increase efficiency. Thus, firms were able to become larger quickly through horizontal and vertical mergers.

Another factor that encouraged mergers was deregulation of the transportation, telecommunication, financial services, and energy industries. The increased competition in these industries was instrumental in consolidation within the industry.

Characteristics

Acquisitions in the 1990s were both a continuation of and a divergence from acquisitions in the 1980s. Although the 1980s saw many large deals, those made during the fifth merger wave were even larger. The largest one until recently in the telecommunications industry was the MCI WorldCom takeover of Sprint, valued at $115 billion (Weston, Siu, and Johnson, 2000).

Strategic LBOs were popular during the fifth merger wave (Wasserstein, 1998), but they were not LBOs in the classic sense. In the classic variant, an investing group buys a private company or a division of a public company often with large amounts of debt. Efficiency is improved, and a glamorous management is put in place, after which the company is taken public in an initial public offering (IPO). With the second variant, the owners purchase several small units and put them together to form a larger company. The package is then sold to the public in an IPO.

The 1990s saw a reemergence of the junk bond market. Investment firms other than Drexel now made a market in junk bonds, and it surpassed its 1988 peak. Unlike the previous merger wave when many acquisitions were financed with cash, in the 1990s many transactions were stock-for-stock transactions. In addition, globalization continued, and strategic acquisitions continued to provide the primary motivation.

Energy Industry

In the energy industry, vertical mergers were common, with natural gas producers entering the marketing and distribution side of the business with mergers. For example, in 1994 Panhandle Eastern acquired Associated Natural Gas, a marketing concern. Because of deregulation, utilities needed the marketing expertise of natural gas companies, which they acquired by buying the companies. Houston Industries acquired NorAm Energy and Duke Power bought Panenergy for their marketing expertise. Product extension mergers have also played a role in the mergers of utilities. Utilities have name recognition and a customer base that other companies can employ to bundle services so that the customer has one bill and several services offered by the same company.

Oil company acquisitions continued with Exxon's acquisition of Mobil in December 1998 and Total Fina's acquisition of Elf Acquitaine in July 1999. The Exxon-Mobil deal amounted to $78.9 billion, while the Fina-Elf takeover totaled 53.5 billion, with both deals making the list of the top 10 acquisitions for the decade (Weston, Siu, and Johnson, 2000).

Financial Sector

In the 1990s the lines between the different financial services began to blur. Commercial banks made loans and extended credit; savings and loan associations collected savings from individuals and made mortgage loans; investment banks underwrote and distributed securities; brokerage houses engaged in retail sales of securities; and insurance companies managed risk.

In the 1980s several attempts were made to diversify across the financial services industry (Wasserstein, 1998). In 1981 Prudential, an insurance company, acquired Bache Group, a brokerage company. Between 1982 and 1984, Kemper acquired several regional brokerage firms. GE Capital bought Kidder Peabody, an investment bank, and Sears, Roebuck bought Dean Witter and Coldwell Banker, a real estate broker. The most aggressive acquirer in the 1980s was American Express, which purchased Shearson Loeb Rhoades, a brokerage firm (1981), a private Swiss bank (1983), Investors Diversified Services (1983), Lehman Brothers, an investment bank (1984), and E. F. Hutton, a retail brokerage house, (1987). Almost all of these acquisitions were failures. Financial supermarkets had trouble managing and coordinating the units and managing the risks. American Express sold the Swiss bank, Fireman's Fund, and Shearson;. Sears sold Dean Witter, Discover, Coldwell Banker and Allstate Insurance; and GE sold Kidder Peabody. After the first attempts at a financial supermarket failed, companies came back with better management in Smith Barney and Merrill Lynch. Smith Barney acquired Primerica in 1988, Shearson in 1993, Travelers Insurance also in 1993, Aetna Property and Casualty in 1995, and Saloman Brothers in 1997. The financial supermarket was reborn in the 1990s.

Banks also continued to acquire other banks, so that the 1990s saw the evolution of the super-regional bank. NationsBank, a North Carolina bank, acquired First RepublicBank in Texas after it failed in 1988 and Mcorp, also a failed Texas bank in 1989. In 1991 NationsBank acquired Citizens & Southern/Sovran operating in Atlanta; both banks had branches in South Carolina and Florida. In 1996 NationsBank acquired Boatman's Bancshares in Chicago. Together, NationsBank and Boatman's had branches in 16 states with branches from Maryland to Texas and from Florida to the Mexican border. NationsBank was truly a super-regional bank. Since 1996 other banks have also become super-regional banks. Perhaps the largest deal occurred in 1998 between NationsBank and BankAmerica, totaling $61.6 billion. The super-regional bank had the advantages of size to improve efficiency, to put technological innovations in place, and to compete globally. Until the advent of super-regional banks, U.S. banks were among the smallest in the world and were in no position to compete globally with European and Far Eastern banks. With the phenomenal growth by acquisition in the 1990s, however, U.S banks became global in scope.

To improve performance, in 1997 several commercial banks acquired securities firms including investment banks. In 1988 Federal Reserve rules limited ownership of securities firms to 10% of holding company revenues, but in 1996 this limit was raised to 25%. Dean Witter, Discover & Co. acquired Morgan Stanley Group; Bankers Trust New York acquired Alex Brown & Sons; SBC Warburg bought Dillon, Read & Co.; and BankAmerica acquired Robertson, Stephens & Co. Investment banks found it advantageous to meld with the larger commercial banks to smooth out their volatile earnings and to secure the necessary capital to globalize their operations. Commercial banks found it beneficial to offer more investment products to customers, to improve profitability, and to bulk up in size to compete globally. So, a bank merger wave that actually began in the late 1980s continues through the present day.

Insurance companies—primarily property and casualty, and life insurance companies—consolidated (Wasserstein, 1998) for many reasons. Some property and casualty insurance companies had under-reserved for losses, making them weak and ripe for takeover. Competition for customers tightened as some large corporations began to self-insure. Life insurance companies also faced problems because they had made some deteriorating value investments in real estate and junk bonds. In addition, instead of buying life insurance policies as an investment, the public now turned to mutual funds. With sinking profitability from few customers and bad investments or liability losses, the property and casualty and life insurance companies were ripe for takeover and many of the acquisitions were horizontal.

Telecommunications

By the early 1990s, the combination of digital technology and fiber optics became commercially viable. Digital technology converted voice, video, and data into computer signals so that much more data could be transmitted over a system. Fiber optic cable reduced the noise in the system through laser transmission. All these innovations promised voice, video, and data transmissions at very high speeds and over the same lines.

Along with two legal decisions, these innovations spawned several large acquisitions. Under one ruling, the phone companies were permitted to carry television signals, but they still were not allowed to buy nonoverlapping cable companies. Under the other ruling, cable companies could provide local phone service. The stage was therefore set for one company to provide multiple services.

For the first marriage of a phone company and a cable system operator, in

1993 Southwestern Bell purchased Hauser Communications, a company with two cable systems (Wasserstein, 1998). U.S. West answered with a joint venture with Time Warner. In December 1993 Southwestern Bell Partnered with Cox Enterprises, a major cable partnership, and BellSouth invested in Prime Cable. In a combination of content with cable, Viacom purchased Paramount Communications to the chagrin of QVC. After the mini-boom of 1993, most companies avoided acquisitions of cable companies because the FCC had re-regulated the cable companies, forcing rate decreases. With large amounts of debt, this endangered cash flow from the cable companies and led to the failure of several joint ventures and Southwestern Bell's sale of Hauser Communications. Later in the decade, some alliances between cable and phone companies proceeded. AT&T purchased Tele-Communications Inc. (TCI) in 1998, giving AT&T a huge cable system and high-speed Internet access. In 1999, Comcast bought MediaOne to take advantage of broadband services and positioning itself for the future of the Internet. The combination will permit millions of households to receive digital services through fiber optic cables.

The combination of phone companies and cable systems was not the only innovation in the decade; now the combination of long-distance and local phone companies was also possible (Wasserstein, 1998). The Federal Communications Act of 1996 essentially deregulated telephone and related industries by opening up local telephone markets to competition by other companies, including long-distance providers. When they have competition in local markets, local phone companies can enter the long-distance market. To meld long-distance and local phone services, in 1997 SBC purchased Pacific Telesis and Bell Atlantic purchased Nynex so that each company had regional long-distance and local phone service. Also in 1997, WorldCom acquired MCI to become the second largest national telecommunications provider and the largest Internet provider.

Media

Radio stations continued their consolidation effort. Westinghouse purchased Karmazin's Infinity Broadcasting in 1996 and American Radio Systems in 1997, becoming the nation's largest radio chain. Consolidation continued as Evergreen Media purchased Chancellor Broadcasting in 1997 to become the second largest radio chain.

In addition to radio consolidation, very large vertical combinations became important with Viacom's purchase of Paramount, putting together cable channels, television and movie production, video distribution, and publishing. In 1995 the fin/syn rules were repealed so that networks and studios could combine. Melding content and distribution in a vertically integrated system, Disney purchased Capital Cities/ABC and Time Warner acquired Turner Broadcasting Systems. The vertical integration continued as other content providers acquired distribution channels.

The 1990s was the era of the Internet. In addition to companies that combined hardware such as AT&T and TCI or Comcast and MediaOne, companies also combined software with content. Among the first efforts to join software with content was a joint venture by Microsoft and NBC forming MSNBC, which created an online news service in 1995. Microsoft continued to make inroads into the Internet sphere with its purchase in 1997 of Web-TV, a company with hardware and software interfaces for interactive television. Then Microsoft invested in Comcast, making cable television Microsoft's platform for distributing digital products. Competing with Microsoft in a television–Internet interface were Oracle Corporation and Sun Microsystems. In 2000, America Online's (AOL) purchased Time Warner for $183 billion in the largest ever stock-for-stock transaction, combining the Internet with Time Warner's content, cable systems, and subscriber base. With attractions such as CNN, a huge library of classic movies, as well as online magazines, AOL is far ahead of its competitors.

Health Care

A dramatic shift toward consolidation and vertical combinations among doctors hospitals, pharmaceutical companies, HMOs, and insurance companies was characteristic of the 1990s.

Since physician groups had no bargaining power with HMOs, groups of physicians sold out to a physician practice management company (PPM). In a typical PPM, the PPM owns the assets of the physician group, but the doctors remain independent contractors, signing a long-term contract to provide services for the PPM. Since it represents many physicians, the PPM has bargaining power not only with HMOs but also with suppliers. PhyCor was one such company. It began operation in 1988, and by 1996 it had 12,000 doctors in its network, with revenues of $770 million (Wasserstein, 1998). MedPartners was started in 1993 and acquired independent practice groups as well as other PPMs, including Caremark International.

With the increasing emphasis on cost containment, hospitals also came under pressure. The industry was now plagued with overcapacity. Hospitals were consolidated into hospital chains. Humana and Hospital Corporation were among the first consolidators, but Columbia was the largest with nearly 7,000 hospitals (Wasserstein, 1998). Another competitor, Tenet Healthcare, purchased several other, smaller, hospital consolidators to become the number two firm in the industry.

Pharmaceutical companies also have engaged in horizontal and vertical acquisitions. Expiring patents on existing blockbuster drugs, the shortened life cycle of new drugs as competitors developed clones, as well as the pressure of cost containment from HMOs and the government, were the driving forces behind the acquisitions. In 1989, SmithKline Beckman and Beecham combined in a horizontal acquisition. Beecham had research expertise and several well-known brand names but needed a U.S. presence that SmithKline Beckman could provide. Several other European giants combined with U.S companies. Not only did global consolidations take place, but also consolidations among U.S. firms proceeded. But even with the globalization of pharmaceuticals, each of the five largest companies had less than 5% of the market (Wasserstein, 1998).

Vertical combinations between pharmaceutical companies and biotechnology firms and between pharmaceutical companies and pharmacy benefits management companies (PBMs) were part of the fifth wave of mergers. For biotech firms, bringing a commercial product to fruition took longer than expected partly because the products needed a long time to receive government approval. Since many firms did not have sufficient cash flow to operate, they needed a cash infusion, and the drug companies were happy to oblige. A small number of acquisitions began in 1986, but the first large one took place in 1990 with Roche's purchase of 60% of Gentech. This seemed to start a trend in which drug companies acquired an interest in biotech companies. The pharmaceutical companies provided the cash in exchange for an opportunity to share in the growth and profitability of the biotech firm. Drug companies' acquisitions of part of the biotech firms created a semi-independent entity within a larger company. Not all combinations of biotech companies were with drug companies. Some were horizontal combinations; for example, Chiron acquired Cetus Corporation.

Other vertical combinations involved PBMs, drug distributors. Basically, PBMs were middlemen who bought drugs in bulk to reduce costs for employers and managed care companies. A PBM also had a list of preferred drugs based on cost for most conditions. With the pharmaceutical companies being squeezed by the PBMs they thought they could gain the upper hand by buying PBMs. For a while, it worked. Merck acquired Medco Containment, SmithKline Beecham purchased Diversified Pharmaceutical Services, and Eli Lily bought PCS Health Systems. Other pharmaceutical companies followed suit. With PBMs in tow, drug companies felt they could control drug prices and make sure their products were on the preferred list. The Merck and SmithKline Beecham mergers gained antitrust approval easily, but Eli Lily's deal encountered some difficulty. The government mandated that Eli Lily could not exclude competitors' products from the preferred list and had to maintain a "firewall" between it and its PCS subsidiary so that it did not know its competitors' prices. These rules were made retroactive so that all acquisitions between a pharmaceutical company and a PBM had to follow the rules. Consequently, drug companies did not achieve everything they had intended with the acquisition of PBM's.

At the beginning of the 1990s, insurance policies for health care consisted primarily of the indemnity plans of traditional insurance companies and health maintenance organizations (HMOs). With an indemnity plan, the patient chooses the doctor, hospital, or other provider, pays a deductible, and the insurance company picks up the remainder of the cost. With an HMO, the patient pays a small deductible if he or she uses certain doctors and other health care providers on the HMO's list of acceptable providers. The HMO negotiates with the list of providers to furnish services or products at reduced rates, and the providers receive a volume of business. Thus, everyone gets something from the association. The purpose of HMOs was to cut health care costs in an era when the public and government were concerned with rising health care costs. The HMO therefore had to be large enough to negotiate deals with providers. This led to consolidation among HMOs. In 1997, PacifiCare Health Systems acquired FHP to become the fourth largest HMO, and Foundation Health Corporation combined with Health Systems International to form the fifth largest HMO.

Companies wanted choices for health care and wanted these choices from one company. In 1996 Aetna Insurance Company purchased U.S Healthcare, an HMO, to originate the point-of-service model. With point of service a client can stay with a list of providers and pay a small deductible as in a traditional HMO or may choose a preferred provider plan or traditional indemnity plan. Aetna, an expert in providing indemnity plans, and U.S. Healthcare, an expert in HMOs, combined to give companies an HMO with choice. These cross-care acquisitions continued for the next few years but then waned as several companies had difficulties integrating the two partners.

In the latter part of the 1990s there was a paucity of deals in the health care industry, but merger activity picked in 2000 with 135 deals in the second quarter. Most of these deals were in the hospital, PBMs, and behavioral health care areas. The large deals were Tyco's purchase of Mallinckrodt, a supplier of low-margin medical equipment and products, Orthopedics LLC's purchase of DePuy Orthopedic Technology, and DeRoyal's acquisition of Southeast Medical, a manufacturer of products for anesthesia, respiratory, and surgery. Today's large acquisitions seem to be in the area of medical products.

CONCLUSIONS

All merger waves have some common elements: All proceeded on a rising stock market and a general economic upturn with generally low interest rates. Generally, legislation favored certain types of acquisitions, horizontal, vertical, or conglomerate, and usually some innovations that affected a large number of industries became viable. During the first merger wave, the important innovation was railroads. In the sucessive mergers, the innovations were, respectively, primarily motor vehicle transportation and radio, a business philosophy, personal computers and cell phones, and the Internet.

Each of the four merger waves ended with a common set of factors; notably, a recession and a downturn in the stock market. Legislation and the failure of many combinations also tended to dampen merger activity.

While the waves share some commonalties, there are also differences. For example, during the later merger waves, hostile takeovers along with innovations in defense mechanisms became important. The industries in which mergers took place changed over time, and globalization became much more important during the later merger waves.

REFERENCES

Asquith, P. (November 1983). "Merger Bids, Uncertainty, and Stockholder Returns." *Journal of Financial Economics*, pp. 51–83.

Cooke, Terence E. (1986). *Mergers and Acquisitions*. New York: Basil Blackwell.

Davidson, Kenneth M. (1985). *Megamergers: Corporate America's Billion-Dollar Takeovers*. Cambridge, MA: Ballinger Publishing Co.

Dodd, P. (June 1980). "Merger Proposals, Management Discretion and Stockholder Wealth." *Journal of Financial Economics*, pp. 11–138.

Dodd, P. (Spring 1986). "The Market for Corporate Control: A Review of the Evidence." *Financial Management Collection*, 1, no. 2.

Dymski, Gary A. (1999). *The Bank Merger Wave: The Causes and Social Consequences of Financial Consolidation*. Armonk, NY: M. E. Sharpe.

Halpern, P. (October 1973). "Empirical Estimates of the Amount and Distribution of Gains to Companies in Merger." *Journal of Business*, pp. 554–573.

Langetieg, T. C. (December 1978). "An Application of a Three-Factor Performance Index to Measure Stockholder Gains from Merger." *Journal of Financial Economics*, pp. 365–384.

Leeth, John D., and J. Rody Borg. (June 2000). "The Impact of Takeovers on Shareholder Wealth during the 1920's Merger Wave." *Journal of Financial and Quantitative Analysis*, 35, pp. 217–238.

Livermore, Shaw. (November 1935). "The Success of Industrial Mergers." *Quarterly Journal of Economics*, pp. 68–96.

Mandelker, G. (December 1974). "Risk and Return: The Case of Merging Firms." *Journal of Financial Economics*, pp. 303–335.

Markham, Jesse W. (1955). "Survey of the Evidence and Findings on Mergers." In *Business Concentration and Price Policy*. National Bureau of Economic Research, New York. Princeton, NJ: Princeton University Press.

Markham, Jesse W. (1973). *Conglomerate Enterprise and Public Policy*. Boston: Harvard University.

Ravenscaft, David J., and F. M. Scherer. (1987). *Mergers, Sell-Offs, and Economic Efficiency*. Washington, DC: Brookings Institution.

Rumelt, Richard P. (1974). *Strategy, Structure and Economic Performance*. Boston: Division of Research, Graduate School of Business Administration, Harvard University.

Salter, Malcolm S., and Wolf A. Weinhold. (1979). *Diversification through Acquisition*. New York: Macmillan.

Scherer, F. M. (1980). *Industrial Market Structure and Economic Performance*. Boston: Houghton Mifflin.

Steiner, Peter O. (1975). *Mergers: Motives, Effects, and Policies*. Ann Arbor: University of Michigan Press.

Stigler, George J. (June 1951). "The Division of Labor Is Limited by the Extent of the Market." *Journal of Political Economy*, 59, pp. 185–193.

Taggert, Robert A., Jr. (1988). "The Growth of the 'Junk' Bond Market and Its Role in Financing Takeovers." In *Mergers and Acquisitions*, Alan J. Auerbach, ed. Chicago: University of Chicago Press, pp. 5–24.

Wasserstein, Bruce. (1998). *Big Deal: The Battle for Control of America's Leading Corporations.* New York: Warner Books.

Weston, J. Fred, and Surenda Mansingka. (September 1971). "Tests on the Efficiency Performance of Conglomerate Mergers." *Journal of Finance,* 26, pp. 919–936.

Weston, J. Fred, Juan A. Siu, and Brian A. Johnson (2001). *Takeovers, Restructuring, and Corporate Governance.* Upper Saddle River, NJ: Prentice Hall.

Chapter 3

Large Mergers during the 1990s

Jonathan M. Karpoff and David Wessels

INTRODUCTION

Remember the merger mania of the 1980s? More and larger merger deals than ever before characterized this era. Through much of the 1980s, merger activity spurred the stock market to stratospheric levels. Standard Oil of California acquired Gulf Oil, Philip Morris gobbled up Kraft Inc., and Time Inc. emerged in a struggle with Paramount Communications as the new owner of Warner Communications Inc. In the granddaddy of them all, Kohlberg, Kravis, Roberts & Co. outbid two rivals to acquire RJR Nabisco for $25 billion in 1988. The story became grist for a bestselling book with a title that reflected the fear such deals inspired: *Barbarians at the Gate.*

Pundits and politicians had a field day decrying the insanity of it all. When the Dow Jones Industrial Average broke 2000, John Kenneth Galbraith drew an analogy to the pre-crash market highs of the 1920s and warned of an upcoming recession. Congressman John Dingell and Senator William Proxmire chaired hearings on the dangers to the U.S. economy posed by unbridled merger activity. Senator Paul Simon from Illinois won reelection on a campaign against the allegedly harmful effects of U.S. Steel's acquisition of Marathon Oil. And in state after state across the country, legislators were convinced to help stem the tide of wanton corporate acquisitions by passing state antitakeover legislation.[1] Hollywood chipped in too, immortalizing the conventional judgment of merger activity in such movies as *Wall Street* and Tom Wolfe's *Bonfire of the Vanities.* Owing in part to the perception that corporate acquisitions represented something less than moral, the 1980s became known, at least in some circles, as "The Decade of Greed."

Well, don't look now, but compared to recent experience the merger mania of the 1980s was downright sedate. From 1996 through 1999, the average annual number of mergers involving publicly traded companies was nearly *three times* the average annual number during the heyday of the 1980s. Not only the numbers, but also the sizes of mergers have increased dramatically. Aggregate acquisition transaction values in every one of the past five years exceed that for 1988—the highwater mark for the 1980s. In 1999, the value of all mergers involving publicly traded companies was *five times* that in 1988. The number of transactions worth more than $1 billion has been higher in every year since 1994 than in any year of the 1980s. The 1988 RJR Nabisco takeover, a symbol of mergers gone wild, has been surpassed by 24 other mergers—all since 1997—on the list of all-time largest merger deals.

In this chapter we examine how the merger market has changed over the past 20 years. We show that merger activity, though not new, has involved more and larger companies in recent years than ever before. Large mergers concentrate in several sectors in the economy that are undergoing substantial technological and regulatory change: telecommunications, financial services, and energy. The number and size of all merger transactions reflect in part an overall increase in economic activity, but the increases far exceed the growth in the overall economy.

Even though they have become larger and more frequent, the mergers of recent years share many characteristics with those of previous years. The use of cash in merger transactions has remained relatively stable. The premiums paid reflect higher price-earnings multiples than in previous years, and the growth exceeds the growth in price-earnings multiples of the S&P 500 stocks only in the last two years of available data, 1998 and 1999. And, as in the 1980s, anecdotal evidence indicates that acquiring firm shareholders do not gain and may lose value because of the mergers.

Overall, the picture that emerges is one of a very active market for control of corporate assets. The fact that this market is particularly active in industries that are undergoing fundamental change suggests that acquisition activities facilitate the large reallocation of resources demanded by structural changes in the economy. As in previous decades, however, bidding companies appear to suffer from the winners' curse—paying too much and letting target firm shareholders capture most of the gains created by the mergers.

CHARACTERISTICS AND FREQUENCIES OF LARGE ACQUISITIONS

Throughout this chapter, we rely on information published in the 2000 edition of *MergerStat Review*, which is published by the MergerStat Company. Most of this information refers to "net announcements," which is the number of acquisitions announced in a given year less any previously announced acquisitions that were canceled. We will use MergerStat's "net announcements" as an indication of the total acquisitions during a given year.

In addition to its information on acquisitions of companies of any size, MergerStat also tracks acquisitions worth $1 billion or more. By this measure, large merger activity increased substantially in the 1990s. Figure 3.1 displays the number of $1 billion transactions per year from 1980 through 1999. The number peaked temporarily at 48 in 1988, declined to 14 in 1991, and then increased every year since. There were 354 $1 billion merger transactions in 1998 and 1999, more than during all of the 1980s.

Nearly all of the very largest transactions ever recorded have occurred only recently. Figure 3.2 reports on the 25 largest acquisitions in history. It is topped by America Online's $166 billion acquisition of Time Warner, Inc. announced in January 2000, followed by Pfizer's $82 billion acquisition of Warner-Lambert in 1999, and Exxon's $81 billion purchase of Mobil Corp. in 1998.[2]

Number 25 on the list in Figure 3.2 is KKR's acquisition of RJR Nabisco in 1988 for $25 billion. Other than this, however, all other acquisitions on the list have occurred in the past four years: one in 1997, nine in 1998, and seven each in 1999 and 2000. As shown in Figure 3.3, 11 of the largest 25 have involved telecommunications firms, including SBC Communications' 1998 buyout of Ameritech, Vodaphone's 1999 purchase of AirTouch Communications, and AT&T's 1999 acquisition of MediaOne Group. Five involve financial services firms, four energy firms, three manufacturing firms, and two pharmaceutical companies.

HISTORICALLY, IS ANYTHING UNUSUAL IN THE MERGER MARKET?

As discussed by John Pound (1992), the prevalence of corporate governance activities, including acquisitions, historically have fluctuated over time. However, the data indicate that the merger market has been much more active in the past several years than in recent memory. Figure 3.4, for example, displays the number of net acquisition announcements recorded by *MergerStat Review* (2000) during each year from 1980 through 1999. The count shows a notable increase from the early 1980s to a local peak of 3,336 in 1986, and a decrease to a low of 1,877 in 1991. Beginning in 1992, however, the number of acquisition transactions has increased in every year, reaching a high of 9,278 in 1999.

Not just the count, but also the total value of all acquisitions has increased substantially. Figure 3.5 reports the average aggregate transaction values during the 1980–1999 period. The graph shows a local peak of $247 billion in 1998, the year of the RJR Nabisco buyout battle, reaching a low of $71 billion in 1991. Afterward, the aggregate value of merger transactions follows a pattern much like that shown in Figure 3.4. By 1999, the $1,426 billion in total transaction value represents a 5.8-fold increase over the 1988 value, which represents the highest annual amount of the roaring 1980s.

As is evident from Figures 3.4 and 3.5, merger activity is pro-cyclical, peaking in the 1980s and late 1990s, and dropping around the time of the 1990–

Figure 3.1
Transactions of $1 Billion or Greater, 1980–1999

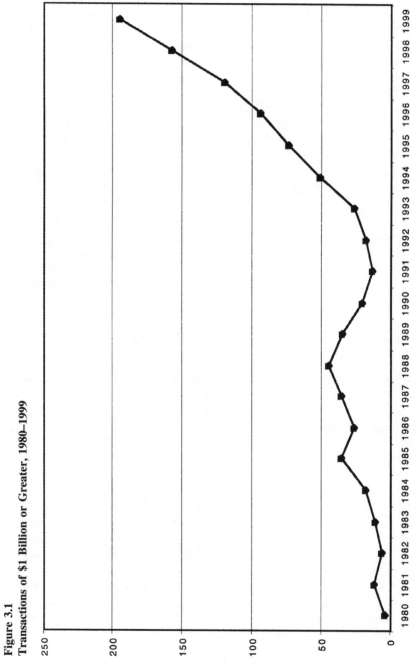

Source: MergerStat, 2000.

Figure 3.2
The 25 Largest Acquisitions in History

Rank	Buyer	Seller	Price Offered* (Millions)	Year Announced
1	America Online Inc.	Time Warner Inc.	$165,937.50	2000
2	Pfizer Inc.	Warner-Lambert Co.	$ 82,399.60	1999
3	Exxon Corp.	Mobil Corp.	$ 81,429.80	1998
4	SBC Communications	Ameritech	$ 75,233.50	1998
5	Vodafone Group	AirTouch Communications	$ 62,768.00	1999
6	British Petroleum	Amoco Corp.	$ 56,482.00	1998
7	AT&T Corp.	MediaOne Group	$ 55,795.40	1999
8	Bell Atlantic Corp.	GTE Corp.	$ 52,845.80	1998
9	AT&T Corp.	Tele-Communications Inc.	$ 52,525.60	1998
10	NationsBank Corp	BankAmerica Corp.	$ 43,158.30	1998
11	WorldCom Inc.	MCI Communications Corp.	$ 42,459.20	1997
12	Deutsche Telekom AG	VoiceStream Wireless Corp.	$ 41,577.27	2000
13	General Electric	Honeywell	$ 40,000.00	2000
14	JDS Uniphase Corp.	SDL Inc.	$ 38,127.56	2000
15	Chase Manhattan Corp.	J. P. Morgan & Co.	$ 36,540.97	2000
16	Travelers Group Inc.	Citicorp	$ 36,031.60	1998
17	Chevron	Texaco	$ 35,100.00	2000
18	Qwest Communications Inc.	US West Inc.	$ 34,748.00	1999
19	Viacom Inc.	CBS Corp.	$ 34,454.00	1999
20	Norwest Corp.	Wells Fargo Co.	$ 31,660.20	1998
21	Daimler Benz AG	Chrysler Corp.	$ 31,156.00	1998
22	CitiGroup Inc.	Associates First Capital Corp.	$ 30,750.68	2000
23	BP Amoco PLC	Atlantic Richfield Co.	$ 26,611.30	1999
24	Monsanto Co.	Pharmacia & Upjohn Inc.	$ 25,760.30	1999
25	Kohlberg Kravis Roberts & Co.	RJR Nabisco Inc.	$ 24,561.60	1988

*Final purchase price may vary from initial estimate.

Figure 3.3
25 Largest Acquisition Announcements, by Industry

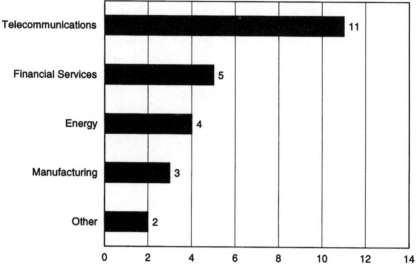

Source: MergerStat, 2000.

1991 recession. To what extent does the recent merger boom merely reflect the strong economy of the latter 1990s? To investigate this issue, in Figure 3.6 we plot the aggregate acquisition value as a percentage of U.S. gross domestic product (GDP) in each year from 1970 through 1999. Throughout the 1970s, a relatively quiet time for merger activity, this percentage was below 2%, rising during the 1980s to a local peak of 4.8% in 1988. After falling to a 1970s-like level of 1.2% in 1991, however, the percentage increased throughout the 1990s, reaching a high of 15.3% in 1999. These data indicate that the recent explosion in merger activity is not due simply to overall economic growth. Rather, it reflects an unusually high number of acquisitions and a high level of acquisition values.

The inference that acquisition values have increased in recent years is further supported by the data in Figure 3.7, which displays the mean and median acquisition values for each year during the 1980–1999 period. Mean acquisition values follow a time path that is similar to those in Figures 3.4, 3.5, and 3.6, peaking in 1988, dropping during the 1990–1992 period, and increasing to very high levels through 1999. In contrast, median transaction values have been relatively flat over the 20-year period.

The discrepancy between the time paths of mean and median transaction values suggests the presence of a growing number of very large mergers in the latter 1990s. Indeed, this is indicated by the data in Figure 3.1. One-billion dollar

Figure 3.4
Number of Acquisition Transactions, 1980–1999

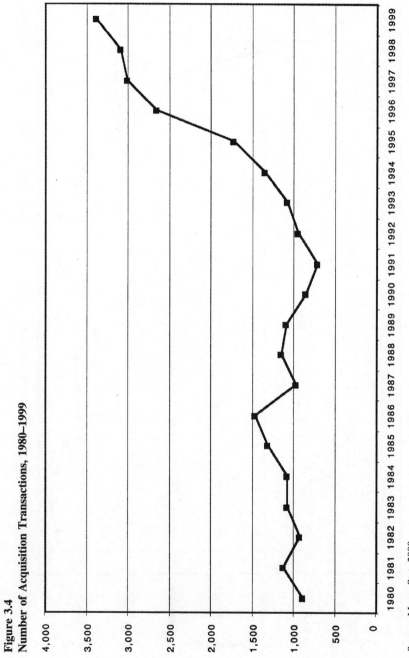

Source: MergerStat, 2000.

Figure 3.5
Aggregate Acquisition Transaction Values, 1980–1999

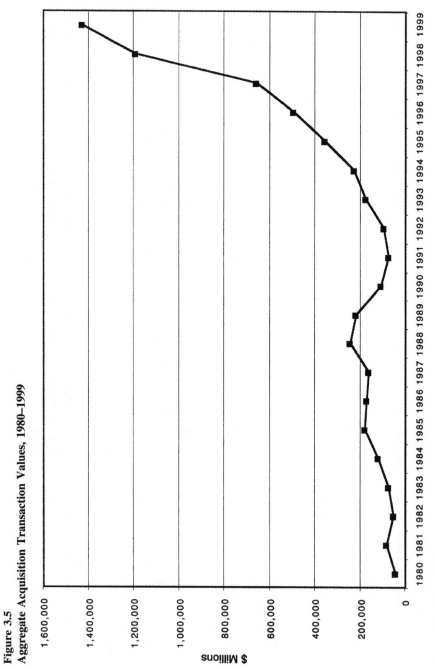

Source: MergerStat, 2000.

Figure 3.6
Aggregate Transaction Value as Percent of GDP, 1970–1999

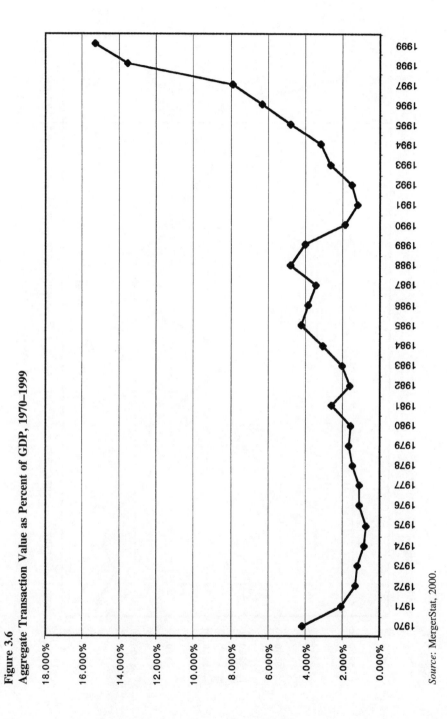

Source: MergerStat, 2000.

Figure 3.7
Average Transaction Values, 1980–1999

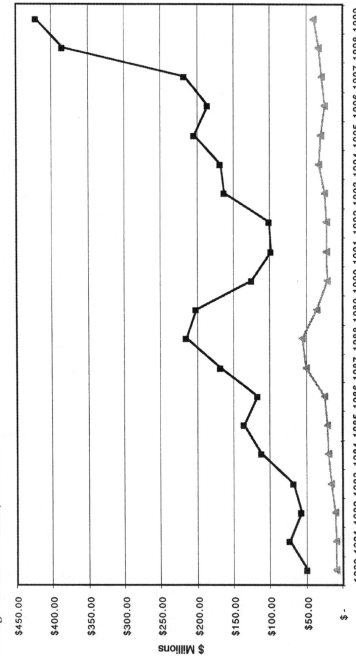

$ Millions

1980 1981 1982 1983 1984 1985 1986 1987 1988 1989 1990 1991 1992 1993 1994 1995 1996 1997 1998 1999

■— Mean ▲···· Median

Source: MergerStat, 2000.

acquisitions, relatively infrequent before the 1990s, have grown in each year since 1991.

In summary, the evidence indicates that the number and size of mergers has increased substantially during the 1990s, especially since 1997. The number of acquisition transactions, their aggregate and mean values, and their aggregate value as a percentage of U.S. GDP all increased substantially during the 1994–1999 period.

OTHER CHARACTERISTICS OF RECENT MERGER ACTIVITY

Figure 3.8 reports the mean and median premiums paid by acquirers in merger transactions from 1990 through 1999. The acquisition premium is defined as the percentage difference between the pre-announcement market value of the selling firm's stock and the amount paid by the acquirer. The data indicate that, although mergers became larger and more frequent during the 1990s, the average premium paid did not change very much. Mean acquisition premiums range from 35 to 45%, while median premiums range from 27 to 35%.[3]

The data in Figure 3.9 indicate that the mean price-earnings ratio paid in acquisitions remained fairly stable from 1990 through 1999, ranging from approximately 20 in 1990 to approximately 25 in the latter part of the decade. In contrast, the price-earnings multiple for Standard & Poor's 500 stocks fluctuated more noticeably. The S&P 500 P/E ratio remained between 15 and 25 until 1998 and reached a decade-long high of 32.6 in 1999. Thus, the market prices of firms fluctuated more relative to earnings than did the prices paid by buyers in merger acquisitions.

A commonly held notion is that their high stock values permitted many firms to use their own stock to acquire other companies during the latter part of the 1990s. The *MergerStat Review* data summarized in Figure 3.10, however, indicate that the proportion of all acquisitions using stock as the payment medium *decreased* during the 1996–1999 period. Thus, for the sample of transactions tracked by *MergerStat Review* (2000), it does not appear that the stock market boom of the 1990s led to an unusual fraction of stock-based merger transactions.

THE HIGH COSTS OF ACQUIRING COMPANIES

Not only have the numbers and sizes of acquisitions increased in recent years, but so, too, have the premiums paid. During the 1990s, the average premium paid for a domestic acquisition was 39.5%. In contrast, from 1986 to 1989, *MergerStat Review* (2000) reports an average annual premium of 30.4%.

Can acquirers afford such high premiums? Apparently not. An acquirer's stock price reaction to an acquisition announcement has always been small, and

Figure 3.8
Acquisition Premiums, 1990–1999

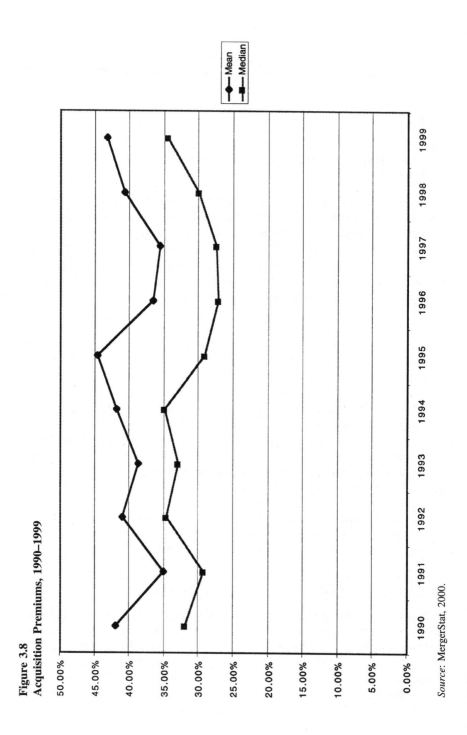

Source: MergerStat, 2000.

Figure 3.9
P/E Ratios—S&P versus Acquisition Prices, 1990–1999

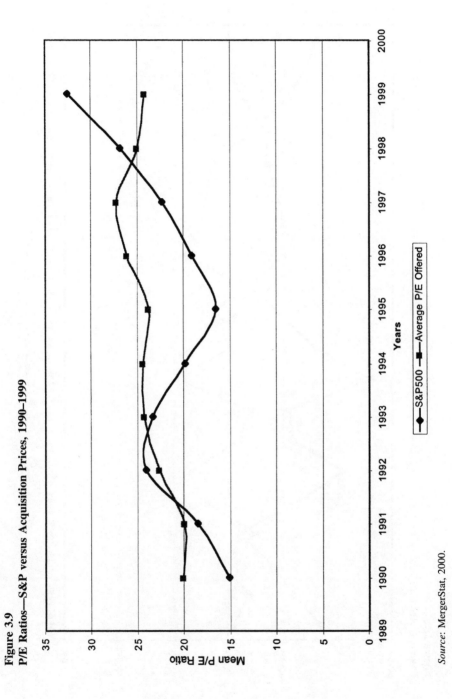

Source: MergerStat, 2000.

Figure 3.10
Payment Medium, 1980–1999

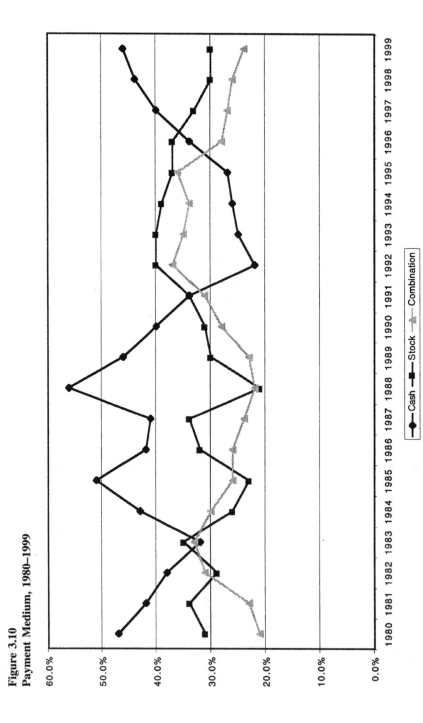

Source: MergerStat, 2000.

Figure 3.11
AOL Stock Price and Trading Volume Surrounding the Time Warner Acquisition Announcement

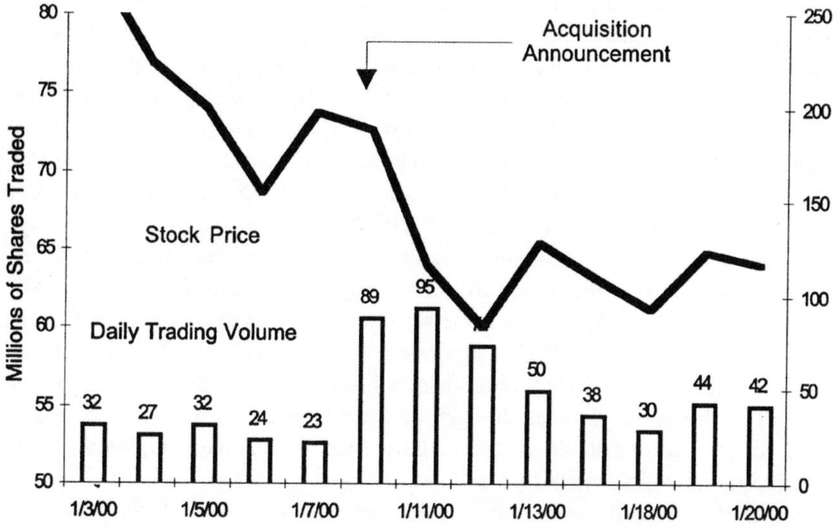

Source: MSN Investor.

anecdotal evidence suggests that recent experiences are no exception. Bradley, Desai, and Kim (1988) report that risk-adjusted excess returns to bidders were a mere 1% in the 1970s and a negative 3% in the 1980s. Acquirers in recent large mergers also have experienced negative announcement period returns. As illustrated in Figure 3.11, for example, the share price of America Online fell $1.125 on the day the firm announced its acquisition of Time Warner. The Nasdaq Index gained 5% on the same day. With more than 1.1 billion shares outstanding, the raw one-day return represents a $1.2 billion loss for AOL's shareholders. The next day's share price drop was even larger, amounting to a $10 billion loss in a single day.

Except for Exxon, which had no change in its share price, all of the acquiring firms in history's five largest acquisitions lost substantial value on the days of their merger announcements. SBC Communications lost $10 billion in market capitalization. While officials from Warner-Lambert were announcing their signed merger agreement with American Home Products for $72 billion, Pfizer announced its own unsolicited bid to acquire control of Warner-Lambert. The $82 billion offer was the largest unsolicited bid ever. Pfizer's announcement prompted heavy trading in its own shares, resulting in an aggregate loss of $5 billion in the aggregate value of Pfizer's stock within one week.[4]

THE GOOD, THE BAD, AND THE UGLY: THREE EXAMPLES

Large target premiums and paltry bidder returns—clearly, investors believe that most large acquisitions tend to be overly expensive for the buying companies. To justify a high takeover premium, the acquirer must significantly improve the target's operating performance or find significant operating synergies following the acquisition. On average, however, such improvements and synergies have been slow to materialize. According to a study by Salomon Smith Barney, the common shares of bidding companies in U.S. mergers worth more than $15 billion underperformed the S&P 500 stock index by 14 percentage points, on average, and underperformed their respective peer groups by 4 percentage points, during the period from their merger date until October 30, 2000.

In January 1999, *Fortune* magazine summarized an analysis by Stern Stewart of six large mergers in 1998. The analysis included AT&T's $52.5 billion problematic acquisition of Telecommunications Inc., and Conseco's $7.1 billion Green Tree Financial disaster. In each of the six cases, the growth required to make the merger profitable to the acquirer was substantially higher than the acquired company's growth history.[5]

One of the acquisitions included in Figure 3.12 is Exxon's 1998 agreement to purchase Mobil Oil at a 34% premium over Mobil's then-current stock price, a premium worth $20 billion. Although smaller in percentage terms than the overall average premium during the late 1980s, the premium was large for a mature oil company. To justify the $20 billion premium, the Stern Stewart valuation formula indicated that Mobil's implied future growth would have to increase from 9.9% to 12.9%. Alternatively, Exxon-Mobil would need to increase the return on capital on its Mobil assets to 17.6% by 2003. According to Stern Stewart, Mobil's *highest* annual return on capital during the five years before the merger had been only 12.2%.

Although the required improvement seems daunting, the Exxon-Mobil merger appears to have proceeded well compared to other mergers. In the summer of 2000, Exxon-Mobil CEO Lee Raymond announced that cost reductions would equal $4.6 billion, 20% higher than the $3.8 billion the company projected in December and 65% higher than the $2.8 billion it originally forecast. Possibly in response to these unexpected gains in efficiency, Exxon shares have increased 17% over the past 18 months.[6]

The merger between AT&T and Tele-Communications, Inc. (TCI) has not gone nearly as well. AT&T paid an $8.7 billion premium for TCI, a cable company. Yet, according to *Fortune*, "it will take AT&T four years and an additional $2 billion to $3 billion or so in expected upgrades to TCI's aging cable infrastructure." The *Wall Street Journal* added,

A hefty $48 billion (later $52.5 billion) sounded like an awful lot to pay for 10 million households, and those are cable households. It would take another $5 billion to upgrade

Figure 3.12
Conseco Stock Price Performance versus the S&P 500 Index Following the Green Tree Acquisition

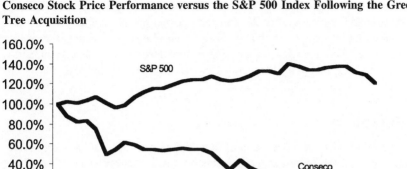

Source: MSN Investor.

the cable network to carry two-way communications, and customers would still have to be sold on switching. Expect more money to fly out the window on loss leaders and discount promotions. Uggh, said shareholders.

Using Stern Stewart data, an AT&T-controlled TCI would need to increase its already extraordinarily high implied perpetual growth rate from 18% to 21% before the deal could start creating value. But there is no evidence that AT&T can produce such growth. To pay for the TCI acquisition, AT&T was forced to double its outstanding debt. Then, with little improvement in earnings or growth, AT&T received intense scrutiny from its creditors and saw its stock value fall 50% since the acquisition. By the end of 2000, AT&T announced it would split into four separately traded entities, in effect unwinding its cable acquisitions altogether.

AT&T's problems pale in comparison to the misery Conseco's investors have been forced to endure. On April 8, 1998, Conseco agreed to purchase Green Tree Financial for $7.1 billion. That day, Conseco shares dropped $8.625, or 15%. The deal would eventually be completed at an 86% premium over Green Tree's pre-announcement share price. Using the Stern-Stewart valuation formula, Green Tree's future perpetual growth rate would have to change from 0% to nearly 10% to allow Conseco to break even on the acquisition.

Over the next two years, Conseco continuously fulfilled the market's worst expectations. Within three months of the acquisition, Conseco announced it was "taking a larger-than-anticipated $350 million after-tax charge to address a surprisingly high level of loan prepayments by customers of its newly acquired lender, Green Tree Financial." Conseco, whose market value once topped $20 billion, saw its stock steadily drop to 10% of its pre-acquisition price (see Figure

3.12). Eventually, major shareholders could no longer stomach the losses. Two years after the acquisition, executives of Thomas H. Lee Partners took the reins of the troubled company after the company posted dismal quarterly results and its founder/CEO resigned under pressure. "The Green Tree acquisition was a disaster," said Tom Goggins, co-manager of John Hancock's Financial Industries Fund, explaining that Wall Street felt Conseco overpaid in the deal.

CONCLUSIONS

The 1990s saw the annoncement of more and larger mergers than ever before. In fact, most of the largest mergers in history have occurred since 1997. These transactions have concentrated among telecommunications, financial services, and energy-related firms, reflecting the large structural changes recently experienced by these industries. Like many mergers from previous decades, however, anecdotal evidence indicates that the gains from recent large takeovers accrue primarily to the shareholders of the acquired companies. Takeover premiums have increased from their levels in the 1980s. Yet, in general, acquiring companies appear to be unable to realize the operating improvements and synergies that would be required to make these large acquisitions profitable.

NOTES

1. For a description of the types, numbers, and effects of state anti-takeover laws during the 1980s, see Karpoff and Malatesta (1989). For a description of the types and frequencies of takeover defenses adopted by many firms, see Danielson and Karpoff (1998).

2. In what would have qualified as the second largest transaction in history, MCI WorldCom announced an agreement to acquire Sprint Corp. in 1999 for $116 billion. The merger ran into antitrust objections in both Europe and the United States, however, and has not been completed.

3. *MergerStat Review* (2000) defines the premium as the percentage difference between the offered price and the selling firm's market price five business days before the initial announcement of the acquisition. These summary numbers are based on a subset of all acquisitions, for which MergerStat had price information.

4. During the week before the announcement, Pfizer's trading volume averaged 7.5 million shares. On the day of the acquisition announcement, 45 million shares were traded. Trading remained higher than normal through the end of the week.

5. The valuation formula used to derive this conclusion was obtained from Stern Stewart, and consists of a slight variation of the following constant growth perpetuity formula,

$$\text{Firm Value} = \frac{\text{EBIT}\,(1 - T)\left(1 - \dfrac{\text{Growth}}{\text{ROI}}\right)}{\text{WACC} - \text{Growth}}$$

The five inputs to the model are earnings before interest and taxes (EBIT), the tax rate (T), growth, return on invested capital (ROI), and the weighted average cost of capital (WACC).

6. During 1999 and 2000, crude oil prices rose from $7 a barrel to more than $30 a barrel. This rise might account for Exxon's success in the stock market. *Source*: Berry Petroleum.

REFERENCES

Bailey, Jeff. (1998). "Conseco Agrees to Acquire Green Tree—Exchange of Stock Valued at About $6.44 Billion; Cross-Selling Plays Role." *Wall Street Journal*, April 8, p. A2.

Blumenstein, Rebecca, Steven Lipin, and Nicole Harris. (1999) "Investors Greet MCI-Sprint Deal Coolly—Firms' Stock Prices Decline on Fears about Delays Linked to Regulators." *Wall Street Journal*, October 6, p. A3.

Bradley, M., A. S. Desai, and E. H. Kim. (1991). "Synergistic Gains from Corporate Acquisitions and Their Division between the Stockholders of Target and Acquiring Firms." *Journal of Financial Economics*, 21 (1988), pp. 3–40. Reprinted in *Empirical Research in Capital Markets*, A. W. Schwert and C. W. Smith, eds. New York: McGraw-Hill.

Danielson, Morris G., and Jonathan M. Karpoff. (1998). "On the Uses of Corporate Governance Provisions." *Journal of Corporate Finance*, 4, no. 4, pp. 347–371.

Karpoff, Jonathan M., and Paul H. Malatesta. (December 1989). "The Wealth Effects of Second Generation State Takeover Legislation." *Journal of Financial Economics*, 25, no. 2, pp. 291–322.

Lipin, Steven, and Nikhil Deogun. (2000). "Big Mergers of '90s Prove Disappointing to Shareholders." *Wall Street Journal*, October 30, p. C1.

Lipin, Steven, Robert Langreth, Gardiner Harris, and Nikhil Deogun. (1999). "In Biggest Hostile Bid, Pfizer Offers $80 Billion for Warner-Lambert." *Wall Street Journal*, November 5, p. A1.

Lohse, Deborah. (1998). "Conseco's Charge Tied to Green Tree Merger Elicits Differing Views from Firm, Analyst." *Wall Street Journal*, July 15, p. C2.

MergerStat, (2000). *MergerStat Review*. Los Angeles: MergerStat.

Pound, John. (Spring 1992). "Raiders, Targets, and Politics: The History and Future of American Corporate Control." *Journal of Applied Corporate Finance*, pp. 6–18.

Raghavan, Anita, Steven Lipin, and John J. Keller. (1998). "Growing Up: SBC Communications to Acquire Ameritech in a $55 Billion Deal—And Then There Were Four." *Wall Street Journal*, May 11, p. A1.

Solomon, Deborah. (2000). "AT&T Plans Big Asset Sales to Cut Debt—Phone Giant Faces Scrutiny from Ratings Concerns over $62 Billion Load." *Wall Street Journal*, November 8, p. A3.

Tully, Shawn, and Eileen P. Gunn. (1999). "Premium Priced—The Monster Mergers of 1998 Claim to Have Big Synergy and Great Strategic Fit. Maybe So. But at the Prices Acquirers Are Paying, Most Deals Still Won't Work." *Fortune*, January 11, 139, no. 1, p. 9.

Weber, Thomas E., Martin Peers, and Nick Wingfield. (2000). "You've Got Time Warner! Two Titans in a Strategic Bind Bet on a Futuristic Megadeal." *Wall Street Journal*, January 11, p. B1.

Chapter 4

Big Bank Mergers in the United States: Motivations, Effects, and Likely Competitive Consequences

Bernard Shull and Gerald A. Hanweck

INTRODUCTION

The deregulation movement in banking has been a victory for the competitive ideal over centuries-old governmental restraints aimed at protecting banks against failure. At the same time, a massive bank merger movement, characterized by megamergers, has materialized over the last two decades in the United States. Megamergers have already gone a long way toward eliminating potential rivals and reshaping the banking and financial system. Passage of the Gramm-Leach-Bliley Act in November 1999, facilitating the combination of banks, insurance companies, and securities firms, is likely to further increase the size and scope of the largest organizations.

Structural reorganization encompasses potentially conflicting developments, some of which are pro- and others which are anticompetitive. Devising appropriate competition policy for the post-deregulation era requires an understanding of both the causes and likely consequences of these changes.

The first section of this chapter briefly describes the scope of the merger movement in the United States. Other sections review causes and empirical evidence on plausible bank motives. The chapter also outlines a model incorporating key structural changes resulting from megamergers and evaluates its implications for competition.

The reorganization can be traced to macroeconomic conditions and institutional changes, as well as to incentives confronting individual institutions. Analysis, based on a modified dynamic limit-pricing model, suggests that combinations of large banks are in the process of changing the competitive relationship between large banking organizations and their smaller competitors. Although empirical testing is needed, some validity can be found in the model's predictions that throw light on a number of puzzling research findings. It may therefore be possible that the irreversible structural changes now underway will have significant adverse effects on competition and on bank customer welfare.

SCOPE OF THE MERGER MOVEMENT AND STRUCTURAL CONSEQUENCES

Between 1980 and 1998, about 7,400 independent commercial banking organizations merged. From 1987 through 1998, there were over 200 mergers in which each of the merging partners held over $1 billion in assets.[1] Since 1991, there have been about 30 so-called megamergers in which each of the partners had $10 billion or more in assets; the total volume of assets acquired in these mergers was over a trillion dollars.[2] Principally as a result of mergers, the number of commercial banking organizations in the United States has declined enormously, from about 12,300 in 1980 to under 7,000 in 1998.[3]

The decline in numbers might be expected to have an impact on the relative size of the banking organizations in local geographic markets. On average, however, concentration in local markets has hardly changed at all. In 1980, the three-bank concentration ratio for Metropolitan Statistical Areas (MSAs) averaged 66.4% and in 1998, 65.8%. In rural (non-MSA) markets, the three-bank ratio averaged 89.6% in 1980 and 88.0% in 1998. A similar stability is reflected in the Herfindahl-Hirschman Index (HHI) for the period.[4]

Nevertheless, when the influence of changing numbers of savings institutions is taken into consideration, average local market concentration shows a substantial increase, albeit from a lower level. Including thrifts, with their deposits weighted at 50%, the average HHI for MSAs increased between 1985 and 1998 from 1,373 to 1,666, with increases in concentration in more than three times as many MSAs as had decreases.

The impact of mergers on future levels of local market concentration remains uncertain in part because the geographic extent of local markets may be changing. At least one study has found that branch banking organizations tend to ignore differences in demand in local markets and to set uniform prices for retail deposit services throughout states or regions.[5] However, the prices of smaller banks in local areas have not converged with these uniform levels.[6]

The trend of aggregate concentration at the national level is, on the other hand, clear. Megamergers, in particular, have increased aggregate concentration substantially, and still higher levels are in prospect. The share of the largest 10 banking organizations increased from 18.6% in 1980 to about 30% in 1998.

Given these changes, the general outlines of the future structure of banking in the United States have become fairly clear. In a decade or so, it is reasonable to expect the existence of a small number of very large multinational organizations, perhaps 5 or 10, that are present in most urban areas, along with a large number of relatively small, local community, or regional institutions. These large organizations will be the product not only of domestic mergers but also of international combinations, such as the acquisition of Bankers Trust by Deutsche Bank. They are likely to include large insurance and/or securities firms, under the terms of the Gramm-Leech-Bliley Act, such as the 1998 Citicorp-Travelers merger. They will almost certainly have a dominant share of the banking and related financial business in many of the local areas in which they operate. As a result of their widespread operations, the number of separate geographic and product markets in which these large organizations meet as rivals will have increased substantially.[7] The number of smaller "fringe" banks in local and regional areas will depend on the size of the "niche markets" they occupy; the relative cost structures of large banking organizations and their smaller rivals; and the strategic pricing arrangements that develop.

CAUSES AND MOTIVES

A number of plausible reasons may be cited for the bank merger movement in the United States and for large bank mergers in particular. It's convenient to separate them as follows: (1) macroeconomic conditions; (2) changes in law, regulation, and policy; and (3) bank-specific incentives. In the 1980s and the 1990s, both good and bad economic conditions, in distinctive ways, have provided the environment conducive to mergers. Deregulation and bank merger policy have been enabling factors. Within the environment so established, a number of bank-specific motives for merger are credible, though their quantitative significance is not easily determined.

Macroeconomic Conditions

The bank merger movement in the United States has occurred in at least two stages. The first was during the 1980s, when many banks experienced large loan losses and poor profits associated with a depressed economy and excessive risk-taking. Many were severely injured by loan losses associated with crises in farming, the real estate and energy sectors, and debt problems in developing countries. As bank failures rose to high levels, so did mergers. At the time, only the better capitalized and profitable banking organizations were in a position to make substantial acquisitions. With the support of the FDIC, they found themselves able to acquire strategically important, though weakened, banks at low cost and risk. Most of the mergers from 1979 to 1992 were the result of failing banks merging with healthier banks.

Commercial bank loan losses and nonperforming loans reached a peak in 1991 and then began to subside. Beginning in about 1993, bank profitability improved dramatically and remained at high levels through the rest of the decade. Better times meant fewer mergers due to failure, but more mergers attributable to the ensuing expansion and stock market boom. Increased profits and market values of large banking organizations after 1991 made possible stock swap-based mergers that were comfortable for the acquirer and highly rewarding to the acquired.[8]

Changes in Law, Regulation, and Policy

Branch banking restrictions in the United States, governed by state and federal law, emerged in the early nineteenth century. Narrow definitions of banking powers were written into the earliest bank charters, beginning in the late eighteenth century. Over the years, both branching and activity restrictions were periodically modified by Congress and by state law, but significant limits were sustained and periodically bolstered—until the last two decades when the movement to deregulate not only attacked the anticompetitive restrictions imposed in the Great Depression of the 1930s but removed the older branching and activity constraints. The Riegle-Neal Interstate Banking and Branching Efficiency Act of 1994 and the Gramm-Leach-Bliley Financial Modernization Act of 1999 are *fin de siècle* legislation that have created opportunities for enormous combinations.

Liberalization of Multiple Office Banking Restrictions

By the end of the 1980s, most states had liberalized their intrastate restrictions on branching; and many were permitting out-of-state banking organizations to acquire or merge with banking companies in their own states. Passage of the Riegle-Neal Act effectively eliminated most of the McFadden Act constraints on interstate expansion, overrode the reciprocal banking provisions of 30 state laws, and permitted bank holding companies to acquire banks in any state, to convert their banks to branches of an interstate bank, and to establish new interstate branches in accordance with state law.

Relaxation of Activity Restrictions

In the 1980s, the FDIC recognized that Glass-Steagall Act restrictions did not apply to the "state-chartered, nonmember insured" banks that the FDIC supervised. By the early 1990s, roughly half the states had authorized affiliates of these typically smaller banks to deal in securities beyond the limits established by Federal law and regulation.[9] In a parallel relaxation of restraints on large commercial banking organizations in the late 1980s, the Federal Reserve Board interpreted Section 20 of the Glass-Steagall Act and Section 4(c)(8) of the Bank Holding Company Act to permit bank holding companies to establish subsidiaries to deal in and underwrite, within limits, a wide variety of so-called ineligible equity and debt securities. These regulatory changes culminated with passage of the Gramm-Leach-Bliley Act in November 1999. The Act repealed or overrode sections of the Glass-Steagall and Bank Holding Company Acts to permit affiliations among commercial banks, securities firms, and insurance companies through newly established "financial holding companies" and "financial subsidiaries."[10]

Revisions to Merger Policy

The existing framework for bank merger policy developed in the 1960s through passage of the Bank Merger Act, by the Supreme Court's decision in the *Philadelphia-Girard Trust* merger case, and by amendments to both the Bank Merger Act and Bank Holding Company Act in 1966. These developments made antitrust standards applicable to bank mergers and gave each federal banking agency prior approval authority, in accordance with the regulatory status of the resulting institution. It required the agencies to deny mergers that violated Section 2 of the Sherman Act, and also Section 7 of the Clayton Act, unless "the anticompetitive effects of the proposed transaction are clearly outweighed in the public interest on the probable effect . . . in meeting the convenience and needs of the community." The agencies were also permitted to take into consideration the "financial and managerial resources and future prospects of the existing and proposed institutions." The Justice Department was given authority to challenge merger approvals by entering suit within 30 days and thereby obtaining an automatic injunction.

The format established by the Supreme Court and Congress established a new kind of bank merger policy in accordance with the structure-performance paradigm that was well established in economics. Following this format, the federal banking agencies periodically denied merger applications, and the Justice Department successfully challenged some approvals. The policy implemented in the 1960s and 1970s effectively precluded horizontal bank mergers among large banks in metropolitan areas.

Policy modifications in the 1980s, however, provided a basis for a less restrictive merger policy. In 1982, the Justice Department overhauled its *Horizontal Merger Guidelines*. The Court, in its *Philadelphia* decision, seemed to have established not only limited geographic and product markets in banking, but also determinative concentration thresholds within the markets so defined. The revised *Guidelines* outlined a more flexible economic analysis for the determination of a geographic and product market that allowed for larger geographic areas and permitted nonbanks to be considered in calculating concentration. It adopted the Hirfindahl-Hirschman Index (HHI) as a more refined measure of concentration, and it established several thresholds based on the HHI that would determine Justice Department reaction to merger proposals. But the *Guidelines* made clear that levels and changes in the HHI were not the only relevant factors. Rather, they were to be viewed as a "screen" for a more thorough examination of proposed mergers. If a merger exceeded the thresholds established, other factors could be considered, including the size distribution of firms, potential competition, and efficiency effects, among others. The *Guidelines* thereby introduced a set of "mitigating factors" that permitted approvals for mergers that exceeded the Department's concentration thresholds. A later development effectively precluded large bank merger denials, even when mitigating factors were insufficient to offset increases in concentration. In the late 1980s and early 1990s, first the Federal Reserve and then the Justice Department began to negotiate divestitures with merger applicants whose proposals would otherwise be denied. Since the advent of negotiated divestitures, the federal banking agencies have denied only a handful of proposals on competitive grounds, and all of these have involved small banks in rural areas.

Bank-Specific Motives

Given economic conditions, deregulation, and merger policy revisions, banks may have multiple and related motives for mergers. Motives may emanate from increasingly intense competition, perceived opportunities to make use of new information technology, increased managerial compensation, and the attainment or retention of regulatory protection against failure.

Competition and Profits

In public announcements and in large bank merger applications, bank officials typically state that their proposals are a response to increased competition and threats to profits from even larger organizations throughout the world. The benefits of such acquisitions might be traced to one or more of the following factors: (1) reduced costs through growth to larger size; (2) provision of additional services; (3) exploitation of new profit opportunities through restructuring less efficient institutions; (4) protection against one or more kinds of operating risk, for example, by diversifying sources of income; as mentioned, (5) protection against unwanted acquisition by larger organizations; and (6) elimination of an actual or potential competitor.

Banks that decide to be acquired may perceive themselves as vulnerable, perhaps because of their size, inadequate management, and/or insufficient profitability. Unable to make acquisitions to eliminate their problems, they find that the acquisition price is right.

Advances in Technology and the Impact on Costs

Advances in the microcomputer and information technologies may have contributed to the merger wave both by increasing competition and by the promise of cost savings. Reductions in cost have permitted the development of new kinds of financial instruments and modes of transactions, including automated teller machines (ATMs), credit cards, debit cards, money market mutual funds, mortgage-backed securities, and complex derivative instruments[11] (Huertas, 1987, p. 143).[12] The new technology has facilitated electronic banking and brokerage relationships through desktop computers and high-speed networks, and facilitated the growth of global financial markets. Declines in cost of processing and communicating information have helped break down entry barriers and increase competition in traditional bank deposit and loan markets. A wider range of institutional and market options have become available to bank depositors. Related developments promise cost savings in maintaining far-flung branches and operating centralized call centers.[13]

Nevertheless, the apparent technological imperative underlying mergers raises questions. With the dramatic decline in the cost of computing and network systems, why are massive resources now required to adopt the latest technologies? It would seem that if substantial resources are required to effectively utilize the technological advances available, then economies of scale must be substantial, and banking must be a declining cost industry. If so, such economies should be observable. To date, they have not been.

Diversification and Risk

Every major banking crisis in the twentieth century produced proposals to liberalize branching restrictions for the purpose of reducing bank risk. It is possible that some bank mergers may be driven by a desire for greater diversification. But the plausibility of diversification as a motive for large bank mergers is, at best, moot. In the modern global economy, large banks have offices throughout the world and have been relatively unrestricted in entering new product markets. Since passage of the Gramm-Leach-Bliley and Riegle-Neal Acts, there is little to restrict diversification in the United States, even without merger.[14]

Managerial Compensation

Managerial salaries are directly related to organizational size. The federal banking agencies, in the course of their bank examinations, scrutinize senior officers' compensation for excessive amounts. Greater compensation at larger organizations has been generally accepted by the agencies as consistent with "safety and soundness."

Too-Big-to-Fail

The banking reforms implemented in the early 1930s were aimed at preventing a recurrence of the massive failures of the Great Depression by restricting competition, constraining risky activities, and establishing federal deposit insurance. In the following three decades, relatively few banks failed each year; by the 1950s, typically only those that suffered from insider abuse failed. All banks were viewed as too important to fail.

Beginning in the 1980s, however, the federal banking agencies made clear that very large banks in trouble would be dealt with differently. Over the last two decades, through financial support and/or by disregarding loan and other asset losses, they have sustained a number of the largest banks, at or near insolvency.[15]

With the realization that the benefits of competition outweighed the potential costs, and the experience of costly regulatory support of failing S&Ls in the 1980s, Congress now views the possible failure of most banks as a "normal" market event that should not require special regulatory intervention. Passage of the FDIC Improvement Act in 1991 (FDICIA) clarified congressional intent that government support for failing banks should be an exceptional event. An exceptional event would be the pending failure of one or more very large banking organizations that would constitute a "systemic threat."[16]

FDICIA thus made clear that the managers, owners, and uninsured creditors of most banks will not be protected from failure, as they previously had. The FDIC is now required to resolve failed banks by the method *least costly* to the insurance fund, precluding the kind of purchase and assumption deals that had protected all depositors in the past. On the other hand, it provided the federal banking agencies with authority, subject to approval by the executive branch, to protect all creditors and stockholders of very large failing banks. In effect, FDICIA codified the too-big-to-fail policy. The most recent evidence that a too-big-to-fail policy remains in effect, and the underlying logic of large size that compels it, can be found in the organization of a loan syndicate for Long-Term Capital Management by the Federal Reserve, presumably to protect, not only financial markets, but also large banking organizations exposed to its possible default.[17]

The continued existence of a too-big-to-fail policy implies an incentive for megamergers either to achieve or sustain a too-big-to-fail status. There is some irony in the willingness of the federal banking agencies to approve megamergers without considering the systemic threats that they pose. When mergers increase market concentration substantially, they do consider mitigating factors, but they do not consider aggravating factors.

EMPIRICAL STUDIES OF BANK MOTIVES AND MERGER EFFECTS

A number of empirical studies have sought to determine the relative significance of bank-specific motives for merger. Such studies typically begin with the conventional economic assumption that mergers are intended to increase net benefits to the acquiring organization's shareholders and/or management by enhancing profits and/or shareholder value and/or management earnings. Higher profits, market value, and management compensation may be derived from decreased costs or increased revenues or, as noted, growth to larger size. The typical approach has been to make inferences from the economic and financial condition of merging organizations before they combine (*ex ante*) and from the condition of resulting organizations after merger (*ex post*). If merging banks, *ex ante*, were too small to reach efficient size, it then might be inferred that their mergers were motivated by the aim to realize economies of scale. If merging banks were differentially specialized, it might be inferred that the merger motive was to expand the range of services offered to achieve better diversification and perhaps economies of scope. If it is determined, *ex post*, that banks have experienced reductions in cost, it might be inferred that the intent was to realize economies of scale or scope and/or greater diversification. If revenues increased, it might be inferred that the intent was to exploit new profit opportunities.

Such studies do shed light on merger consequences but raise more questions on causes. So, for example, in a recent review, Berger, Demsetz, and Strahan concluded that the acquisition of seemingly "inefficient" banks in the 1980s and early 1990s suggest efforts to restructure inefficient banks, thus exploiting profit opportunities. During this period, however, many of the banks in financial distress (more than 2,000 were merged or failed) were in local markets that were experiencing economic recession. Once economic conditions improved, loan losses at the surviving banks in these locations declined, and profitability increased *without change in management.* Were the banks with low profitability that were acquired during this period really "inefficient?" Or were they only temporally impacted by local conditions. Should their acquisition be viewed as efficient banks acquiring less efficient institutions to restructure them, or simply a fire sale motivated by acquiring bank recognition of their long-term franchise value?[18]

Berger et al. found little to support improved cost efficiency as a rationale for mergers, particularly megamergers. They did find evidence that acquiring target banks can provide a significant competitive advantage by increasing market share substantially. They concluded:

The evidence is consistent with increases in market power from some types of consolidation; improvements in profit efficiency and diversification risks [*sic, geographic primarily*], but little cost efficiency improvement on average; relatively little effect on the availability of services to small customers; potential improvements in payments system efficiency; and, potential costs on the financial system from increasing systemic risk or expanding the financial safety net.[19]

So far, then, there is little indication that mergers, on average, achieve lower costs as a result of greater scale, permanent increases in value, or greater cost efficiencies. There is some evidence that large bank mergers lead to greater profit efficiency, possibly emanating from a variety of sources, including asset reallocations, increased market power, and higher prices for retail banking services. Greater bank size does tend to enhance compensation for senior management and directors and to establish or augment a bank's status as "too-big-to-fail."

A problem posed by these results lies in making inferences from findings that are consistent with multiple motives. For example, the same pre-merger conditions that permit an inference that acquiring banks are exploiting profit opportunities by restructuring relatively inefficient banks are consistent with a motive to gain market share, eliminate competitors, and raise management compensation. The same post-merger conditions that permit an inference that the intent of acquiring banks is to reduce costs by reducing risk through diversification and making more efficient use of capital, are consistent with an intent to reduce risk by diminishing competition and/or establishing a status as "too-big-to-fail." Inferences from post-merger findings also raise the possibility that actual motivation may differ from results; that is, interpretation is confounded by the pervasive affliction of "unintended consequences."

The analysis might be rescued from ambiguity if it were viewed as testing independently established motivational hypotheses. So, for example, the cost-reduction projections made by merging banks might be taken as such an hypothesis. In a recent paper, Stephen Rhoades tested a pre-merger motivational hypothesis by examining post-merger results.[20] He examined nine mergers that occurred in the early 1990s. Each was considered a good candidate for improved efficiency, and each involved large banks with substantial market overlap. In all cases, pre-merger projections developed by the merger partners indicated that the combinations would produce substantial reductions in cost. In evaluating these mergers, Rhoades distinguished between cost-cutting by, for example, reducing the numbers of employees, and improvements in cost efficiency (i.e., lower ratios of costs to assets or revenues). He found that all of the mergers resulted in cost-cutting but that only four of the nine were successful in improving cost efficiency.

Even the findings of such studies can be questioned on the grounds that it is not clear that the cost-reduction projections of merging banks can be accepted as an independently established motivational hypothesis. It is difficult to know whether such projections are actual motives for merger or are simply motivated by a need to obtain approval for a merger from a federal banking agency that accepts cost reduction as a mitigating factor. Eliminating competitors, increasing management compensation, and becoming "too-big-to-fail" are not mitigating factors. We should never expect bank officials to mention them in merger applications or in public.

The standard economic assumption that mergers aim to increase profit or market value cannot, then, distinguish among the several distinct motivational objectives for reaching this goal or determine their relative importance. The empirical results of recent investigations are consistent with multiple motivations. It is plausible, in fact, that multiple motives for acquisitions are common and that banks simultaneously aim to reduce costs, eliminate or diminish competitors, achieve higher rewards for management, defend against being acquired, and establish or fortify "too-big-to-fail" status. Although the results of this line of investigation are modest, at bottom, the motivations for merger are less important than their results.

STRUCTURAL IMPLICATIONS FOR BEHAVIOR AND PERFORMANCE

In comparison with causes, it is relatively easy to determine the effect of mergers on bank market structure and on the relative sizes of banks. As noted above, there has been little change in local market concentration, but aggregate concentration at the national level has increased substantially.

For many years, aggregate concentration was a matter of serious concern to legislators and others, even though the proportion of assets or deposits controlled by the largest banks in the nation had no clear economic significance. Concern about aggregate concentration partially explains the long-existing restrictions on branch banking in the United States. The effects on aggregate concentration were focal points in public debates on almost all important banking legislation in the twentieth century, including the Federal Reserve Act of 1913, the Banking Act of 1933, the Bank Holding Company Act of 1956, the Bank Merger Act of 1960, Amendments to the Bank Holding Company Act of 1970, and the Riegle-Neal Interstate Banking and Branching Efficiency Act of 1994.

The integration of antitrust laws and bank merger policy in the early 1960s altered the focus of policy from aggregate concentration to concentration in geographic areas that could be identified as economic markets-at-risk, that is, local areas[21] (Berger and Hannan, 1989, p. 24;[22] Horvitz and Shull, 1964[23]). Serious concerns about aggregate concentration, unrelated to identifiable markets, were thereafter relegated largely to the trash bin of historical curiosities.[24] Today, economic concerns about aggregate concentration are rarely, if ever, articulated in a coherent manner.[25]

Aggregate concentration per se has no economic significance within the structure-performance paradigm that has dominated bank merger policy since the 1960s. Nevertheless, it is possible that megamergers resulting in increased aggregate concentration may affect competition in local markets, independently of changes in the number of banks and concentration in these markets. It may be a reasonable proxy for changes in intermarket structures that affect local market competition. The intermarket changes that merit attention include the emergence of a handful of large banking organizations likely to confront one another in an increasing number of separate geographic and product markets, local banking markets in which one or a few of these large, multimarket banks dominate, and a too-big-to-fail policy that differentiates these dominant organizations from their smaller rivals.

Dominant Firms and Limit Pricing in Banking

Markets characterized by one or a few large firms and a group of fringe firms suggest the relevance of a dominant firm limit-pricing model.[26] Such models analyze the pricing strategy of a dominant firm that must consider the effects of entry and expansion of fringe firms on its profits. The standard (Gaskin's) model indicates that dominant firms with cost advantages and lower rates of discount can retain, and even gain, market share while setting prices to limit entry and/or to drive out smaller rivals.[27] It also indicates that dominant firms face a tradeoff between market share and their discounted future profits, with a determinant optimal maximum market share of less than 100%.

The model implies, among other things, that

1. The market share of the dominant firm will be larger the greater its cost advantage, the lower its cost of capital, and the greater the response rate of new entrants.
2. The optimal price trajectory for the dominant firm will be higher the greater the cost of capital, the greater its average cost, the lesser the initial period fringe output, and the lower the entry-limiting price. With a cost advantage, a lower limit price implies a short-run optimal price that will drive out relatively inefficient fringe firms and increase the long-run market share of the dominant firm.

These results hold in both markets that are growing and markets that are not. The principal distinction is that growing markets are the more profitable for dominant firms, permitting them to maintain a constant market share without a significant cost advantage, and with a higher long-run price above the entry-limiting price.

Regulatory Forbearance

The existence of a too-big-to-fail policy (regulatory forbearance) manifests itself in the ability of large banking organizations to acquire funds at lower costs than other banks. There is empirical evidence that such cost advantages exist.[28] Dominant firms with cost advantages and lower rates of discount can retain, and even gain, market share while setting prices to limit entry and/or to drive out smaller, higher cost rivals. In banking, a too-big-to-fail status constitutes a strategic advantage, comparable to a technological advantage, that augments a dominant market position.

Mutual Forbearance

The pricing model discussed above is confined to a single market. It can be extended to incorporate multimarket linkages among the largest banking organizations, that is, to circumstances in which dominant firms engage in many separate markets, facing a small group of similarly positioned firms ("global rivals"), as well as a competitive fringe ("local rivals"). Assuming all "global rivals" set their prices to maximize the value of their firms in all local markets in which they operate, have similar operating and capital costs, and pursue a "follow the leader" strategy in markets in which they do not dominate, those operating in markets in which they are not dominant will follow the dominant firm's price leadership.

In banking, experience indicates that large organizations do not enter new local markets *de novo* or by small acquisition; rather, they enter by large acquisition. A value-maximizing basis for large organizations to have a large-scale presence can be inferred. If such firms do not face significant cost disadvantages compared to a dominant firm in a local market, then, entry *de novo* at large scale would drive prices below the limit price and possibly close to marginal cost. Mutual forbearance among multimarket banks would involve recognition of this likelihood and would compel entry into new markets by large acquisition. The entry of "global rivals" into local markets by large acquisition and the prospect of mutual forbearance will tend to keep the dominant firms' market share from eroding over time.

Predictions and Recent Evidence

The pricing model, modified by regulatory and mutual forbearance, predicts certain competitive characteristics of retail banking markets and suggests testable hypotheses. Among the predictions are the following:

1. Dominant firms with a funding cost advantage will be able to sustain a substantial market share.

2. With dominant-firm optimal strategy resulting in prices above the limit price, *de novo* entry by small firms will occur.

3. Because the optimal strategy for small firms, below efficient size, is to attract customers and grow, their prices are likely to be lower than those of the dominant firm.

4. In the course of the structural transition now occurring, the negative relationship between local market concentration and prices, often found in earlier cross-section studies, will tend to diminish in significance because of omitted structural variables. Some markets will be characterized by dominant-firm pricing, while others will not. Among the markets characterized by dominant-firm pricing, some will be characterized by mutual forbearance, and others not.

A number of these predictions are consistent with recent research findings:

1. As noted, on average, local market concentration has been relatively stable in the face of rising aggregate concentration. Moreover, a recent study by Pilloff and Rhoades of market-share changes in about 940 MSA and non-MSA counties for the period 1990–1996 found that large, geographically diversified banking organizations did not, in general, increase their market share. The authors interpret this finding as indicating that smaller banks can compete effectively with larger organizations. However, the finding is also consistent with the model's prediction that dominant firms can establish relatively high prices without substantial loss of market share.[29]

2. There has been a substantial increase in *de novo* entry in recent years; and an indication that mergers and acquisitions increase the likelihood of *de novo* entry.[30]

3. While survey reports, noted above, indicate that large banks have posted uniform prices across local areas for a number of retail banking services, pricing by smaller banks in local areas has not converged with these uniform levels. Relatively high prices at large, multistate banking organizations are consistent with the expectation of higher prices for dominant firms, and mutual forbearance.

4. Recent cross-sectional statistical analysis suggests a disappearing positive relationship between local area concentration and deposit prices.[31] At the same time, at least two studies have found that mergers that increase local market concentration also lower deposit rates of interest.[32]

These findings are consistent with the model's implications that intermarket structures will affect local market competition independently of local market structure. However, when the price effects of mergers are directly observed, a positive relationship between increased concentration and prices has been found. Under direct observation, the omitted variables will not be critical. If mergers in a local area have created a dominant firm, concentration will increase and a price increase (above the limit price) will be expected. If mergers have augmented a dominant firm, again concentration will increase and the elimination of an important rival is likely to make a price increase optimal. If mergers have not created or augmented a dominant firm, the relationship found in cross-section studies between concentration and prices will still hold.

5. The model also throws light on the puzzle of relatively high fees at multistate banks, a phenomenon that has been repeatedly reported but has remained unexplained. At least some large banks, as noted, are now posting uniform deposit and consumer loan rates statewide and have apparently reduced the discretion provided local managers in altering them. Their posted uniform prices are public knowledge. For purposes of optimal pricing in the dominant firm–mutual forbearance model, such uniformly set prices would have to exceed the limit prices in the markets in which they apply. The high fees repeatedly reported at multistate banks are consistent with this condition. One characteristic of such centralized decision making is to make "secret" price cuts by any one large bank, in one or more local areas, a relatively conspicuous departure from mutual forbearance. Centralized price-setting also evokes a threat of a massive retaliation through a reduction in the uniform posted prices by other banks.

Policy Implications

Current bank merger policy developed in a period when even the largest banks were limited by restrictions on multiple-office banking. The issues raised could be safely ignored. Bank merger policy at the federal banking agencies and the Justice Department properly focused on local market competition and did not take into consideration the problems raised by supervisory forbearance of large banking organizations, nor the possibility of mutual forbearance.

With the institutional changes of the last two decades, local market concentration may no longer be a reliable measure of the effect of large bank combinations. The concentration measuring rod for market power in local banking markets may itself have changed, ratcheting upward the significance of any given level. While average concentration in local markets has not changed much, concentration has increased in many local markets. Even in those markets in which it has not increased, or even decreased, alteration in the strategic advantage of the largest firms may well have raised the adverse significance of any given level. There is clearly a need for a full-scale reevaluation of current merger policy.[33]

SUMMARY AND CONCLUSIONS

The magnitude of the bank merger movement in the United States is unprecedented. Combinations of large banking organizations in particular portend a monumental structural reorganization of banking and financial institutions.

Large numbers of mergers over the last two decades are traceable to conducive economic conditions, deregulation, and policy changes. Many mergers in the 1980s constituted a resolution of failed banks through combination with healthy banks. After 1991, a booming economy and a rising stock market facilitated the combination of healthy banks and, in particular, large banks. Deregulation and changes in bank merger policy enabled such combinations. Bank-specific motives can plausibly be found in bank managements' efforts to increase profits and shareholder value, as well as to increase their own compensation, thorough a variety of means, including exploiting technological innovations, growing larger to attain or sustain a too-big-to-fail status, and eliminating competitors. Research findings on the relative importance of these factors are not definitive. There is every indication, however, that megamergers will continue into the foreseeable future, effectively establishing new operational parameters for banking organizations and new structural arrangements for the banking and financial systems.

There is reason to question the structural developments now occurring. It has been difficult to find gains resulting from large bank mergers due to greater efficiency or diversification. On the other hand, it is quite possible that megamergers have changed the competitive relationship between large banking organizations and their smaller competitors. Analysis, based on a dominant firm limit-pricing model, modified to incorporate multimarket linkages and regulatory forbearance, indicates that dominant firms will be in a position to charge prices above competitive levels while neutralizing potential competition and sustaining market share. Although further empirical testing is necessary, the model's implications are consistent with a number of otherwise puzzling research findings. Current bank merger policy, developed in an earlier period, is formatted to disregard the competitive problems raised by this analysis. In light of the structural changes underway, a reevaluation of current policy is needed.

NOTES

Note: The analysis in this chapter draws on Shull and Hanweck, 2001.

1. See Rhoades, 1996, 2000; Meyer, 1998.

2. The consolidation of BankAmerica and NationsBank, approved by the Federal Reserve in August 1998, created a banking organization with about $580 billion in assets, the third largest in the world at the time, holding about 8% of the total deposits of all insured depository institutions in the United States. The combination of Deutsche Bank and Bankers Trust created the world's largest banking organization with over $830 billion in assets. More recently, the combination of Sumitomo, Ltd. and Sakura, Ltd., one of several Japanese megamergers announced, resulted in a banking institution with over $927 billion in assets. Clearly, the bank merger movement in this country is not an isolated phenomenon.

3. Extrapolations of current "numbers" and "concentration" trends indicate various outcomes over the next 10 to 15 years, depending on starting and ending dates, and methodology. Most are impaired because they do not, in any way, specify the process that generates structural change. For a more sophisticated methodology, see Shull and Hanweck, 2001, ch. 6, Appendix. Several factors are likely to slow the current decline in numbers and subsequently produce an increase in numbers of banks. These include a decrease in the number of consolidations and mergers as the best "deals" are consummated; and an increase in *de novo* entry by new banks filling niche markets abandoned by the larger, consolidating banks.

4. Concentration data is from Meyer, 1998, Rhoades, 2000, and unpublished data provided by the Financial Structure Section, Board of Governors of the Federal Reserve System.

5. See Radecki, 1998. For a recent review of this phenomenon, and recent data on deposit and loan rates at multimarket banks, see Radecki, 2000. The data indicate small differences in rates by large banks in the same cities.

6. Heitfield, 1999.

7. Shull, 1999; Pilloff, 1999.

8. Both returns on assets and equity rose to record levels after 1991. By 1996, the top 20 U.S. banking companies had price-earnings ratios of 15 to 33 and unprecedented market-to-book value ratios of 1.8 to 3.0. In April 1998, Citicorp stock had a market-to-book value of 3.3.

9. U.S. Department of Treasury, 1991, pp. xviii–16.

10. For a review of the law and its structural implications, see Shull, 2000.

11. About a decade ago, it was calculated that between 1964 and 1987 the decline in the real cost of recording, processing, and distributing information had fallen about 95% what cost $1,000 in 1964 cost $50 in 1987.

12. In 1998, it was calculated that the cost of a microprocessor with computing capacity of one million instructions per second had fallen by over 99.8% since 1982; that is, computing capacity that cost $1,000 in 1982 had fallen to $1.30. The same study projected that over the next 10 years, the cost would likely decline to about one-tenth of one penny. The calculation is reported in "The Changing Landscape for Canadian Financial Services" (1998), p. 13.

13. Broaddus, 1988, p. 5.

14. Opportunities for diversification need not be exploited. For example, if banks do not believe costly episodes of financial distress are likely, a value-maximizing strategy would be to trade lower risk for higher current profits. See Hughes, Lang, Mester, and Moon, 1999, p. 299.

15. These included Continental Illinois in 1984, Interfirst Texas in 1987, Bank of New England in 1989, Sovran and C&S, and Citibank in 1991. In the late 1980s and early 1990s, the regulators did not close Citibank or Bank of New England in a timely fashion, despite substantial losses in real estate loans and derivatives that reduced their book and market value capital below acceptable levels. With respect to Citibank, see Fromson and Knight, 1993, who describe the extraordinary measures taken by the federal bank regulatory agencies, beginning in November 1990, to assist Citibank, at or near insolvency, to the end of avoiding a perceived financial disaster. On the background of the too-big-to-fail policy, see Hetzel, 1991.

16. See Feldman and Rolnick, 1998; Shull, 1995.

17. Raghavan and Pacelle, 1998.

18. Berger, Demsetz, and Strahan, 1999.

19. Ibid., p. 135.

20. Rhoades, 1998.

21. Repeated studies at widely separated points in time, using vastly different samples, a variety of independent variables, and increasingly sophisticated techniques, have reported surprisingly comparable results. A large-scale 1989 study by Berger and Hannan, using 1985 data, found interest rates paid on money market deposit accounts (MMDA) by banks in the most concentrated markets to be 25 to 100 basis points below those in the least concentrated markets.

22. One the earliest studies, in 1964, found interest rates on time deposits in "isolated" one-bank towns to be 17 basis points lower than those in "isolated" two-bank towns.

23. See Horvitz and Shull, 1964.

24. Congress did establish national and statewide deposit-concentration limits on merging banks in passing the Riegle-Neal Act. The limits established were 10% of national deposits and 30% of statewide deposits. For several reasons, including measurement problems, it is as yet unclear whether or not these limits will be binding.

25. However, see Carstensen, 1996.

26. The development of the dominant-firm dynamic price leadership model is reviewed in Gilbert, 1989. The application of this model to banking, outlined in this section, is developed rigorously in Shull and Hanweck, 2001, ch. 6.

27. Gaskins, 1971. For a review of the subsequent literature, see Gilbert, 1989, pp. 475, 511 ff., and Scherer and Ross, 1990, ch. 10.

28. A recent empirical study of the wealth and risk effects of the relevant provisions of FDICIA found large banks benefited as might be expected from a law that provided for the implementation of a too-big-to-fail policy. See Angbazo and Saunders, 1996. Comparison of rates paid on borrowed funds and capitalization rates between 1988 and 1998 also indicates lower funding costs for large banks.

29. Pilloff and Rhoades, 2000.

30. See Berger et al., 1999; and Nisenson, 1999. For a contrary view, see Seelig and Critchfield, 1999.

31. For example, see Hannan, 1992. Using data for 1989 and 1990, Hannan found a significant relationship between local market concentration and business loan rates but could no longer find one for deposit prices.

32. In one, a reduction in rates on local deposit accounts was found resulting from horizontal mergers that raised concentration "substantially"; that is, mergers that produced a *pro forma* increase in the market HHI of at least 200 points to a level of at least 1800 (Prager and Hannan, 1999). The other, using data for the period 1986 to 1994, found that a 1% higher HHI was associated with a 1.2% lower rate on money market deposit accounts and a 0.3% lower rate on certificates of deposit (Simons and Stavins, 1998, p. 24). The study also found that deposit rates of interest dropped after a bank's participation in a merger, for any level of market concentration, at least for sometime thereafter. Further, following the merger, other banks in the same local market first increase their rates, but then lower them in the following year.

33. A reconsideration of bank merger policy may be found in Shull and Hanweck, 2001, ch.7.

REFERENCES

Angbazo, Lazarus, and Anthony Saunders. (1996). "The Effect of TBTF Deregulation on Bank Cost of Funds." Working Paper, Graduate School of Business, New York University.

Berger, Allen N., Seth D. Bonime, Lawrence J. Goldberg, and Lawrence J. White. (1999). "The Dynamics of Market Entry: The Effects of Mergers and Acquisitions on De Novo Entry and Small Business Lending in the Banking Industry," Board of Governors of the Federal Reserve System, Finance and Economics Discussion Series 1991–41. Washington, DC.

Berger, Allen N., Rebecca S. Demsetz, and Philip E. Strahan. (1999). "The Consolidation of the Financial Services Industry: Causes, Consequences, and Implications for the Future." *Journal of Banking and Finance*, 23, nos. 2–4, pp. 135–194.

Berger, Allen N., and Timothy M. Hannan. (1989). "Deposit Interest Rates and Local Market Concentration." In *Concentration and Price*, Leonard Weiss, ed. Cambridge, MA: MIT Press, pp. 255–265.

Broaddus, J. Alfred, Jr. (1988). "The Bank Merger Wave: Causes and Consequences." Federal Reserve Bank of Richmond, *Economic Quarterly*, 84, no. 3, p. 5.

Carstensen, Peter C. (1996). "A Time to Return to Competition Goals in Banking Policy and Antitrust Enforcement: A Memorandum to the Antitrust Division." *The Antitrust Bulletin*, 41, no. 2, pp. 489–504.

"The Changing Landscape for Canadian Financial Services: New Forces, New Competitors, New Choices." (September 1998). In *Competition, Competitiveness and the Public Interest*. Research Paper Prepared for the Task Force on the Future of the Canadian Financial Services Center, Ottawa.

English, William B., and William R. Nelson. (1998). "Profits and Balance Sheet Developments at U.S. Commercial Banks in 1997." *Federal Reserve Bulletin*, 84, pp. 391–419.

Feldman, Ron J., and Arthur J. Rolnick. (1998). "Fixing FDICIA: A Plan to Address the Too-Big-to-Fail Problem." Washington, DC: Federal Reserve Bank of Minneapolis, *1997 Annual Report*, pp. 3–22.

Fromson, Brett D., and Jerry Knight. (1993). "The Saving of Citibank." *Washington Post*, June 16, p. A1.

Gaskins, Darius W. (1971). "Dynamic Limit Pricing: Optimal Pricing under Threat of Entry." *Journal of Economic Theory*, 3, pp. 306–322.

Gilbert, Richard J. (1989). "Mobility Barriers and the Value of Incumbency." In *Handbook of Industrial Organization*, Richard Schmalensee and Robert D. Willig, eds. Amsterdam: Elsevier Science Publishers.

Hannan, Timothy H. (1992). "The Functional Relationship between Prices and Market Concentration: The Case of the Banking Industry." In *Empirical Studies in Industrial Organization: Essays in Honor of Leonard W. Weiss*. Amsterdam: Kluwer Academic Publishers.

Heitfield, Erik A. (1999). "What Do Interest Rates Say about the Geography of Retail Banking Markets?" *The Antitrust Bulletin*, 44, no. 2, pp. 333–347.

Hetzel, Robert L. (1991). "Too Big to Fail: Origins, Consequences and Outlook." Federal Reserve Bank of Richmond, *Economic Review*, 77, no. 6, pp. 3–15.

Horvitz, Paul M., and Bernard Shull. (1964). "The Impact of Branch Banking on Bank Performance." *The National Banking Review*, 2, no. 2, pp. 143–188.

Hughes, Joseph P., William W. Lang, Loretta J. Mester, and Choon-Geol Moon. (1999). "The Dollar and Sense of Bank Consolidation." *Journal of Banking and Finance*, 23, pp. 291–324.

Meyer, Lawrence H. (1998). Statement before Committee on Banking and Financial Services, U.S. House of Representatives, April 29. Reprinted in *Federal Reserve Bulletin* 84, pp. 438–451.

Nisenson, Richard. (1999). "The Recent Resurgence of De Novo Banks." Washington, DC: Office of the Comptroller of the Currency.

Pilloff, Steven. (1999). "Multimarket Contact in Banking." *Review of Industrial Organization*, 14, no. 2, pp. 163–182.

Pilloff, Steven, and Stephen A. Rhoades. (2000). "Do Large Diversified Banking Organizations Have a Competitive Advantage?" *Review of Industrial Organization*, 16, no. 3, pp. 287–302.

Prager, Robin A., and Timothy H. Hannan. (1999). "Do Substantial Horizontal Mergers Generate Significant Price Effects? Evidence from the Banking Industry." *Review of Industrial Economics*, 46, pp. 433–452.

Radecki, Lawrence J. (1998). "The Expanding Geographic Reach of Retail Banking Markets." Federal Reserve Bank of New York, *Economic Policy Review*, pp. 15–34.

Radecki, Lawrence J. (2000). "Competition in Shifting Product and Geographic Markets." *The Antitrust Bulletin*, 45, no. 3, pp. 571–613.

Raghavan, Anita, and Mitchell Pacelle. (1998). "To the Rescue: A Hedge Fund Falters, and Big Banks Agree to Ante Up $3.5 Billion." *Wall Street Journal*, September 24, p. A1.

Rhoades, Stephen. (1996). "Bank Mergers and Industrywide Structure, 1980–94." *Staff Study* no. 169. Washington, DC: Board of Governors of the Federal Reserve System.

Rhoades, Stephen A. (1998). "The Efficiency Effects of Bank Mergers: An Overview of Case Studies in Nine Mergers." *Journal of Banking and Finance*, 22, pp. 273–91.

Rhoades, Stephen A. (2000). "Bank Mergers and Banking Structure in the United States, 1980–98." *Staff Study* no. 174. Washington, DC: Board of Governors of the Federal Reserve System.

Scherer, F. M., and David Ross. (1990). *Industrial Market Structure and Economic Performance*. Boston: Houghton Mifflin Co.

Seelig, Steven A., and Timothy Critchfield. (1999). "Determinants of De Novo Entry in Banking." FDIC Division of Research and Statistics, Working Paper 99–1.

Shull, Bernard. (1995). "The Limits of Prudential Supervision: Experience in the United States." *Economic Notes* (Monte dei Paschi di Siena), 26, no. 3, pp. 585–612.

Shull, Bernard. (1999). "Merger Policy in the United States: Is There a Need for a Change." In *Modernizing the Global Financial System*, Dimitri Papdimitriou, ed. New York: St. Martin's Press.

Shull, Bernard. (2000). "Financial Modernization in the United States: Background and Implications." UNCTAD, *Discussion Paper* No. 151.

Shull, Bernard, and Gerald A. Hanweck. (2001). *Bank Mergers in a Deregulated Environment: Promise and Peril*. Westport, CT: Quorum Books.

Simons, Katerina, and Joanna Stavins. (March–April 1998). "Has Antitrust Policy in Banking Become Obsolete." Federal Reserve Bank of Boston, *New England Economic Review*, pp. 13–26.

U.S. Department of Treasury. (1991). *Modernizing the Financial System*. Washington D.C.

Chapter 5

Megamergers: Causes and Effects— A European (Swiss) Perspective

Rudolf Volkart

INTRODUCTION

In this chapter, we examine the subject of "megamergers" primarily from a Continental European perspective, especially looking at transactions in Switzerland and Germany. We present not only the author's views, but also a range of opinions found in the European literature (e.g., see Siegwart and Neugebauer, 1999) and practice. Some conclusions are derived from general considerations in the field of mergers and acquisitions (M&A), in particular the theoretical background that may explain the causes of conceivable megamerger transactions.

It is not possible to give an exact definition of what is generally regarded as a "mega" merger. Is the critical size of such transactions 1 billion, 5 billion, 10 billion or even more U.S. dollars? We could say that transactions in excess of U.S. $10 billion may definitely be classified as megamergers. Furthermore, it is important not to look at the megamerger phenomenon from the narrow economic angle but in a broader context, taking into consideration behavioral aspects, pure qualitative considerations, and irrationalities as well.

MEGAMERGERS IN THE ECONOMIC CONTEXT

Looking at the current wave of megamergers, we should bear in mind the fundamental changes that are at work in the world economy. These are primarily ongoing globalization, the technological revolution, and the developments in the European Union, where the creation of the single European currency—unexpectedly weak since its introduction—is causing major upheaval, in the European capital markets, for instance. In addition, the more global, broader, and deeper nature of today's financial markets is playing an important role; there are even some voices that interpret these developments as a major factor driving these merger waves.

The most remarkable economic and noneconomic factors underlying the current megamerger scenery landscape are the following:

• division of labor, "dis-integration" of value and production chains
• cross-border mergers (Europe: 50%), half of them intercontinental mergers
• phenomenon not new (U.S.), but size and speed
• open, global, private competitive markets
• factor mobility, especially capital (excluding human capital in general)
• information and communication technology
• European Union, the euro
• effects on competition and on innovation
• institutional investors, capital markets, corporate governance
• consequences for regional and national employment
• political power of merged firms, corporate taxes, regulation.

The dis-integration of value and production chains as well as globalization is most important for the financial sectors of the economy (banks and insurance), for telecommunications, and—to some degree—for commercial services (B2B and B2C e-commerce). The pharmaceutical and petroleum sectors are primarily affected by competition, technology, capital needs, and the general merger wave.

MOTIVES AND "THEORIES" FOR MERGERS

There exists a broad and interdisciplinary literature that analyzes the motives for mergers and constructs theories to explain M&A processes (see Sundarsanam, 1995). In this section, we look at nine more or less different approaches. They have been put together based on a broad set of existing theoretical contributions to a research project at the Swiss Banking Institute of the University of Zurich (see Kerler, 1999). The various theories and theoretical approaches are the following:

• Synergy theories
• Market power and competition
• Corporate taxes
• Inefficient management
• Information theory
• Diversification
• Manager theories

- Process theory
- Economic disturbance theory

Synergy Theories

A significant volume of research has dealt with the question of classifying the different potential synergy effects caused by mergers. Some of the most significant contributions were presented by Penrose (1959), Ansoff (1965, 1987), Chatterjee (1986), Porter (1986), Coenenberg and Sautter (1988), Pursche (1989), Sandler (1991), and Sundarsanam, Holl, and Salam (1996). If we summarize these very briefly, we come up with four important areas of potential synergies:

- Operational synergies (economies of scale, economies of scope, product-market-strategies, expansion, benefit of restructuring)
- Financial synergies (debt capacity and tax shield, possible mismatch of growth and financial resources, coinsurance effect, bankruptcy costs)
- Synergies of power (collusive synergy, market power, and competition)
- Management synergy (managerial skills, management capacities).

Synergies are the most important reason for successful mergers, in particular megamergers, and are the most critical argument (Sirower, 1997), often overstated at the same time. In the latest wave of megamergers, synergies have been occasionally overshadowed by the need, or wish, for sheer size and growth (see among others Garai and Pravda, 1993), as dealt with under another category of merger motives, manager theories.

Market Power and Competition

Market power and competition are often seen as a separate aspect—apart from the types of synergy mentioned. They play a central role in the currently observable horizontal mergers, such as those in the banking sector (see Bernet, 1999; Ramaswami, 1997). This may still be partly true for vertical mergers, although the dis-integration of chains and the tendency to outsource and to spin off is an argument against vertical integration in the modern economy.

Some controversy has arisen over the judgment of "market power." Some argue that even the biggest market players do not achieve a dominant market share. Helmut O. Maucher, for example, the former president of the board of Nestlé, offers strong arguments for this position. Nestlé as the biggest corporation in the food sector worldwide controls no more than some 2% of the world's food market, though this figure may be higher in some individual national markets. On the other hand, why do we need an effective antitrust law and control? The answer is just to avoid too big a concentration in market share, be it international or national! Independently of the above-mentioned considerations, market power may play an important role in many megamergers.

Corporate Taxes

Besides the advantage of a higher tax shield because of an increase in debt capacity, mergers may offer other potential tax advantages under certain circumstances (Scharlemann, 1996; Volkart, 1999). Examples are the acquisition of firms with loss carry forward potentials or acquisitions of targets with "step-up" tax valuation potentials. There is no strong argument why corporate taxes should play a significant role in megamergers. Of course, taxes are a value-driving feature in any transaction, and so they will therefore influence the concrete structure of every deal to a substantial degree.

Inefficient Management

The "inefficient management approach" plays a central role in light of the problems and functioning of corporate governance in a globalized free market system in today's world's economy. Several different mechanisms are required to ensure a sound management behavior in the best interest of the shareholders (Suter, 2000). One very important aspect—at least for listed companies—is the disciplinary effect of the market for corporate control (see Shleifer and Vishny, 1997). If inefficient managements of target firms are exposed to more or less unfriendly takeovers, there is a better chance for a shareholder-value-oriented managerial behavior.

While this is a strong point for M&A transactions and for corporate governance in general, it should not have a significant impact on the incidence of megamergers. A special phenomenon may, however, be the inability of a company or its management, to change a suboptimal corporate culture or the social impossibility of initiating a fundamental restructuring process—especially under the socioeconomic conditions of several Continental European countries. Merger transactions can then be an effective instrument of inducing the necessary evolutionary steps in an underperforming firm (see Hummler, 1999). This can partly be observed as a motive for transactions even in megamergers. The merger of UBS and Swiss Bank Corporation in Switzerland in 1997 may serve as a good example, when the UBS management was under serious pressure from a major shareholder (Martin Ebner) to change strategy, culture, and the structure of the board of directors and enforce a more stringent shareholder value approach by the bank. After the merger, the controversy between the bank and the shareholder evaporated immediately.

Information Theory

The idea behind the information theory approach is the existence of substantial market inefficiencies. Under this perspective, the acquirer's management believes it has superior information about the value of specific target firms, compared to the information available in the market.

Given the many empirical research results showing a low financial success rate in M&A transactions—stemming partly from overpriced acquisitions—the information theory approach has to be viewed with skepticism, at least as far as the results are concerned. On the other hand, managerial arrogance may well be a considerable source of unsuccessful transactions. In an international context, this argument is even more important (Eun, Kolodny, and Scheraga, 1996), where managers have to handle cultural differences between different countries and continents. This was visible, for instance, when the leading Swiss food retailer encountered serious problems some years ago trying to enter the Austrian market. The disinterest of the company's former management in the specific problems associated with internationalization led to substantial losses amounting to hundreds of millions of Swiss francs.

Diversification

As the capital asset pricing model (CAPM) and modern portfolio theory (MPT) tell us, the risk-return position of investment portfolios can be optimized by diversification. In these models, risk is not considered as total volatility of specific asset returns, but only as the nondiversifiable volatility of the expected return of each asset. In a single-factor model such as that of the traditional CAPM, beta mirrors this interpretation.

The wave of mergers in U.S. markets during the late 1960s (1965–1969) was based primarily on the idea of corporate diversification. In most cases, this was or even had to be an unsuccessful concept. (An impressive example of the opposite case is General Electric [GE], which is currently diversifying into the financial sector, for instance, in Continental Europe.) From a theoretical standpoint, financial investors (shareholders) can diversify their investments themselves at the portfolio level. Corporate diversification is therefore not only unnecessary but inefficient and more costly than the financial investors' diversification (see among others Lang and Stulz, 1994). Furthermore, the risk of suboptimal management decisions is increased as well as are corporate governance costs in general. High free cash flows from existing business and unused resources were the basis for many bad M&A decisions in the past.

Modern research shows that reality does not correspond to the neoclassical financial theory ideal of perfect and complete capital markets. One of the main conclusions stemming from this observation is the need to alter our understanding of financial risk (see Stulz, 1999). If we do this and consider total volatility as relevant risk, especially in capital budgeting and M&A decisions, the diversification argument regains some of its merit. This is especially true whenever we look at a company's downside risk, mainly the liquidity and bankruptcy risk. The cash-flow diversification is therefore relevant not only from a valuation perspective, but also in the light of a pure cash-flow considerations relating to a company's short-term survival.

The big universal banks in Europe are a good example of this, especially in Switzerland. It is one of the clearly articulated goals of Credit Suisse (CS) or UBS group strategy to achieve stable operating cash flows from diverse areas of activity in modern banking (and insurance—CS Group). Interestingly enough, this argument is cited by large organizations, UBS having gone through a huge megamerger starting in 1998. For smaller companies, it should be of even greater importance.

Manager Theories

Whenever we accept the existence of market imperfection, information asymmetries, and certain information inefficiencies in markets, manager theories may rate quite high in explaining the motives and reasons for M&A transactions, and megamergers in particular. The well-known shareholder wealth maximization (SWM) approach finds a rival in a second possible view and reality, the management welfare maximization (MWM) approach. Agency problems—and above all information asymmetries—provide an environment in which managers pursue their own interests, which may have more or less to do with the main goal of shareholder value creation. Depending on the disciplinary effects of sound corporate governance, this can cause serious aberrations in management decisions from what should be done under the pure shareholder wealth perspective. The MWM aspects are covered not only by the principal agent theory but also by the transaction theory (Williamson, 1996).

As already mentioned under Diversification, high free cash flows from existing businesses and unused financial resources increase managers' temptation to engage in doubtful acquisitions and adventures. Or as Schumpeter (1934) told us, "the dream . . . of creating a private kingdom" (see Müller-Stewens, 2000, p. 54).

Hirshleifer (1993, p. 143) sees managers as having "an incentive to use investment choices as a tool for building their personal reputations" (Suter, 2000, p. 68ff.) Mueller (2000, p. 61) leaves no doubt as to what he thinks about mergers and managerial welfare:

Efficiency-reducing mergers come about because managers have the discretion to invest corporate income in ways that reduce shareholder wealth. Whether this occurs because managers consciously realize that the mergers are likely to lose money, but undertake them anyway for the private gains they generate, or because they are swept away by the excitement of a booming stock market, the self serving advice of an investment banker, or their own animal spirits and hubris is of no consequence for merger policy.

Another important aspect under of the manager theories is the fact that total management compensation is positively correlated to company growth and size.

Managers' "egos" indeed seem to be one of the driving forces in the ongoing present megamergers wave. Taking into consideration other aspects such as the "herd instinct" or "lemming" effect (doing what everybody does or what is fashionable at the time), the picture we receive of the current changes in the world's economy is a critical one. At least the rationality behind the economic processes, megamergers in particular, is perhaps being constantly given more importance than human, irrational, egocentric, and other aspects.

Process Theory

What process theory tries to consider is closely related to the manager theories and the information theory. The process theory assumes managers to be arrogant (the so-called hubris theory) (Roll, 1986) in their strategic decision making, to judge by the valuation abilities they perceive in themselves. Together with the "winner's curse"—the fact, that information in bidding processes causes further increases in acquisition prices (Varaiya, 1988)—the hubris theory offers an explanation for the overvaluation, overpricing, and financial failure of M&A transactions. Combined with the suboptimality of (overly) big organizations, these aspects should be kept in mind in the discussion of the pros and cons of megamergers.

Economic Disturbance Theory

The economic disturbance approach (Gort, 1969) focuses on a company's business environment. Under the revolutionary changes in the new economy, this has to be seen as one of the key issues of the present megamerger processes, especially in telecommunications, biotechnology, and banking.

Economic shocks alter the structure of expectations. Rapid changes in technology with direct and indirect implications, such as the consequences of the new economy in "old" sectors and businesses, cause fast and dramatic changes in share prices coupled with increased volatility.

As mentioned under Inefficient Management, different kinds of restructuring needs may represent one of the important reasons for M&A transactions and in particular megamergers. In a times of radical evolution and technological revolution, the need for restructuring expand increases dramatically.

Motives for Mergers—A Practitioner's View

In practice, managers often view the motives for acquisitions in a nontheoretical, less stringent way. These views may provide valuable practical insights from a theoretical perspective into the character of mergers. The following motivation factors with their respective examples appear in Achleitner, 2000 (here translated from German into English):

Motivation Factor	*Example*
Brand	Ford/Jaguar
Product	Novo/Ferrosan
Rationalization	Krupp-Hoesch/Thyssen
Cost synergies	Postkonsortium/TNT
Distribution	Sanyo/Luitpold
Technology	Roche/Genentech
Customers	Roche/FDO
Suppliers	OMV/Beryl Oil Field
Workforce	Deutsche Bank/Morgan Grenfell
Market share	Du Pont/Herberts
Market defense	Siemens/Nixdorf
Ego	Daimler/Chrysler

MEGAMERGERS IN THE "VALUE LOOPS" FRAMEWORK

These theoretical approaches will now be applied to megamergers in a summary form and in the context of modern value-based management. Figure 5.1 shows the "Value Loops" framework, which was developed in a series of research projects in corporate finance and valuation at the Swiss Banking Institute of the University of Zurich (Volkart, 1998, p. 94). The basic idea is simple: management must make its strategic decisions in a way that maximizes (optimizes) the enterprise value, or shareholder value, respectively. This leads us to the need for a sound valuation and value-controlling concept to indicate the internal value generation. The corporate value creation then has to be transformed into the share price. Only if this precondition is fulfilled will shareholders have the full benefit of the internal value creation. We will leave aside another aspect at this point: the value transfer (dividends, increase in share price, share buybacks, etc.) to the investors.

The horizontal view in Figure 5.1 shows us the "management–investors" relationship with its inherent agency conflicts. The vertical view, on the other hand, shows the relationship between a firm's intrinsic and the market value. Informational and communicational aspects play a central role in the whole framework.

Figure 5.2 shows the same framework (slightly simplified), within which we try to position the nine theoretical approaches previously described. Those theories that play—objectively and partly subjectively—a more significant role in the megamerger context are shown in bold characters, in contrast to the others that may be of less significance in really big merging processes. In the center of Figure 5.2, the surrounding micro and macro implications are indicated by Corporate Governance, Shareholder Wealth Orientation (micro aspects) and by Globalization, Technologies, Euro, Financial Markets (macro perspective)—im-

Figure 5.1
The "Value Loops" Framework

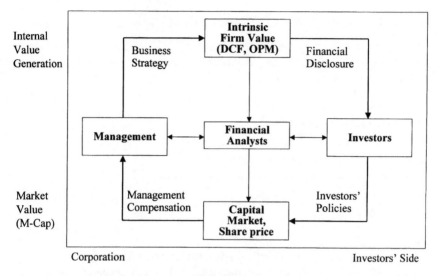

Source: © Swiss Banking Institute, University of Zurich.

Figure 5.2
Megamergers in the "Value Loops" Framework

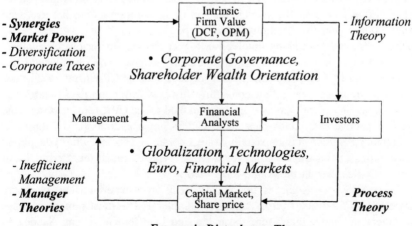

Source: © Swiss Banking Institute, University of Zurich.

portant phenomena in understanding the currently ongoing wave of megamergers wave of the time being.

MERGERS IN SWITZERLAND AND GERMANY

Before we focus on the megamerger activities in Switzerland and Germany, it is worthwhile to recall the five main merger waves in the United States since the end of the nineteenth century:

1897–1904: Industrial revolution

1916–1929: Market power, market share, competition

1965–1969: Diversification, conglomerates

1984–1990: Merger mania, synergies, corporate governance

1995–   : Megadeals, new financial instruments; globalization, European Union, value-based management.

M&A processes are clearly a cyclical phenomenon but with short-dated changes, different structures, and probably increased risk-return potentials over time. Compared to the developments in the U.S. economy, M&A in Continental Europe, especially in Switzerland and Germany, is a more "recent," newer phenomenon. Generally, we can observe an ongoing growth in M&A transactions since 1982 for a period of 20 years. A substantial number of cross-border deals took place, primarily with U.S. firms. Germany experienced a surge in M&A transactions between 1982 and 1989 from about 1,000 transactions per year to about 3,000; since then, the average number of annual transactions has averaged about 2,000 a year (Müller-Stewens, 2000, p. 489).

The main industries being involved in bigger transactions or even megamergers are financial services (banks, insurance), chemicals and pharmaceuticals, computer and telecommunications, and services such as CPA firms or utilities. A strong influence exerted by consulting firms, M&A boutiques—partly aggressively acting in the market—investment banks, and CPA firms is observable in the respective M&A landscapes (see Müller-Stewens, 2000, p. 51). Based on a Continental European understanding of economic and social culture, the pluses and minuses of this ongoing merger wave are viewed much more critically in these countries than in the Anglo-Saxon world.

Figure 5.3 shows some of the biggest deals in Switzerland and Germany between 1996 and 2000 (year 2000 is incomplete). The most remarkable megamergers in Switzerland were those realized by Ciba-Geigy and Sandoz to form Novartis (1996) and by Union Bank of Switzerland (UBS)/Swiss Bank Corporation (SBC) to form the new UBS (1997)—after the earlier cross-border "big bang" of BBC and Asea to form ABB. Looking at the German

Figure 5.3
Megamergers in Switzerland and Germany (in billions of U.S. dollars)

Year	Companies	Business/Industry	New Name	Total Value
1996	Ciba-Geigy/Sandoz	Pharmaceutical	Novartis	28.0
1997	(old) UBS/SBC	Banking	UBS	23.0
1997	Zurich/BAT Industries	Insurance	Zurich Allied	18.4
1997	Hoffman-Roche/Corange	Pharmaceutical	Roche	10.2
1997	Credit Suisse/Winterthur	Insurance	CS Group	9.7
1998	Daimler-Benz/Chrysler	Automobile	Daimler Chrysler	40.5
1999	Hoechst/Rhone-Poulenc	Chemistry	Hoechst	28.5
1999	VEBA/VIAG	Energy/Chemistry	E.On	16.3
1999	Deutsche Telekom/ Wireless Media One	Telecommunications	Deutsche Telekom	13.6
2000	Zurich Allied/ Allied Zurich	Insurance	Zurich Allied	21.4
2000	Mannesmann/Orange	Industry/ Telecommunications	Mannesmann	34.2

Source: Thomson Financial Services data.

merger landscape, we find that the most impressive megamergers were those of Daimler Benz/Chrysler (Daimler-Chrysler) (1998) and of Hoechst/Rhone-Poulenc (Hoechst) (1999), both as international deals.

The Novartis (pharmaceuticals) and UBS (banking) megamergers profited from a positive reaction of response from the stock exchange. In the case of Novartis, the huge financial sums necessary to develop new products in the pharmaceuticals sector seemed to convince the investor community as the main motive for the merger. In the UBS merger, the goal of this international bank to rank among the top financial sector services groups in the world and the requirement of a global presence were reason enough for a positive reaction. Nevertheless, both megamergers had to deal with serious cultural and managerial problems. Qualitative observations and deeper internal insights by the author in one of these cases revealed many negative internal reactions and feelings among the staff. UBS suffered a substantial loss of staff and—in the private banking area—even customer defections. UBS management may have underestimated the problems caused by overlaps in Swiss commercial and private banking as well as investment banking in London, which created serious internal conflicts.

The question arises as to how the success of an M&A transaction can be measured on a quantitative or qualitative basis. The following section offers a closer look at the success rate of M&A transactions in Switzerland in the years 1995–1997 based on empirical testing.

ANALYZING THE SUCCESS OF MERGERS IN SWITZERLAND

Several different approaches are suitable for analyzing the success of M&A transactions. The main categories can be described in the following way:

• Event Studies: Empirical analysis of stock prices and stock price reactions some time before and some time after the transaction
• Analysis of annual reports: EBIT, EBITDA, net profit, ROI, ROE, EVA, etc.
• Subjective management judgment: Questionnaires answered by the managements of acquiring and target companies
• Analysis of specific indicators: Examples: future divestitures; fluctuation of personnel
• Qualitative observations and evaluation: Ad hoc observations, longitudinal studies, etc.

Kerler (1999) analyzed 200 acquisitions in Switzerland between 1995 and 1997, using the event study approach. In this study 26.5% were national and 73.5% were international acquisitions; 30.5% of the acquirers viewed themselves as experienced acquirers; and 55.5% of the transactions took place between related product/industry sectors. The 200 transactions were analyzed based on the CAPM, calculating cumulative abnormal returns 50 days before and 100 days after the transaction date. To check the statistical significance, the usual t-tests were applied to the samples.

The results of this analysis can be summarized as follows:

• Slightly negative abnormal returns were observed.
• In the sample as a whole, no positive synergies and/or other positive effects seemed to be mirrored in the share price.
• The results indicated some support for the managerial welfare position, which does not result in optimal shareholder wealth creation.
• The sample of merging firms in the same industry (related products/industries) showed positive abnormal returns, supporting the synergy hypothesis.
• The sample of transactions in different sectors showed highly negative abnormal returns.
• There was no significant difference between national and international transactions.
• Companies with acquisition experience showed a slightly better performance than the others.

These results in general do not differ substantially from other empirical analysis done for transaction samples in different countries. The financial success of mergers and acquisitions remains doubtful and may be good as well as bad in many cases. Bühner (1992, p. 705) analyzed 28 empirical studies of the profitability of mergers and concludes that 43% of the studies showed negative performance, another 43% no change, and only 14% resulted in positive performance. When we look at the financial services sector, for instance, the current mergers do not seem to have increased the overall efficiency of the financial system (Berger and Humphrey, 1997; Bernet, 1999).

QUALITATIVE AND OTHER CONSIDERATIONS

Some special aspects of true megamergers seem to be important for big transactions. First, legal aspects have to be considered carefully as big mergers are often seriously affected by antitrust regulations—as, for instance, under the U.S. law or, EU regulations. Then, megamergers are a nonroutine business, causing specific questions and problems in big unique transactions. Megamergers entail huge financial operations and financing volumes, which partially explains why the acquirer's shares are often used as the acquisition "currency" in large deals. A further aspect is the need to divest noncore business units after the merger—a good example at this point in time is the spin-off of Ciba SC after the Novartis megamerger.

The success of a megamerger largely depends on professionalism in every stage of the transaction process, in particular on the quality of integration, be it more of an economic or a qualitative nature, for instance, cultural. Megamergers may be the result of overcapacity and a strong need for restructuring in a whole industry or sector, as the bank mergers in Continental Europe, in particular the UBS case in Switzerland, clearly show. Another example is the intercontinental merger of Daimler-Benz and Chrysler in the automotive industry.

From a macroeconomic point of view, the transaction may be "successful" or at least "reasonable," even if the "micro" analysis does not show a positive result. The latest developments in the Swiss banking sector emphasize this point of view: What restructuring process would have arisen if UBS and SBC had not merged into the new UBS? Several competitors, for example, the Zurich Cantonal Bank, a big domestic financial services operator, benefited from the UBS merger, gaining new customers as well as new employees with substantial professional experience.

As mentioned earlier, criticism of the latest wave of megamergers is relatively vociferous among the populations of Continental Europe. Two statements may stand as examples for many other recent criticisms in this region. Kaden (2000) (editor of *Manager Magazine*, a German monthly journal; translated by the author of this chapter) points out the following critical aspects concerning mergers and megamergers in particular:

- events and adventures for managers
- follow the trend and reduce personal risk
- company size does not mean market power: $1+1 < 2$

- neglecting human values creates anxiety, fear
- acquisitions (cash buys) are better than mergers
- avoid mergers of "equals"!
- economies of scale as main driver in several industries
- management capabilities as bottleneck

A second statement, formulated by Slembeck (1999) (translated by the author of this chapter), may complete Kaden's considerations:

- motives: power, prestige, autonomy
- increase of personal income due to firm company size
- manager's career, reputation, influence
- "neutralization" of bad management through merger and acquisition activities
- securing autonomy by proactive merger strategy
- lemming effect, market forces, fashions
- agency conflicts, asymmetric information

In summarizing the "dark side of mergers and acquisitions" (megamergers in particular), we can draw the following conclusions based on careful observation in the practice of M&A:

- Low rate of success: empirical analysis in different countries shows failure rates of > 50%.
- Benefits for the target's shareholders: there is clear empirical evidence that the target's shareholders benefit from mergers and acquisitions.
- (Overly) high acquisition prices: high premiums of 20–40% and more above the stock prices result in overpricing of acquisitions.
- Most important causes of M&A failures: poor strategy—overestimated synergies—unrealistic company valuation—poor integration management—bad timing—cultural problems—organization too big—insufficient internal communication—frustration.

Thinking of the causes and important aspects of successful megamergers, one can conclude the following. First, a clear strategy has to be formulated. This seems to be self-evident, but practical experience shows the opposite. Then, a tightly organized integration process is an absolute "must." There is some evidence that mergers in which one partner is stronger may be more successful than those between "equals." The quality of top management is very crucial, and the personality of the responsible CEO plays a decisive role. Decisions must be taken and implemented fast, and the timing should be as optimal as possible. Joint visions and strategic goals can be immensely helpful in managing megamergers with less risks, and harmonizing the often quite different cultures often seems to be a "bottleneck." And without excellent communication at every stage and in all respects, the success of mergers is in serious doubt. A special aspect is the decentralization of big, megamerged groups, as the successful "experiment" of ABB unmistakably shows us. In the long run, management has to focus on an appropriate value-based management system, including a value-oriented management compensation scheme.

Let us summarize with the "three key principles" of a successful merger:

- First principle: be at the right place at the right time: choose the right partner.
- Second principle: be quick in decision making (human resources, structure) and quick in implementation.
- Third principle: communicate the right information to the right addresses.

The third point—the importance of reliable information—may never be underestimated in megamerger processes. Information builds the basis of investors' decision making. Furthermore, providing true and fair information to the workforce is essential for the success of a merger. And the central role and influence of the press should never be overlooked, at least in big transactions. A positive example of a sound communication concept is the UBS megamerger in Switzerland, where fast and accurate information was provided for all the stakeholders (shareholders, employees, public, press, financial analysts, etc.). A negative example is the failed merger plan of Deutsche Bank/Dresdener Bank in Germany, where wrong and misleading information turned out to be the major fault. Rolf E. Breuer, the CEO of Deutsche Bank, said: "Dresdner Kleinwort Benson is a jewel which we are not going to sell." A few days later he recognized that it was impossible to keep this promise, and the merger failed.

What final conclusions can be drawn, considering the consequences of the (mega)merger phenomenon at the beginning of the twenty-first century and looking at the potential future developments? We can make the following concluding statements (based on Hummler, 1999, p. 245):

- The current merger wave will not create bigger and bigger mega-firms.
- Mergers help to restore nonoptimal firm corporate and financial structures.
- Mergers justify extraordinary actions without causing management to lose face.
- The above argument also applies to re-dimensioning the workforce.
- Often actions to reposition firms could or would not be undertaken without merger effects.
- Therefore, a merger is a generally accepted means of implementing extraordinary strategic measures.

Whatever we think of the current megamerger wave, it is an indisputable fact, and for many managers, there seems to be no alternative but to follow the trend. Whether the phenomenon as a whole leads to sustainable structures is very questionable. Excessively large organizations are a source of serious disadvantages and suboptimality; even the history of nature tells us that dinosaurs died out in one way or another. But the evolutionary process of economies, in particular in the globalized world we encounter today, probably leaves us no alternative but to embrace the process of deep radical change we currently see around us.

REFERENCES

Achleitner, P. (2000). "Bewertung von Akquisitionen." In *Management von Akquisitionen*, A. Picot, A. Nordmeyer, and P. Pribilla, eds. Stuttgart: Schäffer.

Amihud, Y., and G. Miller, eds. (1998). *Bank Mergers & Acquisitions*. Boston: Kluwer Academic Publishers.

Ansoff, H. I. (1965, 1987). *Corporate Strategy*. London: Penguin Books.

Barnes, P. (1995). "Why Do Bidders Do Badly Out of Mergers? Some UK Evidence." *Journal of Business Finance & Accounting*, 25, nos. 5/6, pp. 571–593.

Berger, A., and D. Humphrey. (1997). "Efficiency of Financial Institutions: International Survey and Directions of Future Research." *European Journal of Operational Research*, no. 98, pp. 175–212.

Bernet, B. (1999). "Warum fusionieren Banken." In *Mega Fusionen: Analysen, Kontroversen, Perspektiven*, 2nd ed., H. Siegwart and G. Neugebauer, eds. Bern/Stuttgart/Wien: Haupt, pp. 131–145.

Black, A., P. Wright, and J. E. Bachman. (1998). *In Search of Shareholder Value: Managing the Drivers of Performance*. London: Financial Times Management.

Bradley, M., A. Desai, and H. Kim. (1988). "Synergistic Gains from Corporate Acquisitions and Their Division between the Stockholder of the Target and the Acquiring Firms." *Journal of Financial Economics*, 21, no. 1, pp. 3–40.

Brush, T. (1996). "Predicted Change in Operational Synergy and Post-Acquisition Performance of Acquired Business." *Strategic Management Journal*, 17, no. 1, pp. 1–24.

Bühner, R. (1990). *Unternehmenszusammenschlüsse: Ergebnisse empirischer Analysen*. Stuttgart: Poeschel.

Chapman, T. L., J. J. Dempsey, G. Ramsdell, and T. E. Bell. (1998). "Purchasing's Big Moment—After the Merger." *The McKinsey Quarterly*, no. 1, pp. 55–65.

Chatterjee, S. (1986). "Types of Synergy and Economic Value: The Impact of Acquisition on Merging and Rival Firms." *Strategic Management Journal*, 7, no. 2, pp. 119–139.

Choi, D., and G. C. Philippatos. (1983). "An Examination of Merger Synergism." *Journal of Financial Research*, 6, no. 3, pp. 239–256.

Coenenberg, A., and M. Sautter. (1988). "Strategische und finanzielle Bewertung von Unternehmensakquisitionen." *Die Betriebswirtschaft*, 6, pp. 691–710.

Doukas, J. (1995). "Overinvestment, Tobin's q and Gains from Foreign Acquisitions." *Journal of Banking & Finance*, 19, no. 7, pp. 1285–1303.

Eun, C., R. Kolodny, and C. Scheraga. (1996). "Cross-Border Acquisitions and Share-holder Wealth: Tests of Synergy and Internationalization Hypothesis." *Journal of Banking & Finance*, 20, no. 9, pp. 1559–1582.

Garai, G., and S. E. Pravda. (1993). "Defusing Emotions of Buyers and Sellers in Getting a Deal Done." *Mergers & Acquisitions*, 28, no. 4, pp. 23–28.

Gort, M. (1969). "An Economic Disturbance Theory of Mergers." *Quarterly Journal of Economics*, 83, no. 4, pp. 627–642.

Hirshleifer, D. (Summer 1993). "Managerial Reputation and Corporate Investment Decision." *Financial Management*, 22, no. 2, pp. 145–160.

Hummler, K. (1999). "Mega-Fusionen im Lichte finanztheoretischer Überlegungen." In *Mega Fusionen: Analysen, Kontroversen, Perspektiven*, 2nd ed., H. Siegwart and G. Neugebauer, eds. Bern/Stuttgart/Wien: Haupt, pp. 233–245.

Jensen, M. C. (1992). "Market for Corporate Control." In *The New Palgrave Dictionary of Money and Finance*, P. Newman, M. Milgate, and J. Eatwell, eds. London: W. W. Norton & Co., pp. 657–665.

Kaden, W. (2000). "Internationale Zusammenschlüsse: Welche Chancen, welche Gefahren beinhalten sie?" In *Management von Akquisitionen*, A. Picot, A. Nordmeyer, and P. Pribilla, eds. Stuttgart: Schäffer, pp. 219–220.

Kerler, P. (1999). *Mergers & Acquisitions and Shareholder Value*. Bern/Stuttgart/Wien: Haupt.

Lang, H. H., and R. M. Stulz. (1994). "Tobin's q, Corporate Diversification and Firm Performance." *Journal of Political Economy*, 102, pp. 1248–1280.

Mills, R. (1998). *The Dynamics of Shareholder Value: The Principles and Practice of Strategic Value Analysis*. Lechlade: Price Waterhouse.

Mueller, D. C. (1992). "Mergers." In *The New Palgrave Dictionary of Money and Finance*, P. Newman, M. Milgate, and J. Eatwell, eds. London: W. W. Norton & Co., pp. 700–705.

Müller-Stewens, G. (2000). "Akquisition und der Markt für Unternehmenskontrolle: Entwicklungstendenzen und Erfolgsfaktoren." In *Management von Akquisitionen*, A. Picot, A. Nordmeyer, and P. Pribilla, eds. Stuttgart: Schäffer, pp. 41–61.

Neumann, A. (1994). *Fusionen und fusionsähnliche Unternehmenszusammenschlüsse: Unter besonderer Berücksichtigung finanzieller Aspekte*. Bern/Stutgart/Wien: Haupt.

Penrose, E. (1959). *The Theory of the Growth of the Firm*. Oxford: Oxford University Press.

Picot, A., A. Nordmeyer, and P. Pribilla, eds. (2000). *Management von Akquisitionen*. Stuttgart: Schäffer.

Porter, M. E. (1986). *Wettbewerbsvorteile (Competitive Advantage)—Spitzen-leistungen erreichen und behaupten*, 4. Frankfurt/New York: Auflage, Campus.

Pursche, W. R. (Summer 1989). "Building Better Bids." *The McKinsey Quarterly*, pp. 92–97.

Ramaswami, K. (1997). "The Performance Impact of Strategic Similarity in Horizontal Mergers: Evidence from the U.S. Banking Industry." *Academy of Management Journal*, 40, no. 3, pp. 697–715.

Roll, R. (1986). "The Hubris Hypothesis of Corporate Takeovers." *Journal of Business*, 59, no. 2, pp. 197–216.

Sandler, G.G.R. (1991). "Synergie: Konzept, Messung und Realisation." Dissertation an der Universität St. Gallen, Bamberg.

Scharlemann, U. (1996). *Finanzwirtschaftliche Synergiepotentiale von Mergers und Acquisitions: Analyse und Bewertung nicht güterwirtschaftlicher Wertsteigerungseffekte von Unternehmenstransaktionen.* Bern/Stuttgart/Wien: Haupt.

Schumpeter, J. A. (1934). *The Theory of Economic Development.* Cambridge: Transaction Publishers.

Seth, A. (1990). "Sources of Value Creation in Acquisitions: An Empirical Investigation." *Strategic Management Journal,* 11, no. 6, pp. 431–446.

Shleifer, A., and R. W. Vishny. (June 1997). "A Survey of Corporate Governance." *Journal of Finance,* 52, no. 2, pp. 737–783.

Siegwart, H., and G. Neugebauer, eds. (1999). *Mega-Fusionen: Analysen, Kontroversen, Perspektiven,* 2nd ed. Bern/Stuttgart/Wien: Haupt.

Sirower, M. L. (1997). *The Synergy Trap.* New York: Simon & Schuster.

Slembeck, T. (1999). "Wo liegt die ökonomische Logik von Fusionen? Vom Eigeninteresse des Managements bei Firmenzusammenschlüssen." In *NZZ Fokus.* Zürich: Fusionen, pp. 9–11.

Stulz, R. (Fall/Winter 1999). "What's Wrong with Modern Capital Budgeting?" *Financial Practice and Education,* 9, no. 2, pp. 7–11.

Sundarsanam, S. (1995). *The Eessence of Mergers & Acquisitions.* London: Prentice Hall Europe.

Sundarsanam, S., P. Holl, and A. Salami. (1996). "Shareholder Wealth Gains in Mergers: Effect of Synergy and Ownership Structure." *Journal of Business Finance & Accounting,* 23, nos. 5/6, pp. 673–697.

Suter, R. (2000). *Corporate Governance & Management Compensation.* Zürich: Versus.

Varaiya, N. P. (1988). "The Winner's Curse Hypothesis and Corporate Takeovers." *Managerial and Decision Economics,* 9, no. 3, pp. 175–184.

Volkart, R. (1998). *Shareholder Value & Corporate Valuation.* Zürich: Versus.

Volkart, R. (1999). "Finanzielle Wertgenerierung durch Grossfusionen?" In *Mega Fusionen: Analysen, Kontroversen, Perspektiven,* 2nd ed., H. Siegwart and G. Neugebauer, eds. Bern/Stuttgart/Wien: Haupt, pp. 211–223.

Walter, I. (1996). "Mergers and Acquisitions in the Financial Services Industry." In *Schweizerisches Bankwesen im Umbruch,* H. Geiger, C. Hirszowicz, R. Volkart, and P. Weibel, eds. Bern/Stuttgart/Wien: Haupt, pp. 97–112.

Williamson, O. E. (1996). *The Mechanisms of Governance.* New York: Oxford University Press.

Chapter 6

Mergers "Down Under": An Australian Perspective on Mergers in Financial Services

Ian R. Harper

The financial services industry is gripped by merger mania. Worldwide, more than 4,000 mergers have taken place annually in each of the last few years. In many countries, including France, Italy, Germany, Japan, the United Kingdom, and Canada, major mergers among the largest banks have either been announced or mooted subject to legislative approval. Not only is the number of deals growing, so too is the average value of merger deals. The merger of CitiBank with Travelers Insurance and Salomon Smith Barney to form CitiGroup created the largest financial institution in history. In 1997, merger deals in the financial sector in the United States were worth more than U.S. $500 billion. The merger of BankAmerica and NationsBank alone was worth more than U.S. $60 billion.

AUSTRALIA'S EXPERIENCE

Australia has not been exempt from merger pressure in the financial services arena. Mergers among small to medium-size financial institutions are commonplace. Higher-profile mergers have also been permitted in special circumstances, including the merger/takeover of the ailing State Bank of Victoria by the Commonwealth Bank of Australia in the early 1990s and the merger of the Colonial Mutual Life Assurance Society with the State Bank of New South Wales in 1994.

Government policy has prevented some of the largest potential mergers from taking place in Australia. Prior to 1997, the Australian government maintained the so-called six pillars policy introduced by Finance Minister Paul Keating in the late 1980s to block the announced merger of the ANZ Bank and the National Mutual Life Assurance Society. The six pillars policy was so named because it banned mergers among any of the four major banks in Australia or the two largest life insurance companies. These six institutions were to remain independent of one another by government decree.

In May 1996, the Australian government established a public inquiry into the Australian financial system known as the Wallis Inquiry, following the Australian convention of naming public inquiries after their chairpersons, in this case, Stan Wallis. The Inquiry reported in March 1997, recommending the repeal of the six pillars policy on the grounds that Australia's competition policy regulator had sufficient authority to test the potential anticompetitive effects of mergers in financial services. A separate government-imposed ban on mergers in the financial services sector was neither necessary nor desirable in the Inquiry's view.

Receiving the Wallis Inquiry's Final Report, Finance Minister Peter Costello announced the *partial* repeal of the six pillars policy. Mergers would henceforth be permissible (subject to review by the competition regulator) between any of the major banks and either of the two largest life offices but not among the four major banks themselves. The six pillars policy thus became a four pillars policy that, to this day, prohibits mergers among the four major banks in Australia.

THE URGE TO MERGE

What explains the rash of merger activity in financial services around the world? If mergers were allowed, it is highly likely that two each of Australia's four major banks would seek to merge, producing two moderate-sized institutions by world standards but very large by Australian standards. Where is the pressure coming from? Just what do banks, both in Australia and elsewhere in the world, hope to gain from merger?

The financial services industry is living through a technological revolution. Financial services are information-intensive, and the digital revolution in information processing is profoundly affecting the production and distribution of financial services. Financial services are in the eye of the e-commerce storm.

Banks and other financial intermediaries owe their existence to information asymmetry. Information asymmetry impedes the use of markets to fulfill intertemporal exchange, and financial intermediaries step in to fill the breach. As information asymmetry subsides in the face of increasingly low-cost and ubiquitous access to information, financial intermediaries find themselves increasingly in competition with financial markets. Financial markets force the *disintermediation* of intertemporal exchange as well as encouraging the *securitization* of claims that were previously held to maturity on the balance sheets of financial intermediaries.

The increasing reliance on financial markets forces financial intermediaries to make a stark choice: they must find ways to incorporate financial market activity within their traditional operations, or they must face extinction as their business disintermediates. The wave of merger activity in financial systems worldwide is the manifestation of this evolution. The transformation of financial systems from the traditional reliance on balance sheet intermediation toward market exchange is releasing capital from the balance sheets of intermediaries, predominantly banks and life offices.

The capital that once underpinned the classic risk, liquidity, and maturity transformation undertaken by intermediaries is no longer needed, at least not in such large volumes. Trading securities on open markets simply does not require as much capital. Risks are traded on markets rather than absorbed through capital held on a balance sheet. The importance of liquidity and maturity transformation wanes as the depth and breadth of financial markets increases.

The chief factor driving mergers and acquisitions in financial systems is the industry's need to rationalize its use of capital. Old-style balance sheet intermediation is a capital-intensive business, whereas new-style market exchange requires significantly smaller amounts of capital. This leaves financial intermediaries facing the need either to release surplus capital or to raise the rate of return to the capital they retain. The first option is achieved as firms leave the industry following their acquisition by another player. Capital is returned to the shareholders of the acquired party. Merger is a means of raising the rate of return to the consolidated capital base of the merged entity.

Either capital is released from the industry, or its productivity within the industry is improved. The competing technology does not employ capital as intensively as traditional balance sheet intermediation. A firm that refuses to release capital or to raise the internal rate of return on the capital it retains will be outcompeted by those who substitute the use of market exchange for balance sheet intermediation.

THREE WAYS FORWARD

Acquisition is one way for a firm or industry to release surplus capital. A merger retains capital but aims to improve its marginal efficiency. There are two other ways in which the financial services industry might adjust to the need for lower capital. (1) Firms can simply repay their shareholders; this is a common tactic in the financial services industry. Many banks have re-purchased shares from their shareholders, both in Australia and elsewhere, in recent years. (2) The demutualization of mutual life assurance societies is another manifestation of the same phenomenon. Demutualization both releases capital locked up in the capital reserves of a mutual life office and facilitates its merger with, or acquisition of, another entity. All of Australia's large life offices have demutualized in recent years, AMP Limited being the most recent. Demutualization was a prerequisite (imposed by the regulatory authorities) of the merger between Colonial Mutual and the State Bank of NSW.

If a firm fails to adjust its capital usage by releasing capital or improving its performance, the most likely outcome is failure. A firm's insolvency represents the dissipation of its capital through operating losses. In this respect, if capital is not willingly given up to the market through acquisition or share-repurchase, or its rate of return is not raised to meet the higher industry standard, capital will be taken forcibly through the failure and subsequent liquidation of the firm and its assets.

Faced with competition from a new technology for the production and distribution of financial services, one that requires far less capital than traditional balance sheet intermediation, banks and other intermediaries have only three alternatives:

• Merge with, acquire, and/or be acquired by one or more competitors

• Adopt the new technology and repay surplus capital to existing shareholders.

• Maintain the status quo, dissipate capital through persistent losses, and eventually fail.

MERGERS AIM TO RAISE CAPITAL EFFICIENCY

Although many intermediaries have opted to repay surplus capital to their shareholders, the desire to merge with and/or acquire other intermediaries is also a popular choice. The aim of a merger is to raise the productivity of capital deployed within the firm. This can only occur if a firm raises the risk-adjusted rate of return to capital. To do so, it must raise revenue, lower cost, and/or lower risk for a given rate of return. Mergers are intended to achieve all three.

Cost reductions through economies of scale and scope are the time-honored justification for mergers. It must be conceded that the evidence for such cost economies arising from mergers in the financial services sector is at best ambivalent. Most studies of financial intermediaries, especially banks, show constant returns to scale over large ranges of output. The evidence for economies of scope is more encouraging but only slightly. This evidence should be expected to apply broadly to the major Australian banks with one exception. A merger between two major Australian banks would facilitate substantial rationalization of bank branches. Notwithstanding significant branch closures in recent years, there is still duplication of branches of the major banks in most centers. A merger is arguably the only way in which branch duplication can be addressed, since each bank acting independently is reluctant to be the first to leave town. A merged bank can close one in two branches while still maintaining a presence in all centers.

The scope for enhanced branch rationalization is an effect unlikely to be fully captured in research findings based overwhelmingly on U.S. data. Interstate branching was illegal in the United States from the 1930s until quite recently. U.S. bank mergers, especially large mergers, would add state-based branch networks together, with minimal branch duplication. The branch networks of Australia's major banks are national, giving rise to considerable duplication (and therefore scope for efficiency gains following amalgamation). Comparatively few mergers in the United States would entail amalgamation of national branch networks.

While academic studies of bank mergers tend to downplay the significance of cost economies, they are more sanguine on the revenue side. Merged entities gain from the capacity to cross-sell to their respective customer bases. Generally speaking, the two parties to a merger will bring complementary skills in different parts of the financial services business. These skills can be used to offer services to the "captive" market represented by the customers of the other firm. Even before the merged entity begins to offer a full suite of services to outside clients, it can profit by cross-selling to its existing customer base.

Size enhances revenue-earning capacity in yet another respect. As corporate finance moves increasingly off the balance sheets of banks into open capital markets, banks find themselves competing to lead-manage or underwrite corporate securities. This is a lucrative source of fee income with which to replace lost margin income as corporate finance disintermediates. However, size matters in the business of taking corporate securities to market. A bank that is large enough to manage a substantial corporate fund raising without the expense and effort of forming a syndicate has a significant advantage in any tender. Larger banks win larger tenders and earn significantly larger fees.

Size is also a major factor in establishing and maintaining a brand name. Brand recognition is increasingly important in a world dominated by information technology and e-commerce. Information goods, which include financial services, are "experience goods." To a large extent, the buyer cannot know the quality of the goods/services until after they have been purchased. This is clearly true of a financial product like a home mortgage. Firms compete in such markets by establishing brand names that consumers use to discriminate among alternative suppliers. As the range of suppliers accessible by the average consumer grows, through continuous extension of the worldwide web, for example, firms will need to spend more on establishing and maintaining a brand name. Larger firms can afford to spend larger absolute amounts on advertising and promotion. The same is true of the technology required to reach larger numbers of consumers and deal effectively with their needs. Larger firms can afford to spend larger absolute amounts on the necessary technology platforms.

Mergers raise the return to capital if they lower operating cost or raise operating revenue or both. Lowering risk can also raise the *risk-adjusted* return to capital. Larger firms have the potential to diversify risk across a wider class of assets. This is especially true of financial conglomerates, which combine banking risks with those normally associated with insurance. But even large banks or large insurance companies tend to benefit from risk diversification through size. In the case of banks, this is evidenced by the fact that the largest 25 banks in the United States have the lowest Tier 1 risk-weighted capital adequacy ratios. Their capacity to absorb risk through diversified portfolios enables them to economize on capital, thus raising its risk-adjusted rate of return.

Size also reduces the so-called risk of ruin. Modern financial institutions carry enormous financial risks, many of which are magnified due to trade in financial derivatives. Losses large enough to ruin a financial institution can accumulate with frightening speed, as Barings discovered to its cost. Larger institutions simply have greater capacity to absorb large losses and hence to survive unforeseen disasters. In this respect also, sheer size has a risk-reducing effect on the firm's capital base. The risk of insolvency through massive unforeseen losses is mitigated.

MERGERS MIGHT BE GOOD FOR BANKS, BUT . . .

It is clear why banks are under pressure to merge. It is also clear why a policy of outright prohibition of bank mergers places banks under unnecessary stress. Banks must adjust to the increasing pressure placed upon them by the twin forces of disintermediation and securitization. Blocking mergers rules out one means of effecting this adjustment. Banks will be forced to cut costs and raise revenue in other ways or risk persistent losses and the prospect of failure. The irony is that banning bank mergers, as both the Australian and Canadian governments have done, may well deliver outcomes that will be far less palatable to the general public than allowing mergers to proceed. There may well be more branch closures and staff reductions than otherwise, as well as faster increases in bank fees. Blocking these avenues of adjustment in addition to mergers (which the Australian government has not yet contemplated but could easily be forced by political pressure to do) would be extremely ill advised. Bank distress is one way to release capital from the industry but cannot be a rational choice given the inordinate social cost involved.

Yet it remains true that mergers raise potential concerns that must be weighed against the putative benefits to the institutions involved. The two chief concerns are the potential impact on the competitiveness of the financial system and its prudential soundness.

The Wallis Inquiry in Australia recommended that mergers within the financial system be tested for their potential anticompetitive impact by the competition policy regulator. The Inquiry saw no justification for a separate test, let alone an outright ban, to be applied to financial mergers but not to mergers outside the financial system. The Inquiry's recommendation that the six pillars policy be abolished was thus a vote of confidence in the capacity of the regulator to guard the public interest by weighing the potential benefits of mergers, both to the merging parties and to the public, against the potential costs.

The logic of the Inquiry's opposition to the six pillars policy applies with equal force to its successor, the four pillars policy. Concerns about the potential anticompetitive effect of bank mergers should be addressed by the competition regulator. Such an approach gives the merging parties an opportunity to address concerns raised by the regulator through undertakings. An outright ban blocks all possibility of a negotiated outcome. Although it is possible that bank mergers raise more problems for the community at large than they solve for the banks, this needs to be tested. The four pillars policy assumes either (1) that nothing is to be gained from bank mergers or (2) that any potential benefits are clearly outweighed by potential social costs. The machinery of competition policy in Australia is considered adequate for testing such propositions in other industries. The financial services sector should be treated no differently.

A second issue of concern to public policymakers is the prudential soundness of the Australian financial system. The Wallis Inquiry acknowledged that mergers within the financial system would impinge upon prudential soundness but considered such effects to be manageable and unlikely to warrant blocking mergers. Mergers would need to be cleared by Australia's prudential regulatory authority, the body responsible for regulating deposit-takers and insurers in Australia.[1]

The prudential regulator's chief concern in the event of a merger among Australia's major banks would be the effect on its ability to protect depositors of the merged entity. On the one hand, as argued above, a larger bank would benefit from greater diversification and hence lower the risk to depositors of losing their funds. On the other hand, larger banks become "too-big-to-fail"; that is, it is effectively impossible for governments to allow them to fail, given the potential political backwash from subsequent losses to depositors. Bank directors know this and may well adopt riskier lending policies in the knowledge that gains would accrue to shareholders while, in the worst case, losses would accrue to taxpayers rather than depositors. Managing a "moral hazard" of this type would be a priority for the regulator but is relatively easily addressed by maintaining or enhancing capital requirements on a merged entity. These would limit a merged bank's ability to reduce its capital base and focus its attention on raising the return to capital.

A further concern would be the pragmatic issue of managing distress in a large merged bank. On the only two occasions since 1945 that Australian bank regulators have had to manage bank failure, they have successfully arranged the takeover of the failed bank by another Australian institution. This becomes more difficult the larger the failed institution and the fewer healthy large institutions remain to be "asked" to pick up the pieces. Again, the prudential regulator would need to consider the likely difficulty of managing the failure of a large merged bank in setting the regulatory standards for the merged institution. As in the case of competition policy, it would seem unnecessary to ban mergers among major banks so as to avoid potential difficulties in prudential policy. Appropriate prudential standards need to be formulated and implemented.

"FOUR PILLARS" SHOULD GO

Australia's major banks need flexibility to adjust to revolutionary forces for change sweeping the financial services industry worldwide. The regulatory changes recommended by the Wallis Inquiry were predicated on those same forces for change bearing down on Australia's outdated system of financial regulation. It is hardly fair or sensible to change the regulatory apparatus while blocking necessary change in some of the largest regulated institutions.

It is no answer to say that mergers among Australia's major banks may compromise the competitiveness or prudential soundness of the Australian financial system. Australia's competition and prudential regulatory agencies are more than capable of assessing these effects and imposing conditions, as necessary, on merger proposals. The present position in which major bank mergers are simply ruled out of court (as is also the case in Canada) is untenable. The stakes are too high for the banks and ultimately for the depositing public.

NOTES

An earlier version of this chapter, written for an Australian audience, appears in "Mergers in Financial Services: Why the Rush?" *Australian Economic Review*, 33, no. 1 (March 2000), pp. 67–72.

1. In Australia, this body is separate from and independent of the central bank. The Wallis Inquiry recommended separation of prudential regulation and monetary policy to the Australian government.

REFERENCES

Amihud, Y., and G. Miller. (1998). *Bank Mergers and Acquisitions.* Boston: Kluwer Academic Publishers.

Berger, A., R. Demsetz, and P. Strahan, eds. (1999). "The Consolidation of the Financial Services Industry" (Special Issue). *Journal of Banking and Finance*, 23, nos. 2–4.

Dymski, G. (1999). *The Bank Merger Wave: The Economic Causes and Social Consequences of Financial Consolidation.* New York: M. E. Sharpe.

Financial System (Wallis) Inquiry. (1997). *Final Report.* Canberra: Australian Government Publishing Service. Also available at www.treasury.gov.au/publications/fsi.

Whittington, L. (1999). *The Banks.* Toronto: Stoddart.

Chapter 7

Bank Consolidation in Japan: What Can We Learn from It?

Benton E. Gup

Bank consolidation in Japan is epitomized by the Mizuho Financial Group (MHFG), a financial services holding company formed in 1999 by the consolidation of three major Japanese banks: Dai-Ichi Kangyo Bank, Fuji Bank, Ltd., and the Industrial Bank of Japan. When the consolidation is completed in 2005, the MHFG will be the world's largest bank, with total assets of about $1.3 trillion. It is also the first bank with assets exceeding $1 trillion![1]

The term *mizuho* can be translated as "fresh ears of rice," or "fresh harvest of rice." Japan used to be known as "the Land of Mizuho," which translates into "the land of vigorous rice plants." Thus, the name of the new organization suggests growth opportunities for Japan. Did this consolidation arise out of growth opportunities or out of necessity? Were bad loans the motive for the merger, or was it the desire to have a megabank that could compete internationally with the banks in the United States and Europe? An examination of the events leading up to this and other Japanese bank megamergers of the period helps to answer these questions. Whether these megamergers add value is an equally important issue, but only time can provide a definitive answer. Nevertheless, we can shed some light on that issue too.

BACKGROUND

Japan has a rich history in terms of emperors, shoguns, and samurai warriors dating back to its feudal (Kamakura) period, which began in 1185. After the American occupation (1945–1952) at the end of World War II, a democratic government was established, but Emperor Hirohito retained his position until his death in 1989. In the 1950s Japan experienced great economic growth and became an industrial power producing cars, cameras, computers, electronics, and other products that sparked trade wars with industrial nations. Nevertheless, it still retained some old traditions such as lifelong employment.

During the growth period, from the early 1950s until the early 1970s, the Japanese financial system was heavily regulated and the financial markets were repressed. Starting in the late 1970s, the government began to deregulate the financial system, a process that has continued into the twenty-first century. For example, the cross-selling of banking and insurance will remain illegal until the law is changed in 2001. Hoshi (2000) argues that the slow and incomplete pace of deregulation was one of the most important factors behind the banks' problems. He claims that as corporations in keiretus began to use the capital markets as a source of funds instead of their "main banks," the banks increasingly engaged in real estate lending. However, he explains neither why there was increased demand for real estate loans nor the fact that real estate loans are the most common feature of bank crises around the globe (Gup, 1998, 1999).

Real Estate

The 1980s were an economic boom period in Japan. The boom was fueled in part by bank loans that were highly concentrated in real estate. Direct and indirect lending for real estate and construction loans increased from about 9% in 1981 to about 15% in 1991. Additional real estate loans were made by bank subsidiaries, such as mortgage companies. Thus, real estate prices soared. It was estimated that the value of land in Tokyo exceeded the value of the land in California or that the value of land in Japan was worth four times the value of land in all of the United States (Kindleberger, 1996).

The Bank of Japan (BOJ) became concerned about soaring asset prices and a very tight labor market, and it aggressively raised interest rates to forestall inflation. Friedman (1997) observed that in 1990, the Bank of Japan reduced monetary growth from 13% to 3%, which resulted in lower asset prices, stock prices, incomes, and growth. By 1994, the low inflation had turned into actual deflation and economic stagnation.

Real estate values peaked in 1990, following the tightening of monetary policy. It was the beginning of a decade-long recession. By 1997, real estate values plunged an estimated 70 to 80%. And the Japanese banking sector suffered from nonperforming loans in the real estate market. The key point here is that bank profits and bad loans mirror the level of economic activity.[2] The combination of deflation and bad loans contributed to the sad state of the banks that were near collapse by the end of the 1990s. To help relieve the pressure of bad loans on the Japanese banks, more than $283 billion in distressed assets have been sold at deep discounts to foreign investors (Tett, 2000b).

Stock Values

The Japanese banking system is highly concentrated, and the large "city banks" hold about one-third of the total assets. Several of the city banks also serve as "main banks" in *keiretsus*, which are corporate groups of banks, insurance companies, trading companies, manufacturing companies, and marketing firms. The firms are linked together though cross-holdings of stock. Japanese banks are permitted to own up to 5% of the shares in other companies in the group, and the value of the shares is considered part of their Tier 2 capital. The keiretsus own about 70% of the shares of publicly traded companies in Japan. When stock prices declined 56% from their peaks in 1990, the bank's capital ratios suffered. Moreover, the write-off of their bad debts is financed primarily by the sale of stocks held by banks.

Government Support

The Japanese government tried to stimulate the lagging economy and stabilize the banking sector. The Bank of Japan kept interest rates near zero to help the banks reduce their funding costs. In January 2000, the range of interest rates for the three-month yen TIBOR was 0.187% (January 4) to 0.133% (January 27) (*Fuji Monthly Market News*, February 2000). However, banks have had problems retaining depositors with interest rates near zero. To deal with this problem, the banks are trying to entice their customers with financial products from related companies in their keiretsus and are offering new services. Although the policy succeeded in keeping the cost of borrowing low, it had an adverse effect on the earnings of insurance companies that played a key role in the bank mergers. It also may have contributed to a "liquidity trap" and "credit crunch" that forestalled economic recovery (Hutchison, 2000).

By early 2000, the government had injected nearly $1 trillion into the economy in 10 separate stimulus packages that provided only very short-term benefits. It deregulated and bailed out the large banks that for some time were considered too-big-to-fail (Spiegel, 1999). The revised Foreign Exchange Law in 1998 was the first step in the Big Bang financial reforms that were designed to reform the financial system in order to open the banking, insurance, stock exchanges, and superannuation markets to global competition. It allows banks to engage in the securities and trust businesses as well as lifting the ban on holding companies. Hoshi and Kashyap (2000) argue that the deregulation had an unintended side effect. It allowed large Japanese borrowers to borrow directly in the capital markets, thereby reducing their dependence on banks. The banks, now serving the smaller borrowers, became more closely tied to property loans than in the past. The property loans did not fare well in the 1990s. The Big Bang also contributed to a shift in savings out of Japan into U.S. and other foreign stock and bond markets. Accordingly, the Big Bang did not help the banks to the extent anticipated. The 17 largest banks had total bad debts of about $172 billion.

In October 1998, the government enacted two laws dealing with restructuring the financial system: the Law Concerning Emergency Measures for Reconstruction of the Functioning of the Financial System (the Financial Reconstruction

Law) and the Law Concerning Emergency Measures for Early Strengthening of Financial Function (the Bank Recapitalization Law). It also instituted tax reforms to stimulate the economy (Hall, 1999; Hiroshi, 1999). The restructuring included the use of about $73 billion in public funds to be injected as bank capital in the form of preferred stock and subordinated debt into selected large banks, including Dai-Ichi Kangyo, Fuji, and IBJ. The banks are expected to retire or convert the preferred stock and repay the subordinated date on or before 2010.[3]

In early 2000, the Japanese government was considering an additional spending package to boost the economy if economic growth was not satisfactory (Tett, 2000a). In April 2000, weak consumer sentiment contributed to declining retail sales that had fallen for 36 consecutive months (Nakamae, 2000b). Declining retail sales contributed to the bankruptcy of the Sogo department store, and the fear was that the retailer's collapse could trigger additional bankruptcies. More will be said about this matter shortly.

The additional spending may stimulate the economy. However, it should be noted that Japan's debt levels are projected to be 130% of their GDP, the highest relative debt levels in the industrialized world.

Although the national government is trying to stimulate the economy, the Tokyo prefecture government is going to tax the large banks to raise revenue to stave off a fiscal crisis in the city. The Tokyo Metropolitan Government tax is 3% of gross profits (Kashiwagi, 2000b; Tett, 2000c). It is feared that Osaka and other cities might follow suit with local taxes.

Asian Financial Crises

The financial crises that began in Thailand in 1997 and spread to other Southeast Asian countries adversely affected Japanese banks. Japanese banks played a major role in funding the growth of Thailand, and they were major creditors in Southeast Asia when the economies faltered (Gup, 1999). Thus, the Japanese banks suffered from losses both at home and abroad. According to Hall (1999), the bad loans in the Japanese banking sector increased from about 8,000 billion yen in 1992 to about 35,207 trillion yen in 1998. In relative terms, Hoshi and Kashyap (2000) estimated that in September 1998, bad loans in Japan's banking sector exceeded 7% of GDP.

CONSOLIDATION

There is a pattern of consolidation of the biggest banks in Japan that began in the 1970s. This section reviews the consolidation process in chronological order.

Dai-Ichi and Kangyo

Dai-Ichi Bank, Ltd., founded in 1873, was the first bank established in Japan. The Nippon Kangyo Bank, Ltd. was formed in 1897.

Dai-Ichi and Kangyo banks merged in 1971 to form Dai-Ichi-Kangyo Bank (DKB). The merger process did not go well between the staffs of the two banks because of conflicting cultures and turf wars between them. In addition, many managers resisted laying off employees who were accustomed to lifetime employment. Until the mid-1990s, the bank maintained separate personnel departments for employees of Dai-Ichi and Kangyo banks.

DKB serves more than 12 million individuals and 100,000 business concerns through a network of 350 or more branches in Japan and 37 overseas. In March 1999, DKB had a −25.62% return on equity and a debt-equity ratio of 323%.[4]

Bank of Tokyo and Mitsubishi

In 1996, the Bank of Tokyo and Mitsubishi combined to form the Bank of Tokyo-Mitsubishi, Ltd. In Japan, the bank's network of more than 300 offices are located primarily in Tokyo and Osaka. The Mitsubishi bank group serves Japanese and foreign clients in more than 80 offices worldwide. This group includes Union Bank of California, which is ranked among the top 30 banks in the United States in terms of assets.

In January 1999, the Bank of Tokyo-Mitsubishi announced that it needed $2 billion for affiliated keiretsu companies. The combination faced huge losses from the Mitsubishi keiretsu. Mitsubishi Electric lost $330 million, Mitsubishi Chemicals Corp. and Mitsubishi Materials Corp. both forecast losses of more than $200 million, and Mitsubishi Motors Corp. was in bad shape.[5] In March 1999, the bank's return on equity was −3.64%, and its debt-equity ratio was 515%.[6] It too was having financial problems.

In April 2000, the Bank of Tokyo-Mitsubishi announced that it planned to merge with Mitsubishi Trust & Banking Corporation in the first half of 2001. The new organization will be called the Mitsubishi Tokyo Financial Group, Inc. Both banks are part of the Mitsubishi keiretsu. This combination is the first to combine a commercial bank with a trust company, and it will be the largest trust company in Japan. At the time the deal was announced, the bank will be the fifth largest in the world.

Two other members of the Mitsubishi group (Tokio Marine & Fire Insurance Company and Meiji Life Insurance Company) are expected to join the holding company. In addition, Mitsui Marine & Fire Insurance Company is expected to join as well (Dvorak, 2000b). Although the primary focus of this article is on banks, consolidation in the banking industry is closely related to consolidation in the insurance industry. In that connection, Tokio Marine & Fire Insurance formed an alliance with Asahi Mutual Life and Nichido Fire and Marine. More will be said about the insurance industry shortly.

Mizuho Financial Group

Next was the combination of Dai-Ichi Kango Bank (DKB), Fuji Bank, and the Industrial Bank of Japan (IBJ) to form the Mizuho Financial Group (MHFG), a holding company. Collectively, the banks had assets of about $1.3 trillion, bad debts of $45 billion, and 1998 losses of $8.5 billion.

Fuji Bank was established in 1880. It offers banking services through about 300 branches in Japan and about 20 overseas. It also has 182 subsidiaries overseas that offer securities, trust, and lease operations. In March 1999, its return on equity was −31%, and it had a debt-equity ratio of 716%.[7]

IBJ is the largest long-term credit bank in Japan—a "wholesale" bank that makes long-term loans as well as underwriting both public and private bond issues. Its services include derivatives-based products, leasing, asset management, and more. It has 67 subsidiaries worldwide. In March 1999, the bank had a −13.73% return on equity and a debt-equity ratio 2,207%.[8]

The data presented in Table 7.1 reveals that the three banks are quite different in their operations as reflected in sources of income for fiscal 1999.[9]

Both DKB and Fuji were seeking government bailouts. DKB's ex-chairman tried to commit suicide after 11 of its top executives were indicted in 1997 in a payoff scandal. Fuji had been subject to a speculative attack by fraudulent loan applicants in 1998. It also made a failed attempt to enter the Osaka market, and it was having difficulty attracting funds from other banks.

Equally important, IBJ was about to lose the exclusive right it enjoyed as one of Japan's three long-term credit banks to issue five-year debentures. The other two long-term credit banks (Long Term Credit Bank of Japan and Nippon Credit Bank) had failed. IBJ's president, Masao Nishimura, said: "We would not have merged if we did not have an extreme sense of crisis" (Fulford, 2000). Part of the crises has to do with the fact that many of the customers of these banks are industries that are suffering from slow economic growth, such as steel and textiles, and the defunct Nagasakiya supermarket chain. The debt rating of the three banks was slightly above that of junk bonds. Thus, this is considered a defensive merger where the banks hope to benefit from restructuring.[10]

Fulford (2000) claims that the real reason for the merger is information technology (IT). Citibank and Chase have been spending about $1.5 billion per year on IT while the big Japanese banks have only been spending about $500 million, and most of that was on accounting systems. By merging, the MHFG hopes to spend about $2 billion on IT. Following the merger announcement in August 1999, IBJ's president, Masao Nishimura, stated: "This will make us the only group in Japan that can match American banks in IT investments" ("Sumo-sized Bank Created," 2000). However, because most of the IT budget is spent on integrating systems rather than on retail banking systems, the banks are still

Table 7.1
Income Distribution for DKB, Fuji Bank, and IBJ, March 1999

	DKB	Fuji Bank	IBJ
Loan interest income	63%	49%	32%
Other interest income	20%	22%	34%
Non-interest income	17%	29%	34%

vulnerable to competition from nonbanking firms such as convenience stores and others that offer retail banking services ("Only Connect," 2000).

The MHFG was formed on the basis of a stock-for-stock exchange, based on an equal stock exchange ratio between the banks. The merger process began in August 2000, and it is expected to take several years to complete.

The MHFG announced five basic principles of consolidation:[11]

1. Offer a wide range of the highest-quality financial services to customers.

2. Maximize shareholders' value and, as the leader of Japan's financial service industry, earn the trust of society at large.

3. Offer attractive and rewarding job opportunities for employees.

4. Fully utilize the advantages and strengths of each bank and maximize the benefit of the consolidation through cost reduction.

5. Create a new corporate climate and culture.

In this combination, the maximization of shareholder wealth is a goal of management. Equally important, the MHFG state that in order to increase performance and to create a management structure that places an emphasis on creation of shareholder wealth, they are planning to introduce a compensation structure that includes stock options.

Another feature that makes the MHFG deal unique is that the three banks formed a single holding company while the other banks merged into one company. Masao Nishimura, president of the Industrial Bank of Japan, stated that their customers are becoming more specialized, diverse, and sophisticated. A holding company allows them to establish legally separate companies to serve the specialized needs of their customers ("Forging the New Financial Group," 2000).

The holding company will oversee the various business units (consumer banking, corporate banking, securities and investment banking, public sector banking, International banking, dealing and trading, settlement and clearing, securities and investment banking, trust and asset management) that will be consolidated into the following businesses: The Mizuho Bank, Ltd.; The Mizuho Corporate

Bank Ltd.; The Mizuho Securities Co. Ltd.; The Mizuho Trust & Banking Co., Ltd.;[12] and other financial subsidiaries.

The holding company organization is expected to facilitate decision making and resource allocation. Another expected benefit is that it will give the subsidiaries autonomy and the ability to respond to customer needs. This is why the three original banks will be reorganized and combined into the new subsidiaries, each with its own new corporate culture. Stated otherwise, the three original banks will no longer exist. They will be integrated into business units, and a new culture is expected to emerge in each business unit. Thus, the culture of the consumer banking business will differ from that of the investment banking and trust businesses. While the concept is good, the implementation of this strategy is not easy. An October 2000 article in the *Nikkei Weekly* stated that "the Mizuho merger could go bust due to internal conflicts as officials try to protect their own interests and those of their banks" (Suzuki, 2000).

The MHFG is increasing their investment in information technology. They hope to provide these services and others, such as online banking, to their commercial and retail customers (Sims, 1999). They also intend to play a role in business-to-business (B2B) and business to consumer (B2C) information technology.

It is also expected that one corporate leader will be in charge of the combined companies. However, during the transition phase, there are three chief executives, two chairmen, and one president. More than 100 committees have been organized to facilitate the merger. Each committee has exactly the same number of staff from each of the three banks. In the early phase of the consolidation, one article commented that there appears to be "little leadership from the top," and "strife is spreading below."[13]

The notion of lifetime employment is still part of Japan's corporate culture, but it is slowly changing. The principal change is early retirement, which will facilitate the elimination of 7,000 or more jobs out of the combined payroll of 35,000, and closing about 150 of the 740 branches to eliminate duplications and reduce overhead expenses. These cuts are to be spread over five years. The reduction in the bank's labor force is relatively small, in part because of resistance to layoffs due to the depressed level of economic activity. In addition, there is substantial overlap between DKB's and Fuji's branch systems; this suggests that layoffs will be heavier in some parts of the country than in others. The branch consolidation is likely to begin overseas, which represents a pullback from abroad.

In summary, the ability of the MHFG consolidation to add value depends on the willingness and ability of three banks to cut costs, to integrate their systems, and to overcome corporate cultural differences. Cutting costs will occur as their combined labor force is reduced by 7,000 over a five-year period. The integration of information technology and other operating systems is a daunting task for two, let alone three, banks. The meshing of three distinctly different corporate cultures is even more challenging. Only time will tell how effective they will be in these areas.

Sumitomo-Sakura

In October 1999, the Sumitomo Bank Ltd. and the Sakura Bank Ltd. announced a "strategic alliance" and their intention to merge by April 2002, which was later updated to April 2001 ("Japan Banks Speed up Ties," 2000; Landers, 1999). The completion date was accelerated because of the increased pace of consolidation in Japan and because of competitive threats from convenience store chains that offer banking services.

The Sumitomo-Sakura merger will result in the world's third largest bank, with combined assets of about $926 billion. The new bank will be called the Sumitomo Mitsui Banking Corporation. Sakura Bank is the main bank for the Mitsui kerietsu, and Sumitomo is the main bank for the Sumitomo group.

The merger is considered a rescue for Sakura, although both banks were in poor shape financially. In March 1999, the returns on equity for Sumitomo and Sakura banks were -34% and -29%, respectively. Their debt-equity ratios were 626% and 406%.[14] Sumitomo has a network of more than 330 branches in Japan and 42 offices overseas. The banks provide wholesale and retail banking as well as capital market services.

Mitsui Taiyo Kobe Bank Ltd. was formed by the merger of Mitsui Bank Ltd. and Taiyo Kobe Bank, Ltd. in 1990. The name was changed to Sakura Bank Ltd. in 1992. It has over 450 domestic branches and 78 overseas offices. It is a full-service bank.

As shown in Table 7.2, the relative loan interest incomes are about the same in both banks, but substantial differences exist in their other sources of income, reflecting their different lines of business.[15] Sumitomo has a strategic relationship with Daiwa Securities, the nation's second largest brokerage firm.

Both Sumitomo and Sakura are main banks in their respective keiretsus. The major stockholders of Sakura keiretsu include various life insurance companies, Toyota Motor Corporation, and the Chase Manhattan Bank, N.A. (London). The major stockholders in the Sumitomo keiretsu include life insurance companies, Matsushita Electric Industrial Company, and Sanyo Electric Company. The two banks have about 30,000 employees and expect to cut more than 9,000 jobs by 2004. They also plan to cut 151 domestic and 32 overseas branches.

Of particular note here is that the bank wants to "go beyond the conventional context and boundaries of traditional banking and transform ourselves into a network and financial services company" ("Partners in the Formation," 2000). Sakura is forming an Internet portal to promote its products online. This direction flows from the difficulty in attracting deposits when interest rates are near zero and from the desire to sell customers related financial products.

Table 7.2
Income Distribution for Sumitomo and Sakura Banks, March 1999

	Sumitomo Bank	Sakura Bank
Loan interest income	41%	45%
Other interest income	26%	36%
Non-interest income	33%	19%

Sanwa-Tokai-Toyo Trust (Asahi)

The formation of the MHFG was followed in October by the merger announcement of Tokai and Asahi, two regional banks.[16] Tokai is headquartered
in Nagoya, which is considered Japan's industrial heartland. Asahi has 380
branches concentrated in the Tokyo area and also has some offices overseas.

In March 2000, it was announced that Sanwa Bank Ltd. would join with
Tokai and Asahi to create the world's second largest bank holding company
with total assets of just under $1 trillion. Sanwa has a market capitalization
about twice that of the other banks and will likely take control of the group.
This is consistent with Sanwa's reputation of being "profit oriented" and with
its decisive management style. The new bank will focus primarily on domestic
operations that cater to retail depositors and small and midsize businesses, although Sanwa does some international business (Kashiwagi, 2000a). Sanwa,
headquartered in Osaka (the western part of Japan), is a key market. Sanwa
established a specialized financial keiretsu, with cross-holdings of shares and
business relationships with Toyo Trust and Banking, Taiyo Mutual Life, Daido
Life, Nippon Fire & Marine, Koa Fire & Marine, and Universal Securities ("The
Ties That Bind," 2000). The ultimate goal of these firms is to share information
about customers and cross-sell their products.

Tokai and Asahi had planned to establish the holding company in October
2000, and Sanwa would join the group in April 2001 (Dvorak, 2000a). However,
in June 2000, Asahi announced its intention to drop out of the merger, citing
the inability to agree on how the three banks should combine their operations.
Ashahi could not accept a full-scale merger. It preferred integrating the operations under the umbrella of a holding company. Ashahi had overlapping
branches and businesses with the other two banks. There was also concern about
its ability to form a large-scale regional alliance and to strengthen its share of
the Tokyo market (Moules, 2000; Szep, 2000).

In July 2000, Toyo Trust and Banking agreed to join with Sanwa and Tokai
to form a holding company that will be called UFJ Holdings, Inc. The holding
company will focus on middle-size corporate and retail customers.

OBSERVATIONS

Eastern Culture

Schwartz, Leyden, and Hyatt (1999) state that the experience in Japan highlights key differences between the economic and political systems of the East and West. The eastern methods of resolving economic problems are dependent on politics and government actions such as bailouts. To some extent, the old culture remained in Japan, and politics played a larger role in industrial development there than it did in the United States and Europe. There were commitments to lifelong employment, protection of markets, old school ties to government jobs, move of government retirees to corporate jobs, and so on. A study by Anderson and Campbell (2000) investigating corporate governance at Japanese banks from 1977 to 1996 found very little executive turnover, and it was not related to bank performance. This is in sharp contrast to the United States where performance and executive turnover are closely related. The western methods tend to be *self-correcting* because they are transparent and they are designed to gather feedback and change directions when circumstances warrant. Thus, Anderson and Campbell claim that the delays in restructuring the Japanese banking sector were attributed to weak corporate governance. While that may be correct, it was part of the culture to do it that way.

Schwartz, Leyden, and Hyatt (1999) argue that healthy economic systems always have at least two good options to choose from, economically and politically. They maintain that Japan's system of financial management was so closed that the actual problems could not be detected, much less solved, until it was too late.

Another aspect of eastern culture may be found in corporate goals and values. The Bank of Tokyo-Mitsubishi's corporate philosophy was expressed in its 1997 long-term business plan, which included the following corporate values, guiding principles, and corporate objectives:[17]

Corporate Values
The Bank of Tokyo Mitsubishi Group places primary emphasis on satisfying its customers, preserving its own integrity, and contributing to the communities in which it operates worldwide.
Guiding Principles
1) Ensure customer satisfaction by valuing professionalism,
2) Develop the skills and knowledge necessary to respond to challenges,
3) Observe professional ethics and act with responsibility and pride.
Corporate Objectives
1) Build on our solid domestic management base to provide quality, diversified financial services in Japan and overseas.
2) Acquire a reputation for reliability among customers and appeal to shareholders, employees and communities.

Similarly, the 1999 annual report of the Mitsubishi Trust and Banking Corporation is to "Maximize the unique functions of trust banks to contribute to society, help our customers achieve their goals, and ensure Mitsubishi Trust remains the first choice for banking and trust services."[18]

The corporate goal of maximization of shareholder wealth is conspicuous by its absence from statements made by the Bank of Tokyo Mitsubishi Group. This is in sharp contrast to the mission statement in the merger agreement between Sumitomo Bank and Sakura Bank. Their mission is[19]

- To provide even greater value added services to our customers, and to achieve growth together with our customers.

- To continuously create shareholder value through the achievement of sustainable business growth.

- To provide a challenging and professionally rewarding work environment for diligent and highly motivated employees.

Corporate culture also differs. Each corporation has a unique culture, and two or three corporations may not work well together. The broken alliance between Asahi Bank, Sanwa Bank, and Tokai Bank may reflect cultural differences as well as other problems. Similarly, it serves as a red warning flag to the MHFG that it may face similar cultural problems.

Finally, the Japanese government and companies believed in government bailouts. This aspect of their culture appeared to be changing when Sogo Company, a 170-year-old large department store chain, failed in July 2000 and the government did not bail it out ("Bank Shares Tumble," 2000; Landers, 2000; Strom, 2000). Sogo owed more than $17 billion. The bankruptcy was declared after Shinsei Bank refused to restructure or forgive Sogo's debts. Shinsei had recently been acquired by a foreign consortium led by New York-based Ripplewood Holdings LLC. Shinsei's refusal to restructure Sogo's debts was particularly bad news for the Industrial Bank of Japan, which, with a 363 billion yen exposure, was the largest creditor to Sogo. Shinsei's exposure was 205 billion yen ("Japan: Sogo Bankruptcy," 2000). The Ministry of International Trade and Industry, fearing that Sogo's collapse could lead to a new wave of bankruptcies, promised $1.66 billion in low-cost loans to firms affected by the bankruptcy (Nakamae and Tett, 2000d).

When, however, the Hazama construction group had financial difficulties shortly after the collapse of Sogo, a group of Japanese banks, including Shinsei, indicated that they would forgive some of the firm's debts as part of a rehabilitation plan (Tett, 2000c). Banks have also waived more than $1 billion in debt for Kumagai Gumi Co., another major construction firm that got into financial difficulty. Some believe that forgiving some of these debts was due in part to Shinsei's treatment of Sogo. Others believe that the cleanup of bad debts is an illusion and that they still hold many bad loans ($93.4 billion), some of which they may forgive rather than foreclose on them (Kashiwagi, 2000c). Yet others believe that since the construction industry is a major political supporter of the Liberal Democratic Party and since this industry employs 10% of the workforce, the large firms are too important to fail ("Japan's Bail-outs," 2000).

Too-Big-to-Fail

The consolidation of the large Japanese banks appears to be a form of government too-big-to-fail (TBTF) policy. As noted earlier, TBTF refers to government actions that are applied to firms whose failure would have major disruptive effects on the economy. In TBTF, the government steps in to avoid a large-scale economic disruption, and it bails out the firms in one manner or another. Japanese government actions and policies with respect to banks that carry large problem loans and that have customers who are in financial distress represent one form of TBTF.

Thomas Hoenig, president of the Federal Reserve Bank of Kansas City, states that TBTF has three consequences (Hoenig, 1999): (1) It creates competitive inequalities that could threaten the viability of smaller banks and distort the allocation of credit; (2) it provides a moral hazard problem that appears to extend the government safety net beyond insured deposits; and (3) it leads to a less efficient financial system because the banks do not have to face the full force of market discipline and are under less pressure to operate efficiently. Kane (1999) points out that the market's presumption of TBTF lowers the entities' financing costs. Given the government's near-zero interest rates, one wonders how much lower the financing costs can be for these banks. Even if their costs were zero, their problem is not their net interest margins but their large volume of bad loans.

The Economy

A bank's success or failure is closely associated with the state of the economy that it serves. The state of the Japanese economy has been deteriorating since the real estate bubble burst in the late 1980s and early 1990s. In response, the government has tried various stimulus packages and low interest rates hoping to bolster economic activity. Japan's problems were exacerbated by the financial crises that started in Thailand in July 1997 and spread to other Southeast Asian countries served by Japanese banks. In the fourth quarter of 1997 and throughout 1998, Japan's rate of gross domestic product (GDP) growth was negative. In the third quarter of 1998, it was −3.2% ("International Economic Trends," 1999). Moody's downgraded Japan's domestic currency debt rating from AAA in late 1998 to Aa1 in 1999 and was considering further downgrades in early 2000 ("Moody's Warning," 2000) in view of the country's structural problems in the economy and the fact that Japan's government debt was the highest relative to GDP in the industrialized world. Some of that debt was used to support weak banks.

Despite massive fiscal stimuli and near-zero short-term interest rates, the Japanese economy suffered, and GDP grew at a meagre estimated 0.6% in 1999. Even so, that was better than the 1.1% decline forecasters had expected in a mid-year 1999 survey ("Up and Down," 2000). The better than expected, albeit slow, performance, combined with a recovery in the Southeast Asian countries are positive signs for the Japanese economy and for the banks that serve these markets. GDP in Indonesia, Malaysia, the Philippines, and Thailand increased in the first quarter of 1999 and was substantially above their low points in the previous year ("The Tigers," 2000, p. 3).

Strategies for Globalization

As globalization continues, some world-class banks are in danger of taking second- or third-tier roles. According to Kraus (1999), two strategies have emerged to help them avoid that fate. One strategy is to focus on building a huge domestic bank that is very profitable and to ignore the international markets. The other strategy is to build a global powerhouse that can provide financial services to the world's largest corporations. An article in *The Economist* asserts that Japan and other governments should urge banks to merge, which would allow them to compete internationally with the global banks in Europe and the United States ("The Bank-Merger Splurge," 1999). The article also states that bigger banks created by mergers are not necessarily better for three reasons. First, the consolidation may reduce competition and hurt consumers. Second, the bigger banks are not necessarily safer, especially if they are still burdened with bad loans, and they don't have the IT infrastructure to compete effectively. Finally, the alleged benefits of increased profits are often illusory—a fact confirmed by numerous studies (Agrawal and Jaffe, 2000; Kwan and Eisenbeis, 1999).[20]

Is Valued Added?

KPMG surveyed 700 mergers around the world and 107 companies ("Unlocking Shareholder Value," 1999) and found that only 17% of the deals added value to the combined companies, 30% made no difference, and 53% destroyed value. A study by Houston, James, and Ryngaert (1999) reported that most of the expected value created by mergers comes from management's overestimating revenue gains and underestimating (or not reporting) losses attributable to mergers, as well as its tendency to exaggerate costs savings from the mergers. For example, Kover (2000) found that estimated earnings from the April 1998 NationsBank/Bank of America merger were $5.59 per share but that actual earnings were $4.46 for 1999. Similarly, estimated earnings for the November 1997 First Union/Core States bank merger were $4.46 but reported earnings were only $3.60, and the April 1998 Bank One/First Chicago merger had estimated earnings of $4.23 but reported earnings of $3.46.

Table 7.3
Golden Parachutes

Acquirer	Acquired	Acquired CEO	Golden Parachute
Deutsche Bank	Bankers Trust	Frank Newman	$74 million
NationsBank	Bank America	David Coulter	$29 million
Vodaphone AirTouch	Mannesmann	Klaus Esser	$16 million
Bank Nationale de Paris	Paribas	Andre Lang-Levy	$15million
Total Fina	Elf Aquitaine	Philippe Jaffre	$6.6 million

Sources: Ferguson and Lee, 1999; Raghavan and Sims, 2000.

Managerialism

Managerialism—the self-interest of managers—may also be a factor in the mergers, as manifested in several different ways. First, there is only one king in every kingdom. Stated otherwise, there is only one head of a corporation after a merger or an acquisition. Nevertheless, some very successful companies have co-leaders.[21] Microsoft's Bill Gates and Steve Ballmer are one example. However, in the megamerger of Travelers Group, Inc., and Citicorp, the co-CEO concept didn't work.[22] Travelers Sanford Weill held all of the financial power, and Citicorp's John Reed decided to retire early. While merging two banks is a very difficult task, merging three is mind boggling in terms of ascertaining who will be boss.

Second, golden parachutes are provided for those who do not become the head of the surviving corporation (see Table 7.3).

Third, review of the extensive body of literature dealing with managerial motives and mergers suggests that managers' interests frequently take precedence over those of stockholders.[23] A study by Bliss and Rosen (2000) found that CEO compensation tends to increase after bank mergers, even when they don't pay off for stockholders. This finding is consistent with the documented link between firm size and executive compensation.

Third, which corporate culture will survive? As previously noted, there were vastly different corporate cultures at the various banks in Japan and elsewhere. The idea of creating new corporate cultures by reorganizing into business units has merit but as of yet is unproven. John Reed, former co-CEO of Travelers/ Citigroup, had the following to say about the clash of cultures in their merger (Sellers, 2000).

We are talking about putting two cultures together that are quite different, quite distinct. I'm trying hard to understand how to make this work. I will tell you that it is not simple and not easy, and it is not clear to me that it will necessarily be successful. Just as the body can sometimes reject an organ that it needs, business systems can sometime reject behaviors that are required for the system's success. As you put two cultures together, you get all sorts of strange, aberrant behavior, and it is not clear whether each side getting to know the other side helps, or whether having common objectives helps, or whether it is just the passage of time.

Goffee and Jones (1998) describe four types of corporate cultures: networked, mercenary, fragmented, and communal. Shedding some light on what this means in terms of physical space are the following considerations: networked organizations have unlocked doors and free movement of people; mercenary organizations allocate space functionally and efficiently to achieve a goal; fragmented organizations design space so that people can work alone, even in their cars or at home; finally communal cultures share space, and there are few physical barriers between workers. Based on the information given about the banks, we cannot tell which culture will emerge or if a new shared culture will result.[24]

Information Technology

MHFG and other banks are just beginning to explore IT markets. As previously noted, MHFGs' spending on IT was inadequate, and it was not focused on the retail market. However, MHFG is focusing on the business-to-business (B2B) IT market, which may prove more profitable. Sakura Bank is launching Japan's first online Internet bank, to be known as Japan Net Bank. It is a joint venture in which Sakura owns 50% and the remainder is owned by Sumitomo, Nippon Life Insurance, Fujitsu, NTT DoCoMo (mobile phone operator), and others (Cameron, 2000).

One of the biggest threats to traditional brick and mortar banks comes from information technology companies that have the funds and expertise to provide financial services. For example, Softbank Corporation, a global Internet investment banking company based in Japan, has a finance subsidiary, Softbank Finance Corporation, that advertises itself as a one-stop online financial marketplace offering payments systems, insurance, mortgages, brokerage services, foreign exchange, and so on.[25] Softbank is the leader of a consortium that will be the new owner of Nippon Credit Bank. Softbank Corporation and a 7-Eleven retail chain plan to offer low-cost, convenient banking services at its 8,230 outlets and over the Internet.

Insurance Connection

As shown in Table 7.4, the principal MHFG stockholders in the three keiretsus are life insurance companies and trust companies. It is interesting to note that Dai-Ichi Mutual Life Insurance Co. is a principal stockholder in all three banks and Sumitomo Trust & Banking is a principal stockholder in two of the banks.[26] These relationships may help to explain why these banks consolidated. The government-enforced low-interest rates adversely affected the investment

Table 7.4
Principal MHFG Stockholders and Percentage Share

Dai-Ichi Kangyo Bank, Ltd.	Fuji Bank, Ltd.	Industrial Bank of Japan, Ltd.
Asahi Mutual Life Insurance Co., 4.58%	Yasuda Mutual Life Insurance Co., 3.07%	Dai-Ichi Mutual Life Insurance Co., 6.21%
Nippon Life Insurance Co., 3.61%	Dai-Ichi Mutual Life Insurance Co., 3.07%	Mejii Life Insurance Co., 3.32%
Dai-Ichi Mutual Life Insurance Co., 2.85%	Yasuda Fire & Marine Insurance Co., Ltd., 2.43%	Nippon Life Insurance Co., 3.32%
The Long-Term Credit Bank of Japan, 2.80%	Yasuda Trust & Banking Co., Ltd., 2.43%	Sumitomo Trust & Banking Co., Ltd., 2.18%
Sumitomo Trust & Banking Co., Ltd., 1.90%	Nippon Life Insurance Co., 2.11%	Daiwa Bank Ltd., 1.87%

Source: "The Dai-Ichi Kangyo Bank, Limited," Fuji Bank News Release, August 20, 1999.

returns of insurance companies, which no doubt influenced their decisions to expand their products and services via banks and by forming alliances with non-life insurance companies, such as marine and fire insurance companies (e.g., Dai-Ichi Mutual Life Insurance Co. with Yasuda Fire & Marine) and health insurance companies (e.g., American Family Life Assurance—AFLAC) ("Japanese Insurers Endgame," 2000; Tett, 2000d). Standard life insurance policies guarantee a return of 2.75% for eight years. If the life insurance companies invest the premium in 10-year government bonds, they will earn less than 2%. The negative spread contributed to the failure of Chiyoda Life, one of Japan's largest life insurance companies, in October 2000. Chiyoda's planned merger with Germany's Allianz was called off, and there were no other potential partners ("Chiyoda Life," 2000). Other failed insurers in 2000 include Kyoei Life, Daihyaku, and Taisei.

Other factors contributing to consolidation in the insurance industry are deregulation and foreign competition.

The strong presence of life and non-life insurance companies in these and other keiretsus suggests that there will be consolidation in that industry as well as integration with the banking industry.[27] The merger of Mitsui Marine (part of the Sakura group) and Sumitomo Marine & Fire suggests that the consolidation of insurance companies will be along bank lines. Thus, in February 2000, Sumitomo Marine & Fire and Mitsui Marine & Fire Insurance agreed to merge ("Japanese Insurers to Tie," 2000). Similarly, Dai-Ichi Mutual Life Insurance and Yasuda Fire & Marine Insurance Co. Ltd., announced in August 2000 that they would form an alliance. In addition, Asahi Mutual Life Insurance Co. and

Tokio Marine & Fire Insurance Company intend to merge (Dvorak, 2000c). In the latter two cases, the mergers are between a life insurance company and a non-life company.

Consolidation in the insurance industry also is occurring in Europe and the United Kingdom.[28] Allianz, the German Insurance giant, holds shares in both Deutsche Bank and Dresdner Bank, which announced merger plans in March 2000 but subsequently scrapped the idea. Allianz was the "prime mover behind the merger" (Harris, 2000). Deutsche Bank planned to spin off the retail unit. Allianz would take a 49% stake in the new combined retail banking unit, marking the beginning of a bank-insurance strategy for the retail side and wholesale and investment banking for Deutsche and Dresdner banks. After the merger fell apart, Allianz indicated that it was willing to sell its 21% stake in Dresdner (Ibison, 2000a). However, the insurance connection goes on. Allianz is a shareholder in Crédit Lyonnais (France), and it was announced in April 2000 that Dresdner was considering bidding for control of that bank (Ibison, 2000a).

In the United States Travelers Insurance merged with Citicorp. ING, the Dutch banking and insurance group, made an offer to buy Crédit Commercial de France (CCF), a French Bank (Iskandar and Muller, 2000). CCF is owned by foreign investors, including KBC of Belgium and Swiss Life. ING also has made a bid for Wellpoint of California, a health insurer. Finally, as previously noted, Sanwa Bank has established a specialized financial keiretsu with various insurance companies for the purpose of cross-selling their products.

In Japan, members of the Mitsubishi Tokyo Financial Group, Inc, will include three insurance companies.

The consolidation reflects a move to expand life insurance company operations away from the sluggish property and casualty business and to be able to sell more financial products to an aging population by integrating with banks. A recent study of large mergers by Anderson Consulting revealed that financial service mergers (banks and insurers) are more successful than most cross industry mergers (Mackintosh, 2000). Nevertheless, two-thirds of those mergers destroyed value.

NOTES

The author benefited from discussions with the following bankers: Takahiro Yazawa (Sumitomo Bank, Ltd.); Masanobu Kobayashi, Takayuki Yokota, and Hiroshi Takahashi (Fuji Bank, Ltd.); and Shigeaki Mori (Industrial Bank of Japan, Ltd.), and with the following academics: Manasori Amano and Kiyoshi Abe (Chiba University), Akio Kuroda (Meiji University), and Yupana Wiwattanakantang (Hitosubashi University). Thanks is also due to Hiroshi Nakaso (Bank of Japan). Financial support for travel to Japan was provided by the University of Alabama, Culverhouse School of Commerce, and the University's International Programs and Services/Japan.

1. This chapter focuses on megabanks. At the other end of the size spectrum, Japan's small shinkin banks, credit co-ops, agricultural co-ops, and fishery co-ops were also in trouble, but they are not considered here (see "Mr. Tanigaki's Augean Stables," 2000).

2. The definition of bad loans has changed over the years. For details, see Hoshi, 2000.

3. Several series of preferred stock were issued, some of which are convertible into shares of common stock.

4. Data are from the *Financial Times* (www.ft.com), Markets/Premium Research (visited 3/11/00).

5. Bremner, Thornton, and Kujnii, 1999.

6. Data are from the *Financial Times* (www.ft.com), Markets/Premium Research (visited 3/11/00).

7. Ibid.

8. Ibid.

9. Ibid.

10. "New Japanese Banking Giant Takes the Slow Road to Reform," 2000.

11. "Foundation of the Mizuho Financial Group ('MHFG') Through Consolidation of the DKB, Fuji Bank and IBJ," December 22, 1999 (a joint statement by the three banks).

12. In June 2000, Dai-Ichi Kangyo sold its corporate trust unit to the Bank of New York (Anderson, 2000).

13. "Only Connect," 2000.

14. Data are from the *Financial Times* (www.ft.com), Markets/Premium Research (visited 3/11/00).

15. Ibid.

16. Only mergers occurring in 1999 or 2000 are mentioned here. However, a number of mergers of smaller financial institutions occurred in the 1990s. For additional information, see Gup, 1998, ch. 3.

17. "The Bank's First Long-Term Business Plan," Bank of Tokyo Mitsubishi News Release, March 24, 1997, www.btm.co.jp/html_e/news/news_10e.htm (visited 2/4/00).

18. Mitsubishi Trust and Banking Corporation Annual Report, 1999 (www.mitsubishi-trust.co.jp/english/annu00.html (visited 4/19/00).

19. Webgate News Release, 4/21/2000, http://news.sumitomobank.co.jp/eng/e00024_01.html (visited 4/21/000).

20. A study by Berger, DeYoung, Genay and Udell (1999) found that improvements in X-efficiency may be a motive for cross-border mergers. X-efficiency—movements toward an optimal point on the best practices efficient frontier—tends to be greater for domestic banks than for foreign banks.

21. For a thorough discussion of this issue, see Heenan and Bennis (1999).

22. Sellers, 2000; Gasparino and Beckett, 2000.

23. For a detailed review of the literature, see Berger, DeYoung, Genay, and Udell, 1999 (Sections 4.2.1–4.2.2).

24. For a discussion on building shared cultures, see Marks and Mirvis (1998).

25. For more information on Softbank Corporation, see www.sbfinance.co.jp/English/ir_e.html.

26. The Sumitomo Trust & Banking Co., Ltd. (Trust Account) also owns 2.05% of the Sumitomo Bank Ltd. (Strategic Alliance, 1999).

27. See Nakamae, 2000a, and "Japan: Sumitomo, Mitsui Marine," 2000, for a discussion of consolidation in the insurance industry and the role of keiretsus.

28. GCU PLC and Norwich Union PLC agreed to an $11.6 billion merger in 2000 (Fuhrmans, 2000).

REFERENCES

Agrawal, Anup, and Jeffrey F. Jaffe. (2000). "The Post-Merger Performance Puzzle." In *Advances in Mergers and Acquisitions*, Cary Cooper and Alan Gregory, eds. Stamford, CT: JAI Press.

Anderson, Amy L. (2000). "Bank of N.Y. Buys Dai-Ichi Trust Unit." *American Banker*, June 16, p. 7.

Anderson, Christopher, W., and Terry L. Campbell II. (2000). "Corporate Governance of Japanese Banks." University of Missouri, Columbia, Working Paper, June 6.

"The Bank-Merger Splurge." (1999). *The Economist*, August 28, p. 15.

"Bank Shares Tumble over Sogo." (2000). *Financial Times* (www.ft.com), July 13 (visited 7/13/00).

Berger, Allen N., Robert DeYoung, Hesna Genay, and Gregory F. Udell. (December 1999). "Globalization of Financial Institutions: Evidence from Cross-Border Banking Performance," Federal Reserve Bank of Chicago, Working Paper Series, WP 99–25.

Bliss, Richard T., and Richard J. Rosen. (February 2000). "CEO Compensation and Bank Mergers." Unpublished paper. http://papers.ssrn.com/paper.taf?abstract_id=210908.

Bremner, Brian, Emily Thornton, and Irene M. Kujnii. (1999). "Mitsubishi: Fall of a Keiretsu." *Business Week* (International Edition). www.businessweek.com/1999/99_11/b3620009.htm (visited 2/13/00).

Cameron, Doug. (2000). "Sakura Going Online." *Financial Times* (www.ft.com), September 7 (visited 9/7/00).

"Chiyoda Life Files for Bankruptcy." (2000). *Financial Times* (www.ft.com), October 9 (visited 10/9/00).

"The Dai-Ichi Kangyo Bank, Limited ('DKB'), The Fuji Bank, Limited ('Fuji') and The Industrial Bank of Japan, Limited ('IBJ') to Get Consolidated to Form a New Financial Services Group ('the New Group')." (1999). Fuji Bank News Release, August 20. www.fujibank.co.jp/pub/news/news-e/news-e8–20.html (visited 12/14/99).

Dvorak, Phred. (2000a). "Three Japanese Banks are Close to Megamerger." *Wall Street Journal*, March 14, p. A25.

Dvorak, Phred. (2000b). "Big Bank Merger Shows Old Ties Persist in Japan." *Wall Street Journal*, April 20, p. A20.

Dvorak, Phred. (2000c). "Tokio Marine Discusses Alliance." *Wall Street Journal*, September 14, p. A22.

Ferguson, Tim W., and Josephine Lee. (1999). "Failing Upward." *Forbes*, October 18, pp. 53–54.

"Forging the New Financial Group." (2000). *IBJ News*, No. SE-1, January 25.

Friedman, Milton. (1997) "Rx for Japan: Back to the Future." *Wall Street Journal*, December 17, p. A22.

Fuji Monthly Market News (February 2000). www.fujibank.co.jp/eng/fb/market/month/html (visited 2/14/00).

Fuhrmans, Vanessa. (2000). "British Merger of $11.58 Billion Likely to Create a Global Insurer." *Wall Street Journal*, February 22, pp. A21, 24.

Fulford, Benjamin. (2000). "Godzilla Bank." *Forbes*, March 20, pp. 132, 136.

Gasparino, Charles, and Paul Beckett. (2000). "How John Reed Lost the Reins of Citi-group to His Co-Chairman." *Wall Street Journal*, April 14, pp. A1, A8.

Goffee, Rob, and Gareth Jones. (1998). *How Your Company's Culture Can Make or Break Your Business*. New York: HarperCollins.

Goto, Shihoko. (2000). "Megamergers Will Boost Japan's Financial Competiveness." Associated Press Newswires, Dow Jones Interactive News Retrieval Service. http://nrstg1p.djnr.com/cgi-bin/DJI (visited 1/27/00).

Gup, Benton E. (1998). *Bank Failures in the Major Trading Countries of the World: Causes and Remedies*. Westport, CT: Quorum Books.

Gup, Benton E. (1999). *International Banking Crises: Large Scale Failures, Massive Government Interventions*. Westport, CT: Quorum Books.

Hall, Maximilian J. B. (1999). "Current Banking Problems in Japan: How Serious and How Might They Be Resolved?" In *Bank Problems: A Global Perspective*, George G. Kaufman, ed. Research in Financial Services, Vol. 11. Stamford, CT: JAI Press, pp. 3–33.

Harris, Clay. (2000). "Michael Dobson First Casualty of Deutsche Merger." *Financial Times* (www.ft.com), March 17 (visited 3/17/00).

Heenan, David A., and Warren Bennis. (1999). *Co-Leaders: The Power of Great Partnerships*. New York: John Wiley & Sons.

Hiroshi, Nakaso. (July 1999). "Recent Banking Sector Reforms in Japan." Federal Reserve Bank of New York, *FRBNY Economic Policy Review*, pp. 1–7.

Hoenig, Thomas, M. (Third Quarter 1999). "Financial Industry Megamergers and Policy Challenges." Federal Reserve Bank of Kansas City, *Economic Review*, pp. 7–13.

Hoshi, Takeo. (March 2000). "What Happened to Japanese Banks?" Institute for Monetary and Economic Studies, Bank of Japan, Tokyo, Japan, Discussion Paper No. 2000-E-7.

Hoshi, Takeo, and Anil Kashyap. (2000). "The Japanese Banking Crisis: Where Did It Come from and How Will It End?" *NBER Macroeconomics Annual 1999*, p. 14.

Houston, Joel F., Christopher M. James, and Michael D. Ryngaert. (1999). "Where Do Merger Gains Come From? Bank Mergers from the Perspective of Insiders and Outsiders." Unpublished paper, University of Florida, Gainesville, FL, October 1.

Hutchison, Michael. (2000). "Japan's Recession: Is the Liquidity Trap Back?" Federal Reserve Bank of San Francisco, *FRSB Economic Letter*, No. 2000-19, June 16.

Ibison, David. (2000a). "Allianz Approves of Dresdner Going It Alone." *Financial Times* (www.ft.com), April 19 (visited 4/20/00).

Ibison, David. (2000b). "Dresdner Fuels Cédit Lyonnais Speculation." *Financial Times* (www.ft.com), April 19 (visited 4/20/00).

"International Economic Trends." (November 1999). Federal Reserve Bank of St. Louis.

Iskandar, Samer, and Emma Muller. (2000). "ING Tells CCF to Accept Offer." *Financial Times* (www.ft.com), March 17 (visited 3/17/00).

"Japan Banks Speed up Ties." (2000). CNNfn, April 21. http://cnnfn.com/2000/04/21/asia/wires/sakura_wg/ (visited 4/21/00).

"Japan: Sogo Bankruptcy." (2000). *Thompson Financial BankWatch*, July 12.

"Japan: Sumitomo, Mitsui Marine to Merge by April 1, 2002." (2000). *Financial Times* (www.ft.com), February 18 (visited 2/18/00).

"Japanese Insurers Endgame." (2000). *The Economist*, September 2, p. 70.

"Japanese Insurers to Tie." (2000). CNNfn, August 28. http://cnnfn.com/2000/08/28/asia/ wires/yasuda_wg/ (visited 8/28/00).

"Japan's Bail-outs." (2000). *Financial Times* (www.ft.com), September 27 (visited 10/2/ 00).

Kane, Edward J. (Forthcoming). "Incentives for Banking Megamergers: What Motives Might Regulators Infer from Event Study Evidence?" *Journal of Money, Banking and Credit.*

Kashiwagi, Akiko. (2000a) "3 Japanese Banks Agree on Merger." *Washington Post Online* (www.washingtonpost.com), March 15, E03 (visited 3/25/00).

Kashiwagi, Akiko. (2000b). "Tokyo Slaps Big Tax on 30 Major Banks." *Washington Post Online* (www.washingtonpost.com), March 31, E04 (visited 3/31/00).

Kashiwagi, Akiko. (2000c). "Japan Rattled by Suicide of Bank President." *Washington Post Online* (www.washingtonpost.com), September 27, E03 (visited 9/27/00).

Kindleberger, Charles P. (1996). *Manias, Panics and Crashes.* 3rd ed. New York: John Wiley & Sons, p. 104.

Kover, Amy. (2000). "Big Banks Debunked." *Fortune*, February 21, pp. 187–194.

Kraus, James R. (1999). "French Merger Fight Highlights Clash of Strategies." *American Banker*, August 10, pp. 1, 4.

Kwan, Simon, and Robert A. Eisenbeis. (Fourth Quarter 1999). "Mergers of Publicly Traded Banking Organizations Revisited." Federal Reserve Bank of Atlanta, *Economic Review*, pp. 26–37.

Landers, Peter. (1999). "Sumitomo, Sakura to Merge into Mammoth Bank Designed to Survive Japan's Transformation." *Wall Street Journal*, October 15, p. A10.

Landers, Peter. (2000). "Japan Drops Big Bailout Amid Public Outcry." *Wall Street Journal*, July 13, p. A18.

Mackintosh, James. (2000). "Banks and Insurers Combine Best." *Financial Times* (www.ft.com), August 6 (visited 8/7/00).

Makin, John H. (July 2000). "Japan Battles the Paradox of Thrift." American Enterprise Institute for Public Policy Research, *Economic Outlook* (Washington, DC).

Marks, Mitchell Lee, and Philip H. Mirvis. (1998). *Joining Forces: Making One Plus One Equal Three in Mergers, Acquisitions, and Alliances.* San Francisco: Jossey-Bass Publishers.

Mitsubishi Trust and Banking Corporation Annual Report. (1999). www.mitsubishi-trust.com.jp/english/annu00.html (visited 4/19/00).

"Moody's Warning Rattles Japan's Markets." (2000). *New York Times on the Web*, www.nytimes.com/reuters/business/buiness-markets-apap.html (visited 2/17/00).

Moules, Jonathan. (2000). "Asahi Explains Merger Collapse." *Financial Times* (www.ft.com), June 28 (visited 6/29/00).

"Mr. Tanigaki's Augean Stables." (2000). *The Economist*, March 4, p. 77.

Nakamae, Naoko. (2000a). "Merger Tries to Cut the Banking Ties That Bind." *Financial Times* (www.ft.com), February 16 (visited 2/17/00).

Nakamae, Naoko. (2000b) "Outlook Bleak as Japan's Economy Worsens." *Financial Times* (www.ft.com), April 28 (visited 4/29/00).

Nakamae, Naoko, and Gillian Tett. (2000). "Sogo Collapse Prompts Cheap Loans Pledge." *Financial Times* (www.ft.com), July 13 (visited 7/27/00).

"New Japanese Banking Giant Takes the Slow Road to Reform." (1999). Knight-Ridder

Tribune Business News, *Daily Mail*, London, August 21. http://nrstg1p.djnr.com (visited 1/27/00).

"Only Connect." (2000). *The Economist*, May 27, pp. 75–76.

"Partners in the Formation of a Leading Financial Services Complex." (2000). Tokyo, Sumitomo Bank, Ltd., www.sumitomobank.com.jp/eng/sakurainfo.html (visited 2/15/00).

Raghavan, Anita, and G. Thomas Sims. (2000). "Golden Parachutes Emerge in European Deals." *Wall Street Journal*, February 14, pp. A17–A18.

Schwartz, Peter, Peter Leyden, and Joel Hyatt. (1999). *The Long Boom: A Vision for the Coming Age of Prosperity*. New York: John Wiley & Sons.

Sellers, Patricia. (2000). "Behind the Shootout at Citigroup." *Fortune*, March 20, pp. 27, 32.

Sims, Calvin. (1999). "Japan Bank Merger Carries Old Burdens." *New York Times*, September 7, www.nytimes.com/library/world/asia (visited 1/30/00).

Spiegel, Mark M. (1999) "Moral Hazard under the Japanese 'Convoy' Banking System." Federal Reserve Bank of San Francisco, *Economic Review*, no. 3, pp. 3–13.

"Strategic Alliance Between Sakura Bank and Sumitomo Bank" (financial data). (1999). News Release, Sumitomo Bank, Tokyo, Japan, October 14. www.sumitomo-bank.com.jp/eng/e00003_01.html (visited 2/22/00).

Strom, Stephanie. (2000). "Clouds Hanging over Sogo Bankruptcy Lift a Bit in Japan." *New York Times*, July 15. www.nytimes.com/library/financial/071500sogotokyo.html (visited 7/15/00).

"Sumo-sized Bank Created." (2000). CNNfn, August 20. http://cnnfn.com/1999/08/20/asia/japan_banks/ (visited 3/14/00).

Suzuki, Yumiko. (2000) "Mizuho Merger Losing Its Luster." *Nikkei Weekly*, October 2, pp. 1, 23.

Szep, Jason. (2000). "Asahi Wants Out of Bank Merger." *Financial Times* (www.ft.com), June 15 (visited 6/15/00).

Tett, Gillian. (2000a), "Japanese Government Suggests Further Spending Package." *Financial Times* (www.ft.com), February 23 (visited 2/23/00).

Tett, Gillian. (2000b). "Japanese Asset Sale Tops $238bn." *Financial Times* (www.ft.com), April 18 (visited 4/19/00).

Tett, Gillian. (2000c). "Japan Banking Woes Linger." *Financial Times* (www.ft.com), August 30 (visited 9/4/00).

Tett, Gillian. (2000d). "US-Japan Insurance Tie-up." *Financial Times* (www.ft.com), August 7 (visited 9/7/00).

"The Ties That Bind." (2000). *The Economist*, February 5, p. 71.

"The Tigers That Changed Their Stripes." (2000). *The Economist: A Survey of South-East Asia*, February 12, pp. 1–16.

"Unlocking Shareholder Value: The Keys to Success." (November 1999). London: KPMG Mergers & Acquisitions Global Research Report.

"Up and Down." (2000). *The Economist*, February 12, p. 17.

Webgate News Release. (2000). http://news.sumitomobank.com.jp/eng/e00024_01.html (visited 4/21/00).

Chapter 8

Bank Mergers in Spain: Are They Unique?

Benton E. Gup

Are the recent mergers and acquisitions of Spanish banks unique? The answer to that question is both yes and no. Cross-border and in-market mergers by banks and firms in other industries have increased dramatically in recent years. In that sense, the mergers in Spain are not unique. What differentiates them from other mergers is their aggressiveness in Europe and the growing presence of Spanish firms in Latin America (Mexico, Central America, South America, and the Caribbean islands with links to Spain). This chapter explains why these mergers are taking place and the implications for the future.

The chapter is divided into seven subject areas: (1) the extent of global cross-border mergers; (2) Spain's evolution as a market economy; (3) the Euro-zone as a catalyst for mergers; (4) bank mergers and alliances in Europe; (5) technology's role in changing the way banks operate domestically and internationally; (6) growth opportunities in the Americas; and (7) the future and speculation on further consolidation in Spain.

CROSS-BORDER MERGERS

The number of cross-border mergers is increasing. In January 2000, *Business Week* published an article which found the value of mergers in Europe in 1999 to be $1.5 trillion compared to $988 billion in the previous year. The predictions were that mergers would exceed $2 trillion in 2000. An Organization for Economic Cooperation and Development (OECD) study of 1999 cross-border mergers revealed that three quarters of them occurred in Western Europe (Lumpkin, 2000; Wessel, 2000). This is consistent with a survey by KPMG Corporate

Table 8.1
Top Global Buyers in 1999

Rank	Country	Value ($billions)
1	United Kingdom	246
2	United States	155
3	Germany	93
4	France	92
5	Netherlands	44
6	Spain	25
7	Japan	20
8	Belgium	17
9	Canada	16
10	Italy	14

Source: "Merging Across Borders," 2000.

Finance of more than 50,000 cross-border mergers and acquisitions which reported that M&A activity increased from $159 billion in 1990 to $789 billion in 1999 ("Merging Across Borders," 2000). Table 8.1 lists the top 10 global buyers, with Spain ranking sixth. Telecommunications mergers accounted for $304 billion during the period under review; oil and gas accounted for $254 billion; and banking and financial services for $226 billion.

Europe's banking landscape is being reshaped by megamergers. According to the OECD, this is an attempt by a fragmented industry to consolidate (Wessel, 2000). The proposed merger between Deutsche Bank and Dresdner Bank did not materialize, but other mergers did. Deutsche Bank had already acquired Bankers Trust in the United States; Royal Bank of Scotland acquired London's National Westminster Bank; and France's Banque Nationale de Paris acquired Banque Paribas. Hypo Vereinsbank (HVB) is the product of a merger between Bayerische Hypothenke-und Weschsel Bank and Bayerische Vereinsbank (Fairlamb, 1999). HVB is acquiring Bank of Austria A.G, making it the third largest bank in Europe after Deutsche Bank and PNP Paribas (Major and Frey, 2000). This was the second largest cross-border merger in Europe after HSBC's acquisition of France's Credit Commercial de France (CCF). The Swiss bank UBS acquired PaineWebber Group (U.S.), and Credit Suisse First Boston acquired Donaldson, Lufkin & Jenrette (DLJ) (U.S.). The Dutch insurer Aegon NV bought Transamerica Corp. (U.S.), and Sweden's Nordenbanken acquired Finland's Mferita. On the other side of the Atlantic Ocean, Chase Manhattan

(U.S.) acquired the merchant bank, Robert Flemming Group, PLC (U.K.,), and Citigroup Inc. (U.S.) acquired the investment bank Schroders PLC (U.K.).

Despite the large number of deals, some resistance to cross-border mergers remains. One major factor in this resistance is cultural differences, which can be minimized to some extent by creating a holding company and by allowing independence of the separate organizations. Another problem is that many European banks are trading at 2.5 times their book value and a large portion of the purchase price must be written off as goodwill (William, 2000a). Finally, some investors are reluctant to accept foreign shares and want to be paid in cash.

TRANSITION IN SPAIN

A major change occurred in Spain's political environment following the death of Francisco Franco in 1975. The government was transformed from a dictatorship to a parliamentary monarchy when the Spanish constitution became effective December 29, 1978. Spain has a king as chief of state and a president as head of government. The monarch's position is hereditary, whereas the president is proposed by the monarch and elected by the National Assembly following legislative elections.

Spain has moved from a closed economy toward an open one by *deregulating* selected sectors of the economy (i.e., electricity, gas, and telecommunications sectors) over a 10 year period (or less) and privatizing some government-owned firms (i.e., Endsa, Repsol, and Telefónica). Although this chapter focuses on bank consolidation in 2000 and beyond, a large number of banking sector mergers took place in the early 1990s (see Table 8.2).

The 1995 reform of corporate income taxes eliminated the double taxation of profits, which opened the door for Spanish firms to invest internationally (Joumard, 2000). These developments set the stage for economic growth, mergers, and international expansion. Spain's success in implementing structural economic reforms was rewarded by Thomson Financial BankWatch, which upgraded Spain's sovereign rating to AA+ from AA in June 2000 ("Upgrades Spain," 2000).

U.S. banks and finance companies have been operating in Spain for many years. In 1991, for example, Bank of America and Citibank España carried out full-service banking operations in Spain (Double, Kohn, and Griffin, 1991). Bankers Trust, Chase Manhattan N.A., Citibank N.A., Manufacturers Hanover Trust, and Morgan Guarantee had wholesale operations there, and American Express and Bank of New York had representative offices. In addition, Spanish banks used major American credit cards. There is no doubt that banks and finance companies from other nations also had a significant presence in Spain.

Table 8.2
Banking Sector Mergers and Acquisitions in Spain, 1991–1992 through 1997–1998

	1991–1992	1993–1994	1995–1996	1997–1998
Number of transactions	76	44	27	30
Value—U.S.$ (billions)	$4.3	$4.5	$2.3	$5.9

Source: Lumpkin, 2000.

EURO-ZONE: A CATALYST FOR MERGERS

Spain became a member of the European Community (EC) in 1986, joining the other 11 member states—Belgium, Denmark, France, Germany, Greece, Ireland, Italy, Luxembourg, Netherlands, Portugal, and the United Kingdom. One goal of the EC is to develop a single internal market by requiring the member countries to liberalize various sectors of their respective economies. Spain has been a leader in this area, but not not all countries have moved forward at the same speed.

The financial markets in Europe were fragmented, each country having its own currency and exchange rates. To deal with this issue, 11 member countries of the European Monetary Union (EMU)—Austria, Belgium, Denmark, France, Germany, Ireland, Italy, Luxembourg, Netherlands, Portugal, and Spain—signed an agreement to create a common currency, the euro.[1] The euro will replace the currencies of the participating countries when the system is fully adopted, and it will eliminate exchange rate risk between the participating countries. The euro began trading on January 1, 1999, and full adoption of the monetary system is expected on June 30, 2002, with the distribution of euro-notes and coins.

Today the euro-zone is a single capital market that has resulted in increased competition. The development of the euro-zone as an open market facilitated cross-border mergers and alliances because having a common currency and common regulations makes such deals easier. Specifically, it allows Spanish firms to tap the markets of the euro-zone members to help finance acquisitions ("Spain's Surge," 2000). Within those markets are fund managers who have access to funds they want to invest in good deals. According to the head of the leverage finance division of Morgan Stanley Dean Witter in London, there is no shortage of money but the scarce commodity is good deals (Reed and Matlack, 2000).

Accordingly, Banco Bilbao Vizcaya Argentaria (BBVA) acquired a small stake in the privatization of France's Crédit Lyonnais and Italy's Banco Nazionale del Lavoro. Banso Santander Central Hispano (BSCH) also has a stake in the Royal Bank of Scotland, which in turn, owns part of Italy's San Paolo IMI and Germany's Commerzank.[2] BSCH and the Italian bank, San Paolo IMI, signed an agreement to offer products jointly to small and medium-sized businesses in Italy and Latin America. BSCH is one of San Paolo's largest stockholders ("Sanpaolo," 2000).

Spanish commercial banks' cross-border mergers and alliances are not always welcomed, as is evidenced by BSCH's planned alliance in Portugal with the Champalimaud group and its investment in France during the takeover struggle of Société Générale. Conversely, the Spanish government has also blocked some mergers, notably, the takeover of Unión Fenosa, the country's third largest electric utility by Hidrocantábrico, a smaller utility, as well as a proposal by Baden-Württenberg (EnBw), a German power company to acquire Hidrocantábrico (Burns and Taylor, 2000). The Spanish government opposed foreign bids, and EnBw is partially owned by the French government, which has refused to open its energy market to foreign firms. It also blocked a cross-border merger between Telefónica and KPN NV because the Dutch government owns a 44% stake in KPN (Vitzhum, 2000).

Cross-border and cross-region mergers by Spanish savings banks (*cajas*) are prohibited by law. Nevertheless, some cross-region merger activity is occurring. The cajas are some of Spain's largest financial institutions, accounting for about 45% of domestic deposits (Burns, "Savings Banks," 2000). Commercial banks account for 50% and loan cooperatives for the remainder. Caja Madrid, a savings bank, bought the Banca Jover, a subsidiary of France's Crédit Lyonnais. Banca Jover's branches are concentrated in Catalonia and the Balearic Islands.

Although Spanish banks are extending their reach into the euro-zone, Germany's Deutsche Banks and the United States' Morgan Stanley Dean Witter are moving into Spain. Deutsche Bank has an agreement with Red Postal to sell its products in the 1,800 units throughout Spain that are operated by the postal service. Deutsche Bank has had a presence in Spain since 1993 when its Barcelona subsidiary, Bancotrans, acquired Banco de Madrid. Morgan Stanley Dean Witter, an investment banking firm, acquired AB Asesores, Spain's largest independent financial group. And in other sectors of the economy, American Airlines in partnership with British Airways acquired a 10% share of Iberia Airlines.[3] The fact that such acquisitions are occurring in other sectors reveals the extensiveness of the merger activity.

It is widely believed that banks need to be large in order to compete internationally. Large banks can achieve economies of scale and scope, and thereby reduce costs and excess capacity in terms of number of offices. Spanish banks have about one branch bank for every 1,000 people, which means they have more branches per capita than any other country in the euro-zone (White, 2000a). By way of comparison, U.S. banks have about one branch for every 4,000 people.[4] BSCH, for example, has 8,473 branches in Spain and 2,400 abroad, and it has more than 90,000 employees who are about equally divided between Spain and Latin America (BSCH, 2000). BSCH has about 10 million customers in Spain and one branch for every 1,180 customers.[5] They have 14 million customers in the Americas and one branch for every 5,833 customers.

During 1999, BSCH closed 425 branches in Spain. They still have a long way to go to match their efficiency in the Americas.

When retail banks merge in the United States and branches overlap, those branches may be sold because of antitrust considerations or closed to reduce costs. It is not clear what happens to overlapping branches in Spain or other euro-zone countries when banks merge. Nevertheless, the European Commission has an active antitrust division, and at some point in time, it may focus on concentration in the banking/financial services industry. Finally, retail banking tends to be local or regional business at this time. That may change with the development of Internet banking.

As is true of most bank mergers, increased operating efficiency means reducing personnel. Operating efficiency also may benefit from investments in information technology (IT). Spanish banks appear to have made significant investments in this area.

BANK MERGERS AND ALLIANCES IN EUROPE

Spanish banks were active in terms of merger activity during the 1990s and before the creation of the euro-zone. A faltering banking sector in the 1980s contributed to consolidation in the industry in the 1990s and beyond.

In 1991, six commercial banks accounted for two-thirds of the total assets of more than 165 commercial banks (Berlin, 2000; Double, Kohn, and Griffin, 1991).[6] The government encouraged bank mergers in order to compete in the EC. For example, BSCH owns a stake in San Paolo IMI SpA, Italy's second largest bank, and San Paolo IMI owns a stake in the Spanish bank (Ball, 2000). San Paolo IMI is launching an online portal to offer financial services and products. More will be said about such technology in the next section.

Since then, further consolidation has occurred, as shown in Table 8.3, which does not reflect the latest mergers of large banks. Banco Español de Crédito (Banesto) was once Spain's largest bank. In February 2000 it was acquired by Banco Santander. Subsequently, Banco Santander merged with Banco Hispano Americano to form Banco Santander Central Hispano (BSCH), which is now Spain's largest bank. BSCH has banking subsidiaries in Germany, Italy, and Portugal, and has alliances with banks in France and the U.K. as well.

Banco Bilbao Vizcaya acquired its next largest competitor, Argentaria, to form Banco Bilbao Vizcaya Argentaria (BBVA). Subsequently, BBVA confirmed that it would acquire Argentaria Caja Postal y Banco Hipotecario. And the consolidation goes on.

THE ROLE OF TECHNOLOGY

Internet banking is replacing and supplementing cross-border bank mergers. Internet banking avoids restrictive labor laws that adversely affect the downsizing of personnel which inevitably follows mergers. It also provides entrants with

Table 8.3
Spain's Commercial Banks, June 1999

	Commercial Banks	Asset Size (Ebn)
1	Banco Santander Hispano	256
2	Banco Bilbao Vizcaya	146
3	Argentaria	77
4	Banco Popular	25
5	Banco Sabedell	15
6	Bankinter	15
7	Deutsche Bank	9
8	Banco Atlantico	8
9	Barclays Bank	5
10	Banco Zaragonzano	5

Source: White, 2000b.

a low-cost way to enter new domestic and cross-border markets. Nevertheless, Internet banks do not appear to be complete substitutes for retail brick and mortar banks. For example, Bank of America Corp. reports that about 7% of its 30 million customers bank online, and there has been about an equal reduction of transactions at its branches ("Online Paying Off," 2000). Consequently, it plans to close about 200 of its 4,500 plus branch network.

Some Spanish banks are taking a leading role in the new Internet technology. In March 2000, BBVA acquired a majority share of Dublin, Ireland's First-E Group PLC. Subsequently, BBVA joined forces with Telefónica to develop Uno-e-com, an Internet banking service. It should be noted that BBVA is one of Telefónica's leading shareholders.[7] Its goal is to have one million customers in the next three years and to operate in France, Italy, Portugal, Argentina, Brazil, and Mexico (Mackintosh, 2000). Telefónica controls 70% of Terra Networks, one of Europe's largest Internet companies (Cha and Streitfeld, 2000). Terra, in turn, has penetrated the Latin American market. In addition, Telefónica's Terra Networks unit is acquiring Lycos, an Internet portal in the United States and Latin America. This gives BBVA a means to penetrate both Latin America and the U.S. markets. Unfortunately, many people in Latin America do not have phone lines or computers.

Meanwhile, BSCH has sold its 30% stake in Airtel, a mobile phone operator, to British Telecommunications (BT) and Vodaphone ("BT, Vodaphone," 2000). This sale by BSCH is surprising in light of WAP (wireless application protocol) technology, which will allow telephones to be used for banking and stock market transactions and to communicate with the Internet. In its *1999 Annual Report,*

BSCH notes that its mobile phone banking utilizes WAP. Nevertheless, BSCH has joined with Italy's Sanpaolo IMI, Germany's Commerzban, the United Kingdom's Royal Bank of Scotland, and France's Société Général to launch an Internet portal for government bonds and other capital market products and services in 2001.

Finally, Spain's Bankinter offers 300 types of transactions online, including banking, stock trading, and taxpaying (Power, 2000). It will compete with BBVA's Uno-e and First-E Group, which was mentioned earlier. However, at the end of March 2001, the First-E Group only offered a single savings account online. Nevertheless, Uno-e offers a wide variety of services.

While Spanish banks are moving outside their borders, other countries are moving into Spain and the EU. Sweden and Finland's Merit-Nordenbanken has more than 1.1 million customers online, and U.K.'s Barclays has more than 600,000 customers online in Germany. In addition, Lloyds TSB (U.K.) plans to open an online bank in Spain that will serve customers in Europe and the U.K.

AMERICA: GROWTH OPPORTUNITIES

The European market is mature. The demographics reveal that the population in Spain and elsewhere in Europe is aging and is expected to decline further in the years to come. The growing economies in Latin America offer growth opportunities that are not available in Europe, but the payoffs may not be immediate. These markets are logical extensions for Spanish banks, telecommunications, and energy firms because of their historic political and economic ties as well as a common language. Equally important, these markets are open to foreign investments. Although some observers view the expansion as Spain's "reconquest" of its former colonies, the primary motive appears to be economic growth opportunities.[8]

As a result of acquisitions in the Americas, Telefónica, for example, has more customers in Argentina, Brazil, Chile, and Peru than it has in Spain. It also operates in El Salvador, Guatemala, and Puerto Rico, and it is acquiring five wireless companies in Mexico (Vitzhum and Harris, 2000).[9] In 2000, BBVA acquired control of Bancomer, Mexico's second largest bank, for $1.4 billion in cash (Fritch, 2000; Tricks, 2000). Previously, BSCH acquired Grupo Financiero Serfin, Mexico's third largest bank. BSCH also has subsidiary banks operating in Argentina, Brazil, Chile, Colombia, Peru, and Uruguay. In June 2000, it extended its influence in Venezuela by acquiring the country's fifth largest bank, Banco de Caracas, and increasing its ownership of Argentina's Banco Rio de la Plata ("BSCH May Be Close," 2000). In October, the Banco de Venezuela, which BSCH controls, acquired more shares in Banco de Caracas. BBVA owns Banco Provincial, one of the largest banks in Venezuela.

Other Spanish firms with large investments in Latin America include, but are not limited to Mapfre (insurance), Repsol (engery), Endesa (power company),

Iberdrola (power company), Iberia (airline), Unión Fenosa (energy), and Grupo Sol Melia (hotels).

Spanish and European banks have been aggressively acquiring investment banking and asset management firms in the United States. France's Société Générale SA and Spain's BSCH were in serious talks to acquire Texas-based Fayez Sarofim & Co., which has about $44 billion under asset management (Raghavan and Brown, 2000).

THE FUTURE: FURTHER CONSOLIDATION

The future holds further consolidation in banking in Spain and the rest of Europe. The demutualization of mutually owned financial institutions will make available firms that were not previously considered merger candidates. For example, Scottish Life was considering demutualizing, and it was courted by GE Capital. However, the merger talk collapsed (Bolger, 2000; Saigol, 2000). Scottish Life is one of the few life insurance companies that has not demutualized.

William (2000a) states that when market share reaches about 40%, competition authorities *may* intervene, leaving cross-border mergers the only viable option for ambitious banks.[10] BBCH is selling at price earnings (P/E ratio) of about 42, while BBVA has a P/E ratio of about 32. BBCH's P/E ratio is sufficiently high to give it the currency to acquire other banks and firms with lower P/Es and not dilute their earnings. BBVA's relatively low P/E suggests that it may become a target for a larger foreign bank or insurance company.

Another possibility is that the European Union's executive body, the European Commission, may block further consolidation in banking and other industries when they see potential anticompetitive effects. The European Commission has blocked some mergers (e.g., WorldCom's takeover of Sprint).[11] In addition, the Spanish government has used 1995 legislation to block corporate takeovers in Spain by state-owned foreign companies (e.g., the French state-owned utility, Eléctricité de France, from taking over a Spanish power company). The Spanish government also put pressure on Telefónica, which led to the breakdown of merger talks with KPN, a partially state-owned Dutch telecommunications company (Hargreaves, 2000). Similarly, German bank regulators (the Bundesaufsichtsamt für das Kreditwesen) have prohibited Cobra—part of a Dutch-based holding company—from exercising their voting rights on the proposed merger between Dresdner Bank and Commerzbank (Major and William, 2000). Cobra owns 17% of Commerzbank's stock. The merger proposal collapsed over disagreements over valuation (Cameron and Felsted, 2000). This was the second failed merger attempt for Dresdner Bank and Allianz (which owns 22% of Dresdner). Dresdner has a strategic alliance with BSCH that it will maintain. Although this bank's attempted mergers were not successful, it would not be surprising to see antimerger activity from the EU or Spain, especially if it involves cross-border activity and foreign ownership.

The growth of Internet alliances and distributive networks may be a substitute for merger-type consolidations or part of the merger process.[12] Some analysts believe that strategic alliances are blocking tactics designed to thwart unfriendly takeovers. Alternatively, these alliances can be viewed as "trial marriages" that allow the potential partners to get to know each other before taking the final step. Finally, they can be considered an "alternative paradigm," allowing major banks to work together while maintaining their separate identities (William, 2000c). Spain's big banks have entered into alliances with telecommunications companies as well as banks in other countries to provide financial services. The headline of a recent *New York Times* article read, "In Europe, Wireless Mergers Losing Ground to Alliances" (Kapner and Sorkin, 2000).[13] Thus, as an examination of such relationships around the world makes clear, strategic alliances are a growing trend that may well reflect the future structure of financial service firms.

NOTES

Another version of this chapter was presented at The Trilateral Relationship: Spain, The United States, and Latin America, held at Universidad de Alcalá, Spain, November 13, 2000.

1. The four remaining countries are Denmark, Greece, Sweden, and the U.K.

2. In an attempt to remain independent, Commerzbank asked BSCH to increase its stake from 5% to 10% or to sell its shares to the German bank's consumer finance unit. In September 2000, BSCH had not yet decided to increase its share and involvement with the Commerzbank or to decrease its shares (Walker and Vitzhum, 2000a, 2000b).

3. Iberia is a subsidiary of the state-owned Sociedad Estatal de Participaciones Industriales.

4. At the end of 1999, there were 62,544 branches of commercial banks in the United States (*Statistics on Banking*, 2000).

5. The BSCH *1999 Annual Report* lists 8,473 branches and 10,200 ATMs in Spain on page 42 (English version) and 6,011 branches and 5,811 ATMs on page 45. Bank of America has 14,369 ATMs, the largest number of any U.S. bank. American Express is the next largest owner with 8,672 ATMs (Stock, 2000).

6. According to Berlin, 2000, there were 165 commercial banks in Spain in 1996.

7. La Caixa, a savings bank, is another leading shareholder of Telefónica.

8. See Baklanoff, 1996, for a discussion of the "Reconquest."

9. Telefónica agreed to buy stakes in phone companies owned by Motorola Inc., which gives it a presence in Mexico (where it is the dominant phone company), Brazil, Israel, the Dominican Republic, and Honduras ("Telefónica to Buy Motorola Mobile Stakes," 2000).

10. Two of Spain's largest power companies, Endesa SA and Iberdrola SA, were considering merging in the fall of 2000. Together, they control 80% of the country's power supply ("Spanish Power Deal Looms," 2000).

11. A discussion of the European Community competition policy is beyond the scope of this chapter. For further information, see The European Commission's web page on competition (http://europa.eu.int/comm/competition/index_en.html; and an overview of the International Affairs Unit of the Directorate General for Competition (DG IV A.3) (http://europa.eu.int/comm/competition/international/overview/.

12. For a discussion of alliances and distributive networks, see Tapscott, Ticoll, and Lowy, 2000.

13. Telefónica, Ipse 2000 S.p.A, and Andala S.p.A., and Hong Kong's Hutchison Whampoa formed an alliance to bid for wireless licenses in Italy.

REFERENCES

Baklanoff, Eric N. (1996). "Spain's Economic Strategy Toward the 'Nation's of Its Historical Community': The 'Reconquest' of Latin America." *Journal of Interamerican Studies and World Affairs*, 38, no. 1 (Spring), pp. 105–127.

Ball, Deborah. (2000). "Italy's San Paolo IMI Considers Tighter Ties with Spanish Bank." *Wall Street Journal*, May 18, p. A23.

Banco Santander Central Hispano (BSCH). (2000). *1999 Annual Report* (Spain).

Berlin, Mitchell. (May–June 2000). "Why Don't Banks Take Stock?" Federal Reserve Bank of Philadelphia, *Business Review*, pp. 3–15.

Bolger, Andrew. (2000). "GE Capital Abandons $1.5bn Bid for Scottish Life." *Financial Times* (www.ft.com), September 15 (visited 9/15/00).

"BSCH May Be Close to Venezuela Deal." (2000). *Wall Street Journal*, June 23, p. A15.

"BT, Vodaphone to Announce Joint Control in Spain's Airtel." (2000). *Wall Street Journal*, June 12, p. A21.

Burns, Tom. (2000). "Savings Banks: Facing Up to the Restrictions." *Financial Times* (www.ft.com), *Financial Times Survey*, Banking Finance & Investment/Alliances (visited 6/13/00).

Burns, Tom, and Andrew Taylor. (2000). "Spain Blocks Electricity Takeover Bid." *Financial Times*, May 27, p. 19.

Cameron, Doug, and Aredea Felsted. (2000). "Commerzbank Merger with Dresdner Bank Collapses." *Financial Times* (www.ft.com), July 25 (visited 7/26/00).

Cha, Ariana E., and David Streitfeld. (2000). "Lycos in Deal with Spanish Firm." *Washington Post*, May 16, p. E01.

Double, Mary Beth, Robert A. Kohn, and Ralph Griffin. (October 1991). "Spain—Overseas Business Report—OBR-91000." U.S. Department of Commerce, International Trade Administration.

Fairlamb, David. (1999). "A Union Between Dresdner and Hypo Vereinsbank Would Create a Global Player." *BusinessWeek Online* (www.businessweek.com), November 1 (visited 6/13/00).

Fritch, Peter. (2000). "Bank Deal to Create New Mexican Behemoth." *Wall Street Journal*, June 13, p. A19.

Hargreaves, Deborah. (2000). "Takeover Court Action Blocked." *Financial Times* (www.ft.com), June 29 (visited 6/30/00).

Joumard, Isabelle. (2000). "The Spanish Bull: How Strong Is It Really?" *OECD Observer* (www.oecdobserver.org), June 13.

Kapner, Suzanne, and Andrew Ross Sorkin. (2000). "In Europe, Wireless Mergers Losing Ground to Alliances." *New York Times on the Web* (www.nytimes.com), August 25 (visited 8/25/00).

Lumpkin, Stephen. (March 2000). "Mergers and Acquisitions in the Financial Services Sector." OECD, *Financial Market Trends*, no. 75, pp. 123–140.

Mackintosh, James. (2000). "Internet Banking: Side-Stepping the Problems of Mergers." *Financial Times* (www.ft.com), February 25 (visited 6/13/00).

Major, Tony, and Eric Frey. (2000). "HVB to Take over Bank of Austria." *Financial Times* (www.ft.com), July 23 (visited 7/24/00).

Major, Tony, and John William. (2000). "German Watchdog Clouds Merger." *Financial Times* (www.ft.com), July 17 (visited 7/18/00).

"Merging Across Borders." (2000). abcNews.com, www.abcnews.go.com/sections/business/DailyNews/bordermergs000223.html (visited 6/13/00).

"Online Paying Off." (July 2000). *U.S. Banker*, p. 14.

Power, Carol. (2000). "Spain's Bankinter Diffuses Web Tech." *American Banker*, April 28, p. 15.

Raghavan, Anita, and Ken Brown. (2000). "French, Spanish in Talks to Buy Money Manager Fayez of U.S." *Wall Street Journal*, September 11, pp. A27, A30.

Reed, Stanley, and Carol Matlack. (2000). "The Big Grab: Deal Mania May Be Even Hotter in Europe This Year." *Business Week*, January 24, pp. 130–131.

Saigol, Lina. (2000). "Scottish Life Mulls Demutualisation." *Financial Times* (www.ft.com), September 6 (visited 9/15/00).

"Sanpaolo, BSCH to Link in Two Markets." (2000). *Wall Street Journal*, July 13, p. A18.

"Spain's Surge." (2000). *Business Week*, May 22, pp. 73–80.

"Spanish Power Deal Looms." (2000). CNNfn (http://cnnfn.com), September 27 (visited 9/27/00).

Statistics on Banking, 1999. (April 2000). Washington, DC: Federal Deposit Insurance Corporation.

Stock, Helen. (2000). "Deal Will Make E-Trade No. 3 in Teller Machines." *American Banker*, March 14, pp. 1, 16.

Tapscott, Don, David Ticoll, and Alex Lowy. (2000). *Digitial Capital: Harnessing the Power of Business Webs.* Cambridge, MA: Harvard Business School Press.

"Telefónica to Buy Motorola Mobile Stakes." (2000). *New York Times on the Web* (www.nytimes.com), October 10 (visited 10/10/00).

Tricks, Henry. (2000). "BBVA Wins Battle for Bancomer." *Financial Times* (www.ft.com), June 12 (visited 6/14/00).

"Upgrades Spain." (2000). Thomson Financial BankWatch, June 18.

Vitzhum, Carlta. (2000). "Madrid Exercises Its 'Golden Shares' on Foreign Deals." *Wall Street Journal*, May 18, p. A23.

Vitzhum, Carlta, and Nichole Harris. (2000). "Telefónica Makes Its Move into Mexico." *Wall Street Journal*, October 5, p. A19.

Walker, Marcus, and Carlta Vitzhum. (2000a). "Commerzbank Is Close to a Deal with Generali on Increased Stake." *Wall Street Journal Interactive Edition* (www.wsj.com), September 1 (visited 9/1/00).

Walker, Marcus, and Carlta Vitzhum. (2000b). "Seeking Deals with Gernerali and BSCH, Commerzbank Aims to Stay a Solo Act." *Wall Street Journal Interactive Edition* (www.wsj.com), August 28 (visited 9/1/00).

Wessel, David. (2000). "Cross-Border Mergers Soared Last Year." *Wall Street Journal*, July 19, p. A18.

White, David. (2000a). "Cross-Border Alliances Are the Next Target." *Financial Times* (www.ft.com), *Financial Times Survey*, Spain: Banking Finance & Investment/Alliances (visited 6/13/00).

White, David. (2000b). "Mergers: Banking on a More Aggressive Strategy." *Financial*

Times (www.ft.com), *Financial Times Survey*, Spain: Banking Finance & Investment/Alliances (visited 6/13/00).

William, John. (September 2000a). "Consolidation: Scope for Further Mergers and Acquisitions." *Financial Times* (www.ft.com), *Financial Times Survey*, Banking in Europe/Mergers (visited 9/4/00).

William, John. (September 2000b). "Cross-Border Mergers: Fear of Becoming Takeover Candidates." *Financial Times* (www.ft.com), *Financial Times Survey*, Banking in Europe/Mergers (visited 9/4/00).

William, John. (September 2000c). "Freeze or Jump? That Is the Question." *Financial Times* (www.ft.com), *Financial Times Survey*, Banking in Europe/Mergers (visited 9/4/00).

Chapter 9

Risk Management Systems for Merging Banking and Casualty/Property Insurance

D. Johannes Jüttner

INTRODUCTION

The triumphant march of capital markets around the globe, continuously emerging new technologies, and advances in financial modeling have forced banks, investment houses, and insurance companies into a process of repositioning, regrouping, and consolidation. Acquisitions, mergers, and takeovers among and across these institutions are engendering ever larger units, culminating in mega-banks and multiproduct financial conglomerates on a scale unimaginable only a couple of years ago. Although the shape of financial institutions and their relationship to financial markets is still evolving, the trend toward larger and more diversified institutions across a wide menu of products appears to be emerging. The risk profile of these new financial units is not simply the sum of its components' parts; some risks may be amplified, others mitigated, and new risk profiles may emerge. As a result, a modified approach to risk measurement and management is called for in the case of across-industry affiliations.

This exploratory chapter focuses on the search for a new mode of risk measurement and management arising out of the affiliation of banks and property/casualty (P/C) insurance companies. The form of the association is of no particular concern; our analysis applies equally, with the appropriate modifications, to mergers, takeovers, or the expansion of product ranges when banks add insurance services and insurance companies in turn complement their palette of products with banking and financial products. For example, banks sell credit insurance, and insurers enter into banking activities by accepting deposits or offering funds management services. The association may also take the form of a financial conglomerate.

These changes began with the Financial Institutions Modernization Act

(FIMA) of 1999, which abolished the historical separation between commercial banking, investment banking, and insurance underwriting. The Act empowers well-managed and well-capitalized bank holding companies to become *financial holding companies* (FHCs). They are authorized to engage, *inter alia*, in insurance agency and underwriting activities.[1] This *convergence* of banking, securities, and insurance activities in financial conglomerates has required a redrawing of the lines between functional regulators, where the Federal Reserve Bank is carrying out the role of an "umbrella supervisor," in the first instance for FHCs. These developments have occurred worldwide and have prompted the establishment of a Joint Forum on Financial Conglomerates (1999), which monitors the supervisory developments from a global perspective.[2] As convergence engenders growing similarities in balance sheets, one would expect a fusing of the involved institutions' risk management and supervisory systems. However, this does not appear to be happening in banking and insurance.

The novel contribution of this study lies in the application of a common value-at-risk methodology to affiliated institutions. As far as their assets side is concerned, our approach grafts the *Market-Value-at-Risk* and the new *Credit-Value-at-Risk* concepts, which are by now ubiquitous in banking, on insurance companies. We include one particular feature of the latter, namely, unexpected credit losses associated with reinsurance assets in the analysis. *Underwriting risk*, by contrast, affects only the liabilities side of the insurance business. Analogously to the market and credit VaR analyses, we apply a Value-at-Risk framework to unexpected underwriting loss reserves. Finally, we discuss liquidity risk, which differs substantially across banking and insurance. Since banks commonly have easier access to central bank funds than insurance companies, regulatory safeguards have to prevent the insurance companies' backdoor access to central bank emergency funds. In addition, such privileged access may jeopardize competitive equity with respect to stand-alone insurers. Our analysis assists affiliated companies in the allocation of risk capital, which protects institutions from unexpected losses from market, credit, underwriting, and liquidity risks. The proposed measurement, structure, and management of the risks of the affiliated companies differ significantly from current practice and supervisory requirements in insurance.

We commence in the first section with a brief discussion of the incentives for affiliations across the banking and insurance industry, examine the evidence regarding diversification benefits accruing to combined institutions, and provide a critique of the results achieved for the traditional, largely hypothetical, mergers approach. The second section contains a detailed analysis of the market, credit, and underwriting risks when combining banking and P/C insurance activities. Care is taken to include the unique risk features in insurance such as solvency predictions and reinsurance asset quality. In the third section we juxtapose the VaR methodology to the insurance industry's loss reserves resulting from underwriting risks, and we contrast our approach with the untidy patchwork of the National Association of Insurance Commissioners' risk-based capital and other regulatory requirements. The next section examines the differing features of the liquidity risks of banks and P/C insurance companies and evaluates implications arising from banks' easier access to liquidity for competitive equity and financial stability. The final section presents conclusions.

MERGERS OF BANKS AND INSURANCE

Incentives

The shift from intermediated to direct finance through capital markets has squeezed the interest rate margins of banks. In order to retain large corporate customers and match interest rates offered in money and capital markets, their net interest income per loan-dollar fell. Furthermore, competitive pressure and product innovation from investment banks diminished the commercial banks' scope for assets and liabilities expansion (Santomero, 1996). Therefore, their only alternative has been to seek new opportunities for earning fee income outside their traditional range of business.

The existing extensive branch system allows banks to cross-sell their customers an increasing array of financial products and services, including insurance products. They are assisted in this endeavor by the commodity-like features of some insurance products (e.g., car insurance). Their standardization requires only limited expert knowledge. These benefits of economies of scale will be reinforced by the selling of banking and insurance products over the Internet to an enlarged customer base. The affiliated institutions can thus defray the fixed costs of the new technology and also benefit from the physical presence of an established bank or insurer in their marketing efforts (the "click and mortar" effect).

Merging banking and insurance activities promises to improve the risk and return profile of the combined institution. The similarities of the asset features in both industries provide opportunities for reaping benefits from economies of scale and scope in portfolio and risk management.

Evidence Regarding Diversification Benefits

In the present context, the risk-return implications of affiliations of banking and insurance activities are of particular interest. Any scope for risk reduction, given returns, is an important consideration in mergers between banks and insurance companies. Useful surveys of studies of potential diversification benefits from merging banking and insurance are provided by Kwan and Laderman (1999) and Laderman (1999).[3] These studies, in the absence of actual mergers, have assessed any diversification benefits on the basis of *simulated merger methodology*. This has been commonly done in connection with exploring the implications of such hypothetical mergers for return enhancement and risk reductions, as measured by the means of ROA and ROE and their distributions.

Diversification benefits are measured by the potential for reducing the variance, standard deviation, or coefficient of variation (standard deviation divided by the mean) of returns on assets or equity. Accounting and market data (for ROE only) for the return and risk measures have been employed. Some authors use the industry averages of these variables on a stand-alone basis as well as for simulated mergers between bank holding companies (BHC) and various nonbank activities. Others carry out the same exercise at the company level, and a few attain optimal diversification benefits by adding nonbank activities to a BHC in the proportion required by the correlation estimates of returns on assets.

Although the results of the studies cited earlier are based on simulations of combined bank/insurance activities, a recent investigation by Whalen (2000) employs *actual* return and risk measures of U.S. banking organizations and those of their foreign subsidiaries active in selling and underwriting insurance products overseas.[4] The company data set, comprising the years 1987 to 1999, is relatively small; in 1999 only eight bank holding companies were involved in insurance activities through foreign subsidiaries, with total foreign assets accounting for less than 1% of the foreign subsidiary assets of U.S. banks. This study confirms the general tenor of the results in the literature. Banking organizations are likely to improve their return-risk opportunities by engaging in banking and insurance activities. Whalen's computations of diversification benefits when combining banking and insurance also take into account return correlations.[5]

While the studies regarding the stability of returns on assets and equity provide some guidance for strategic merger decisions, they fail to convey pertinent information about whether merged institutions are more or less prone to fail than stand-alone companies. The few studies that evaluate the potential merger consequences in terms of reducing the probability of bankruptcy are, however, a step in the right direction. Probability of bankruptcy is defined as losses exceeding capital. Boyd et al. (1993) and Laderman (1999) find that diversification of BHCs into casualty insurance indeed reduces the probability of bankruptcy. Whalen (2000) evaluates the potential risk effects of insurance activities on a firm's likelihood of solvency (the positive of bankruptcy probability) using data from actual combined banking/insurance activities, in the form of a Z-score measure as follows:

$$Z = [E(ROA_j) + K_j]/\sigma_{ROAj} \qquad\qquad (9.1)$$

where

$E(ROA_j)$ = expected ROA for actitivty j

K_j = equity-asset ratio for activity j

σROA_j = standard deviation of ROA for activity j

Assuming ROA to be normally distributed, Equation (9.1) indicates the number of standard deviations below the mean that activity profit would have to fall before the risk capital backing up the activity became negative. A higher ROA and equity-asset ratio and a lower standard deviation of ROA engender higher Z-scores.

Critique of the Traditional Merger Evaluation Approach

The traditional approach to evaluating the benefits of mergers in terms of improved risk-return features does not meet the more exacting standards of modern risk management in financial institutions.

• The analytical methods employed fail to capture *market risk*. The time horizons for the means, standard deviations, coefficients of variation of returns, and the solvency (bankruptcy) models only allow the assessment of longer-term performance measures. This framework is no longer appropriate in an environment where banks and insurance companies trade in securities and hold significant positions in derivatives. Market events emanating from large, unexpected changes in interest rate and exchange rates, and gyrations of asset and commodity prices, can engender huge losses within days for on- and off-balance-sheet positions, while a quarterly solvency model might still indicate a healthy trading position and sound balance sheet. The rapid materialization of market risk can eat up a company's risk capital in a span of a couple of days or weeks without showing up for some time in, say, an equation like (9.1).

• The extant literature cannot distinguish between the impact of market and credit risk on the risk-return tradeoff and on the probability of bankruptcy. Although market risk, as already explained, is relevant in the short term, credit risk emanates from the asset side of both institutions and its negative impact usually materializes more slowly, perhaps over a period of a year or so.

• Market and credit risks are common to both affiliated parties, but underwriting risk is unique to the liabilities side of P/C insurance companies. In particular, the absence of an explicitly computed frequency distribution of unexpected underwriting loss reserves constitutes a serious defect in the merger literature. This important risk component is intermingled with, and only measured as part of, the standard deviation of ROA and ROE. Market, credit, underwriting, and liquidity risks require separate measurement and management.

• Most studies reviewed use accounting data without revealing the accounting methods used. There is, of course, nothing wrong with the application of accounting data, provided assets and liabilities are marked-to-market (MTM), when necessary on a daily basis, and, where no market prices exist, when fair-value accounting is employed. Some studies claim to employ market data for assets and equity. However, since many assets, such as bank loans, are in general not priced in markets, a mixture of accounting and market data would be a more fitting characterization. This is not a quibble but a substantive criticism of the approach. Reliable measurement of market and credit risks has to be based on current and expected future market or fair values of financial instruments.

- All studies ignore the impact of liquidity risk on the operations of hypothetical or actual combinations of banks and insurance companies. A possible liquidity squeeze looms as an ever-present threat to banks and insurers, though they commonly are caused by different events. Bank runs and claims avalanches in the wake of natural disasters are the polar cases.

This critical evaluation of the traditional approach to assessing the risk-return features of combining banking and insurance provides us with an agenda for further research.

MAJOR RISKS AND THEIR MANAGEMENT IN BANKING AND PROPERTY/CASUALTY INSURANCE

The major risks on the asset side of banking and insurance overlap to a large extent; they consist of *market* and *credit risks*. Both industries share a susceptibility to *liquidity risk* that threatens to interrupt from time to time, or even to endanger, the existence of banks or insurers, though important differences remain. *Underwriting risk* affects the liabilities side of insurance companies but is irrelevant for banks if we leave securities underwriting risk on one side. Although market and credit risks impact on banks and insurance companies to a large extent in a very similar fashion, they diverge with respect to liquidity risk, and the insurer's underwriting risk introduces a new risk element into any merger equation.

It is appropriate to look at the first two risk categories in banking and insurance on an affiliated basis and to explore any benefits for risk diversification or potential cumulation of risks. Underwriting risk, on the other hand, is unique to only one of the merger parties and calls for the development of a risk measurement and management mode similar to those pertaining to market and credit risks. Finally, we analyze the separate liquidity risk features of banking and insurance and examine how they could interact.

Market-Value-at-Risk for Banks and Affiliated Property/ Casualty Insurers

The increasing integration of national economies and in particular the globalization of financial markets required a concerted effort by supervisors to introduce uniform prudential norms, initially only for internationally active banks. The Basel Committee on Banking Supervision (BCBS) at the Bank for International Settlements (BIS) in Switzerland, which is owned by the major central banks, was charged with this task.[6] The BCBS's regulatory approach attempts to enhance the stability of financial institutions without intruding in a prescriptive way on their commercial decisions. The Committee accomplishes this objective by essentially adopting world best practices as their regulatory benchmark, which leading banks already followed in their management of market risk. All major banks now embrace these risk management practices.

In recent years, banks have increasingly added the *trading of securities* and *derivatives* to their traditional banking activities.[7] These positions of securities and derivatives are often held for only a very short period. Market or position risk is defined as the risk that the value of on- or off-balance sheet positions will decline as a result of unexpected changes in market prices before the positions can be liquidated, hedged, or offset with other positions. The risk caused by unexpected fluctuations of interest and currency rates as well as asset and commodity price gyrations can affect the market value of these short-term positions appreciably on a daily basis. For this reason, banks in conjunction with their supervisory authorities have developed a new risk management tool called *Market-Value-at-Risk* (VaR) which allows the measurement and management of *market* or *position risk*.[8]

The VaR approach has been grafted onto the risk management systems of insurance companies without major complications, though only a few empirical studies have been done on the topic in this area.[9] As already pointed out, the traditional merger evaluation literature completely ignores market risk. At the operational basis, the assets held for trading by the affiliated insurance arm would have to be marked-to-market. This allows the calculation of daily, continuously compounded rates of asset price changes, and they provide the raw input for frequency distributions of daily price changes. Furthermore, any correlations between asset price changes are taken into account to calculate the portfolio's mean on the basis of, say, a year's historical daily asset price changes. The bankassurance company (which we define as a firm that combines banking and insurance activities) then calculates the maximal losses associated with the regulation-imposed percentile of 99% either for the combined activities or separately for banking and insurance. For example, this percentile might imply a 1.5% loss of the portfolio of assets of, say, $230 million. The resulting loss of $3.45 million (= 0.015 × 230) constitutes the VaR of the portfolio. Together with other regulatory requirements, it determines the amount of risk capital that is assigned to absorb the losses due to major fluctuations in the market value of an institution's portfolio of assets. We cannot think of any reason why one would not apply the VaR procedure to the trading assets and derivatives of insurance companies. The available technological infrastructure and expertise provide incentives for insurers to branch out into trading.

VaR measurement and management systems can be adopted separately by the banking and insurance arms, or they may be applied to the combined portfolios of trading securities in a financial holding company. The former case mandates separate accounts for risk capital, where one dedicated account cannot be used to absorb the trading losses of the other entity. Combined portfolios require common capital provisioning.

Credit-Value-at-Risk of Banks and P/C Insurers

The Basel Committee on Banking Supervision (BCBS) of the Bank for International Settlements (BIS) started from the premise that the *credit risk* of all the various banking risks poses the greatest threat to the viability of financial institutions. While the BCSC initially focused on banks, credit risk threatens the asset side of a broad spectrum of institutions; in addition to banks, they include investment houses, pension funds, insurers, and others with significant financial assets. When the values of assets shrink owing to unexpected credit losses, the capital cushion wears thin, disappears altogether, or becomes negative. The decline in asset values arises from an unexpected deterioration in the credit quality of consumer and commercial loans and from bonds of corporations or those issued by other banks whose credit ratings have been downgraded. Nonperforming loans and defaulting bonds are written down to their recovery value.

At the regulatory level, concern for the banks' vulnerability to credit risk resulted in the 1988 Capital Adequacy Accord. The 1988 Accord did not stand the test of time, however. The Asian financial crisis of 1997–1998 exposed glaring shortcomings in the agreement. The coarse granulation of risk groupings and their inappropriate classification engendered a dispersion of required capital from economically meaningful risk-adjusted capital. The BCBS (June 1999) responded to the defects of its credit risk management system with an improved *New Capital Adequacy Framework*. Banks are now required to use the ratings classification of the major ratings agencies or to develop internal ratings as the basis for the credit risk assessment of their assets.[10]

Although the new Basel approach to credit risk management constitutes an improvement, it still ignores any *diversification benefits* of judiciously composed portfolios of assets, where various credit risks might offset each other, at least partially. In order to more precisely align risk-adjusted and regulatory risk capital, the BCBS (April 1999) issued a position paper asking for comments on the credit risk equivalent to the Market-VaR for the appropriate measurement and management of credit (or default) risk of financial institutions.

Credit-Value-at-Risk for Bankassurance

The general acceptance and rapid spread of the Market-VaR as a superior market risk measurement and management approach for financial institutions[11] suggests that the same methodology be applied to credit risk of banks and nonbank financial institutions such as insurers. Gupton, Finger, and Bhatia (1997) presented a fully fledged Credit-VaR version. The BCBS's position paper captured best risk operating procedures, bestowing the seal of supervisory approval on them. A comparison of various credit risk models is given in Crouhy, Galai, and Mark (2000). Credit-VaR has thus far not been included in the official regulatory arsenal, though it is already an established tool of larger and more sophisticated banks that are likely to possess, or are able to acquire, the demanding data set for this new risk management technique. In principle, Credit-VaR can be applied to financial institutions with a broad array of assets, such as loans, notes, bonds, shares, and derivatives that are held for *investment purposes*. Thus, it applies equally to banks and insurance companies since their asset side shares many similarities with respect to their susceptibility to credit losses.

Credit-VaR-Model and Data Requirements

Credit-VaR is based on measurement of the unexpected credit losses of banks and insurance companies as a result of credit risk migrations, including default risk.[12] The risk manager faces the daunting task of collating a credit loss data set that is forward looking in order to allow the construction of a probability density function (PDF) of credit losses. The unexpected difference between difficult to obtain current and uncertain futures asset values (unexpected credit losses) provides the raw input in the PDF. The PDF serves as the basis for selecting, say, a 99% confidence interval for unexpected losses that are to be covered by an appropriate amount of risk capital. Larger, or extraordinary, losses that have a 1% probability to occur are not covered. Because the credit quality of most assets changes only gradually, the time horizon for analysis is measured in quarters or years rather than in days as with the Market-VaR. However, this is not always appropriate. The unexpected, sudden, and substantial depreciation of the Korean won in 1997, for example, pushed companies with U.S. dollar-denominated loans into liquidations, resulting in huge credit losses of loan-granting banks in a very short period of time.

Current Credit Values

To compute unexpected credit losses, we require current and future values of the assets that banks and insurance companies hold. Current prices of assets such as bonds, notes, and shares that are traded in efficient and liquid markets are available for the different risk categories. All assets in such markets are priced on the basis of their perceived riskiness. For example, the market factors a higher risk premium into the required discount rate of, say, a single-B-rated bond than into one with a triple-A rating. Consequently, the B-rated bond will have a lower price than the A-rated bond, given the same promised cash (coupon flow). The values of such securities in the institution's portfolio may be marked-to-market if required.

Not all assets of bankassurance companies are traded in open market. This applies to their portfolio of commercial and consumer loans, giving rise to a most serious pricing problem. The amortized book values of loans have to be converted into credit-risk-adjusted *fair values*. The company can achieve this by taking advantage of the rating agencies' risk rating of comparable companies. This approach means applying the appropriate bond interest rates of rated companies as the discount rate to the cash flow of loans they hold.

Future Credit Values

Generating the expected future values of assets is the task that awaits us next. The *forward-looking data requirements* of every risk management system pose complex analytical challenges. However, they are of particular concern for the computation of unexpected credit losses associated with all assets of financial institutions because of the relatively long annual time horizon.[13] Credit quality changes have to be projected over a time horizon of a year. The enormity of the assignment unfolds when we examine the factors driving forward asset values. The main influences are as follows:

- Credit ratings migration
- Changes in the term structure of credit spreads
- Interest rate changes
- Exchange rate changes
- Market events

Strictly speaking, only the first two are genuine credit risk factors. However, since market interest rate and exchange rate changes, as well as market events such as regional or global financial crises, can trigger credit risk, they are included here as influences determining the expected credit risk of securities.

We now examine these drivers of credit risk changes. As already mentioned, credit risk measurement and management are hampered by a dearth of data. By relating changes in the above determinants to credit quality changes, we artificially generate a credit loss data set that feeds into a PDF.

Credit Ratings Migration

Credit ratings migration has received the lion's share of attention as the major influence on the future value of securities. Gupton et al. (1997, pp. 65–76) base the probability of a credit rating change of a company with bonds on issue on the historical experience of ratings changes collated by ratings agencies. For example, in the past, B-rated companies had an 83.46% chance of retaining this rating and a 4.07% (6.48%) probability of a downgrade (upgrade) to CCC (BB) during the next year, and so on for other ratings categories. A downgrade would require using higher expected risk-adjusted discount rates for the computation of institutions' relevant bonds and, by implication, for the loans they hold. We discuss the source of the interest rate data below. Since expected ratings changes that are extrapolations of the historical record are associated with risk-adjusted discount rate changes, banks and insurance companies with credit exposure to rated companies are then able to generate a distribution of expected credit value losses (and gains in case of a credit ratings upgrade). These expected credit losses and gains become inputs for the PDF of expected credit losses.[14]

Reinsurance Credit Rating

The credit ratings transition approach is particularly relevant for the valuation of insurers' risky reinsurance claims. The overwhelming majority of P/C insurers, in Australia at least, cede underwriting risk to reinsurers.[15] Applying the transition matrix approach to reinsurers would allow the fair valuation of prospective claims on reinsurers. Any credit ratings downgrade of a reinsurance company lowers the probability that an insurer's claim on the reinsurer will be fully or only partially covered; a poor rating makes it unlikely that cover will be available if needed. The frequently computed distance to default (in standard deviations) would appear to be a particularly helpful piece of information.

U.S. insurance regulators ignore the financial strength of individual reinsurance companies in that only net values (insurance premium minus reinsurance expenses) are used uniformly across all companies to compute risk-based capital requirements. This approach underestimates the amount of risk capital for reinsurers with low credit ratings and penalizes insurance companies with highly rated reinsurance claims on their books, driving a wedge between regulatory and risk capital.

Unrated Companies

For claims on unrated companies, a bankassurance group could conceivably develop its own internal ratings system. Apart from utilizing any information gleaned by experienced credit officers during the loan granting and monitoring process, the institution presumably would base its assessment on factors similar to those that are standard for ratings agencies. In this process econometric evaluations of the work of rating agencies assist in the selection of ratings-relevant variables and their relative importance in the ratings process.[16]

Interest Rate, Yield Spread, and Currency Changes

Earlier we listed changes in interest rates and shifts in the term structure of credit yield spreads among the determinants of future credit values. Both have similar effects on asset values on the balance sheet of bankassurance companies. For example, both a rise in market interest rates and a widening of credit yield spreads along the maturity spectrum increase the discount rates used for expected cash flows and thus depress the relevant asset values. How are expected values of rates and yield spreads modeled? Gupton et al. (1997) do not model the stochastic path of interest rates or of spreads. Instead, they take as given the multiperiod risk-adusted interest rate structures from which they compute in a deterministic way the corresponding risk-adjusted *implied forward rates* as the one-year ahead discount rates. These forward rates are calculated for every ratings grade and maturity of the debt instruments. Subsequently, they are applied to the valuation of every conceivable migration outcome of loans, bonds, and other assets in the portfolio.

When banks and insurance companies hold *foreign currency loans*, their current and future values, in addition to yields and spread changes, are influenced by the change in the exchange rate over the period. Analogously to implied forward interest rates, the future value of exchange rates is deemed to equal their respective forward rates. However, because of interest rate parity, the currency forward rates are implicitly determined by the domestic and foreign interest rates and the current spot exchange rate. As a result, the derivation of future currency rates provides equally deterministic values. Moreover, since forward currency rates are commonly biased predictors of expected future spot rates, the future values of debt claims derived on the basis of currency forward rates have to be treated with caution.[17]

In this way current and expected future values of assets are marked-to-market, and the differences between both provide expected and unexpected credit loss data for the probability density function (PDF) we introduced earlier. The unexpected credit losses are measured as deviations from the mean (expected credit losses) of the density function. Unexpected credit losses are backed by risk capital, while institutions provide reserves for expected credit losses.

The shape of the credit-loss-PDFs for banks and insurers separately and for their combined operations also reflects benefits from diversification, which may be due to a regional, international, and industry spread of loan customers as well as of bonds and shares. It appears that bankassurance companies not only reap considerable synergies in the form of risk reductions but also save on management costs from combining the credit risk management of their banking and insurance affiliates.

Market Events

Unexpected market events presumably pose the greatest threat to the asset side of a bankassurance company in the short term. They include sudden shifts in interest and exchange rates, abrupt ratings downgrades for assets clustered in regions or industries, perilous widening of yield spreads,[18] recessions, or oil price hikes. Scenario analyses and stress testing have to be developed in order to cope with such situations. With institutions holding a diversified portfolio of shares, bonds, and loans, their betas are supposed to measure market risk where the market increasingly transcends national borders. Indeed, bankassurance risk managers can respond to the threat of market events by internationalizing their activities. The business-cycle aspect of a company's market risk appears to be directly related to the credit rating of its debt securities. Ratings agencies stress that they take economic cycles into account in their credit risk assessment. Thus, both types of risk (market and credit risks) are relevant in the present context.

Insolvency Predictions: Traditional versus VaR Approach

In contrast to the traditional literature dealing with the risk-reducing potential of bank-insurance mergers, which focuses, as Equation (9.1) shows, on distributions of returns on assets or equity, the Credit-VaR approach relates the risk capital directly to unexpected credit losses. As the credit-loss-PDF is skewed toward large credit losses, while the ROA or ROE-data are assumed to be normally distributed, the business outcome according to the former might signal illiquidity because the risk capital has been wiped out, while the Z-score still falls short of insolvency. The Credit-VaR is simply a more pertinent measure of the health or otherwise of financial institutions. In addition, the traditional merger evaluation approach ignores Market-VaR completely. Other shortcomings of the traditional approach have been discussed earlier in this chapter.

VALUE-AT-RISK FOR LOSS RESERVES DUE TO UNDERWRITING RISK

In the previous section we analyzed the risks of a bankassurance's *portfolio of assets*. However, for insurance, unlike banking, one of the major risks is concentrated on the *liabilities side* of its balance sheet. Combining banking with insurance would thus tend to increase the total risk of a bankassurance company. However, our understanding of underwriting risk in the VaR context is very limited, and even virtually nonexistent. In the following sections, we examine whether the VaR methodology can be grafted onto the measurement and management of underwriting risk. Our objective is to develop a PDF of loss reserves.

Derivation of Frequency Distributions

Insurance's core business entails underwriting and the bearing of underwriting risk. The premium revenue collected is used to pay out claims and to invest any surplus in order to augment reserves. The accumulated reserves form the insurer's assets. This stylized description of the insurance business ignores the often considerable time delay between the occurrence of a claimable incidence and the payment of the claim even for short-tail business, let alone for long-tail business where it is more pronounced.[19] This necessitates the setting aside of loss reserves. Actuaries have developed a variety of techniques to estimate expected underwriting losses for which reserves provisions are recommended. However, our knowledge of modeling unexpected insurance claims along the lines of VaR models appear to be scant.

Panning (1999), for example, demonstrates that estimates of expected loss reserves are essentially ad hoc because they are not generated by an underlying model.[20] To rectify the situation, he develops a VaR-approach that generates *expected loss reserves* as given by the mean of the distribution of future losses and *unexpected loss reserves* as measured by their standard deviation. Loss distributions are derived from regression estimates of an insurer's current and appropriately discounted expected future claims data. They are caused by past and expected future incidents that trigger claims. The errors of the regression estimates are transformed through Monte Carlo simulation techniques into frequency distributions. Reliance on the error observations alone would provide insufficient data for the PDF of expected (mean) and unexpected (dispersion) of claims payments. The frequency distribution then forms the basis for the *Loss-Reserves-VaR* analysis, that is, for determining a 99% confidence interval. Focusing primarily on expected losses tends to deflect attention from thoroughly analyzing the dispersion of losses of the distribution.

In addition, a fully fledged VaR approach to measuring expected and unexpected underwriting losses allows, in principle, the computation of effective correlations between various risk categories and thus provides a basis for a more reliable quantification of covariance effects. The current risk-based capital model in use in the U.S. P/C insurance industry only includes a general adjustment for diversification between major risk categories.

When insurers are forced to model unexpected underwriting losses, greater precision in the computation of effective risk capital provisions will result. Enhanced understanding of how to measure risk will also diminish premium pricing errors.

The current regulatory approach in non-life insurance practices appears to lack an explicit theoretical risk measurement and management basis. The insurance industry and regulators do not ignore unexpected underwriting losses in the calculation of their required capital provisioning. The current risk-based capital (RBC) model for the non-life insurance industry captures such losses by multiplying reserves with prescribed rule-of-thumb risk factor multipliers. For example, as part of the RBC formula, a company's deviation of its claims ratio from that of the market is taken into account in setting risk capital levels.

Combining the Various VaR Approaches

Let us now put together the main VaR approaches that measure, and are designed to manage, the major risks to the assets and liabilities sides of a bankassurance company.

Market and Credit Risks

Market and credit risks are measured and managed by applying Market-VaR and Credit-VaR. Both types of risk management systems are common to banking and insurance because their asset side and securities trading activities are similar. Moreover, our approach includes the fair value assessment of reinsurance claims (gleaned from their ratings) which are unique to the insurance arm of the combined company. They allow the estimation of frequency distributions of unexpected trading losses and unexpected credit losses, respectively. The specification of a 99% confidence intervals determines the amount that the company will not lose in more than 1% of all possible outcomes. An appropriate amount of risk-bearing capital is then put aside to absorb the unexpected losses corresponding to the chosen confidence interval. Extraordinary losses are not covered by capital. We are concerned with asset risks because their unexpected shrinkage may cause insolvency where assets fall short of liabilities.

The current regulatory risk-based capital concept includes asset and credit risk (though defined differently), besides underwriting risk. However, it fails to develop an appropriate market risk framework. Affiliations between banks and insurers would engender a culture clash that would invariably result in spillover effects. Banking brings a more sophisticated risk measurement and management system to the table where asset risk is dissected into its component parts, one resulting from unexpected market movements and the other from credit risk deteriorations.

Underwriting Risk

The *liabilities side* of the insurance arm of the combined company is mainly subject to underwriting risk which may lead to insolvency. Data from A. M. Best, as quoted in Holzheu (2000), provide a breakdown of the 683 insolvencies in the U.S. non-life insurance industry from 1969 to 1998 into the components of underwriting risk, namely, those caused by insufficient loss reserves, errors in the setting of premiums (22%), too rapid growth (13%), and catastrophic losses (6%). The measurement and management of these underwriting risks are covered in our analysis by a VaR model of loss reserves.

Current Risk-Based Capital (RBC) Requirements and Bankassurance

The National Association of Insurance Commissioners (NAIC) adopted a RBC requirement for property-liability insurers in 1994. The RBC-related formula includes *asset risk* (default and market value risk), *credit risk* (uncollectible reinsurance and other receivables), *credit risk* (pricing and reserve errors), and *off-balance sheet risk* (including guarantees of parent obligations, excessive growth). The various risks are packaged in a compact RBC formula that also allows for a covariance adjustment for diversification benefits obtained from offsetting risk groups.

The NAIC's risk-based capital requirement is completely at odds with the risk capital system initiated by the Basel Committee on Banking Supervision. The NAIC inappropriately amalgamates in its asset risk elements of default with market risk. Although default risk is the ultimate threat to the values of shares, bonds, or loans an institution holds, asset values change far more frequently due to ratings adjustments, as we stressed in our discussion of Credit-VaR. By focusing on the accounting year as its risk time horizon, pervasive shorter-term influences on assets values such as interest and exchange rates changes, share price gyrations, and other market factors are ignored by the NAIC's approach, but they are included in Market-VaR. Credit risk according to the NAIC terminology has a completely different meaning; indeed, it appears to be more appropriately lumped together with underwriting risk.

In addition to RBC, the NAIC also operates a Financial Analysis and Surveillance Tracking (FAST) audit ratio system.[21] However, both evaluation approaches (RBC and FAST) are static, ratio-based solvency testing systems that essentially project the binary status solvent-insolvent of an insurer. In order to overcome the regulator's "snapshot" investigation, Cummins et al. (1999) developed a cash-flow model in the dynamic financial analysis mould to improve insolvency predictions. However, their modeling design is based on scenario projections and not on stochastic probability distributions of cash flows, let alone asset values. For example, because deteriorating, scenario-generated bond qualities do not engender cash outflows, stocks are sold to produce the desired outcome. Bond ratings upgrades are ignored, for they are only concerned with the possibility of negative outcomes. When assets are marked-to-market on a daily basis for risk management purposes, their cash management prescriptions (selling/buing shares) would appear to be nonsensical. The model's focus on runoff modes of insurers under stress-testing conditions may appeal to regulators, but it is of limited use for managerial decisions. This feature stands in stark contrast to Market- and Credit-VaR where the interests of the managers of both regulators and financial institutions' coincide. As mentioned earlier, bank regulators adopted best industry practices.

Thus, the risk management systems of banks and insurers in bankassurance companies appear to be incompatible. At the operational level of the two affiliates, it is almost inconceivable that separate risk systems of differing quality can coexist. Since the two VaR approaches common in the banking industry appear to be far superior to those applying to insurers' asset, a rethink appears to be likely where the spillover effects from bankassurance companies filter into the insurance industry. At the regulatory level, this would necessitate a revamping of the supervisory framework in the insurance industry.

LIQUIDITY RISK

Although both banks and insurers are subject to liquidity risks, risks are commonly caused by different events. Because banks have a privileged access to central bank refinancing, we have to give special consideration to the seeping of this liquidity source into the insurance arm of the bankassurance company.

Liquidity Risk of Banks

A sizable portion of bank assets are very liquid, withdrawable on demand and their nominal values guaranteed, while the majority of their assets are invested in longer term assets that cannot be sold at short notice. Liquidity risk in banking arises when the outflow of funds unexpectedly exceeds the inflow by a large margin and the bank is close to depleting its stock of securities that can be easily converted into cash. This situation commonly occurs when bank customers doubt the safety of a particular bank or of the whole banking system. They are then inclined to withdraw their deposits, virtually all at once, even from solvent banks. Under these circumstances, banks may be temporarily unable to honor their liabilities. Another reason, which often exacerbates a bank run, consists in the drying up of liquidity in securities markets. Where before securities could be sold and bought without significant market impact costs, banks now can only convert assets into cash at distress prices. At times, markets may become illiquid for other reasons, as occurred in the aftermath of the LTCM-crisis when huge losses forced hedge funds and investment banks to hastily liquidate speculative positions during a period of rising investor risk aversion. Moreover, the liquidity squeeze may be the byproduct of an excessively restrictive monetary policy.

Liquidity Risks in Insurance

Liquidity risk arises in property/casualty insurance when the cash-flow patterns of their liabilities and assets change abruptly and unexpectedly. It may take on the nature of a funding of claims crisis. As insurers' contractual liabilities entail commitments for payouts in case of specified damages, funding crises are commonly associated with unexpectedly large claims in the wake of natural catastrophes (hailstorms or hurricanes) or unforeseen damages (asbestos). They are commonly associated with a liabilities blowout.

Liquidity risk may also result when an insurer is threatened from an unexpected writedown of assets at a time when government or corporate bonds, mortgages, or shares need to be liquidated at distress prices because cash is required immediately to meet unexpected claims. Considering the potential for a dramatic turn of events regarding unexpected claims, the insurance industry appears to manage its liquidity risk well. The prevalence of reinsurance in the industry has provided an effective protection against the draining effect of clustered claims. A mitigating effect can also be expected from the implementation of a Market-VaR framework which measures and allows effective management of the short-term loss potential of investments and off-balance sheet items such as securities held for trading and derivatives.

Bankassurance and Liquidity Risk

The impact of an affiliation of banks and general insurance companies on *liquidity risk* has many dimensions.

- *First*, one presumably searches in vain for significant diversification benefits with respect to compensating liquidity effects. It is probably safe to assume no systematic relationship between the offsetting occurrence of heavy net funds outflows (inflows) that banks face from time to time and low (high) claims incidence (natural catastrophes) by the insurance arm. Moreover, P/C insurers do not face the same disintermediation risk of banks where customers withdraw funds in response to competitors offering higher yields or more attractive investment products. In the longer term, policy holders, of course, surrender policies to take advantage of more competitively priced products offered elsewhere.

- *Second*, even if a plethora of liquidities by the banking partner coincided with a claims avalanche in the insurance arm of the group, supervisors might limit the mutual assistance that the bank is allowed to give under crisis conditions. In Australia, any such incidence is complicated by the fact that while the banking and insurance industries have the same regulator, namely, the Australian Prudential Regulatory Authority (APRA), the Reserve Banks of Australia (RBA) is responsible for *financial system stability*. It provides liquidity to the whole system if required but in general does not assist individual banks. It encourages and supports the efforts of other banks to assist an illiquid but solvent bank. However, it is unclear whether this practice also extends to banks and their insurance arms.

- *Third*, whenever a liquidity crisis and solvency risk appear on the financial horizon, the specter of *contagion* starting at one of the affiliates and spreading to other associate entities arises. Clearly, regulators are concerned about the spread of an isolated liquidity or solvency problem to other parts of the financial system, in particular to banks where it could perhaps trigger a *systemic crisis*. Failure of one bank to settle its transactions with other banks deprives other banks of funds that could cause gridlock in the whole settlements system.

- *Fourth*, in its day-to-day implementation of interest rate targeting, the RBA deals with a range of accredited financial institutions. It sells/purchases securities in the market and uses repurchase agreements to calibrate money market cash. To the extent that the insurance arm is not accredited to deal with the RBA, it is still questionable whether a bank can carry out such transactions on behalf of its insurance affiliate. Doing so could interfere with the implementation of monetary policy.

- *Fifth*, normal as well as emergency access to liquidity by an insurance firm via a bank affiliate raises the issue of *competitive equity* as stand-alone insurers do not enjoy this privilege (Marcus, 2000).

- *Sixth, market liquidity risk* in the sense of markets for securities and derivatives unexpectedly drying up, poses an equal threat to banking and insurance operations.

CONCLUSIONS

The merging of banking and P/C insurance activities presents new challenges for the risk management of the affiliated companies. The available empirical evidence regarding any risk-reducing effects of such mergers is almost entirely based on hypothetical affiliations, yields ambiguous results, and relies on a dated risk concept for financial institutions (standard deviation of returns). In addition, theoretical investigations on the matter are scant. This exploratory study applies modern institutional risk management systems to market, credit, and underwriting risks as they arise in bankassurance. We identify *market* and *credit risks* as common risk elements on the asset sides of companies that combine banking and insurance, while *underwriting risk* affects only the liabilities side of the insurance partner. Moreover, *liquidity risk* affects both affiliates, though it emanates from different business events.

The VaR-methodology is our *leitmotif* for analyzing the first three risks. The *Market-VaR* concept, which is established in banking, can be equally applied to the short-term securities trading in insurance. The inputs into the required frequency distributions of daily asset price changes are readily available from market quotations. *Credit-VaR*, with its longer-term time horizon for risk analysis, requires a more involved computation of unexpected credit losses. However, a merging insurer would stand to benefit from its banking affiliate's experience in the implementation of the two asset-side risk measurement and management systems. Transplanting the VaR concept to underwriting risk encounters the obstacle of a dearth of data and the virtual absence of loss reserves modeling approaches. Data and theory provide the foundations on which a PDF of expected and unexpected underwriting losses can be built. The application of a consistent risk system to the assets and liabilities sides of bankassurance allows the assessment of the financial positions of banks and insurers on a continuum ranging from triple-A to near-insolvency, or worse. It leaves behind the limiting dichotomy of solvent and insolvent companies.

This chapter also unbundles the overlapping risk groupings of the NAIC's patchwork approach and enables affiliated institutions to tackle the risk management task in a consistent fashion. Finally, the chapter examines the differing exposures of banking and insurance to liquidity risk and evaluates some implications of banks' privileged access to liquidity. This study does not include empirical estimates; nor does it explore the opportunities for covering insurance risks in capital markets.

NOTES

The research for this chapter was sponsored by the Volkswagenstiftung.

1. Many banks have carried out insurance agent activities for some time. National banks engage in a wide range of general insurance activities in towns with under 5,000 people. Moreover, the Comptroller of the Currency authorized national banks to provide a range of insurance and insurance-like products. As to the future, McDonough, 2000, doubts that more than a few banks will actually be interested in the underwriting of insurance. What is more, the mutual charter of many insurance firms will prevent mergers and acquisitions, unless they incorporate.

2. The Joint Forum was established in 1996 under the aegis of the Basel Committee on Banking Supervision, the International Organization of Securities Commissions (IOSCO), and the International Association of Insurance Supervisors (IAIS).

3. The literature they review and Laderman's (1999) own results include a range of other nonbank activities in their merger simulation tests such as life and agency insurance, real estate development, security broker/dealer activities, and investment advice. These activities are added, in varying proportions, to those of bank holding companies.

4. The general restrictions on banks to engage in insurance activities that were lifted in November 1999 did not apply to U.S. bank holding companies selling and underwriting insurance products overseas to nonresidents.

5. In private correspondence Whalen confirmed that neither foreign earnings nor

assets of U.S. BHCs are purged of the effects of exchange rate changes. However, he believes any bias to be small. The domestic banks in the sample would similarly be impacted by their overall foreign currency exposure. His correlation results bear a close resemblance to those reported previously. However, only a detailed analysis of banks' on- and off-balance sheet currency exposures, their methods used to translate the results of individual lines of foreign business, and the currency translation procedure of assets would settle the issue.

6. In April 1995, the BCBS issued for comment by banks and financial market participants supervisory proposals for applying capital charges to the market risks incurred by banks. See, for example, BCBS, 1995.

7. In addition, banks and insurance companies employ derivatives to manage risk and enhance income. The evidence of property/casualty insurance companies' use of derivatives is investigated by Cummins et al., 1997.

8. See Jorion, 1997, and Gupton et al., 1997, for in-depth analyses of Market-Value-at-Risk. This version is called Market-Value-at-Risk in order to distinguish it from a similar risk management tool for credit risk, that is, from Credit-Value-at-Risk.

9. The April issue of the *North American Actuarial Journal* contains the proceedings of a 1997 conference on "Integrated Approaches to Risk Measurement in the Financial Services Industry," which essentially deals with possible applications of VaR models in the insurance industry.

10. Very few banks so far have developed reliable internal ratings systems, due mainly to the lack of accurate historical ratings migration and default data for their loan portfolios. In addition, very few banks, if any, have consistently marked-to-market the loans on their books. Their loan performance record would therefore not contain useful information about the likelihood of credit risk downgrading or loan defaults of, say, B-rated companies.

11. Panning, 1999, evaluates the alternative risk measures to VaR, such as standard deviation, probability of loss, expected loss, and worst case scenario, and finds them wanting.

12. Expected credit losses are calculable with a reasonable degree of certainty. Loan loss reserves provide the capital cushion for such losses. Credit risk deals with unexpected credit losses, which are covered by risk capital.

13. The data requirements are in general less demanding for Market-VaR. Current and historical market prices (daily for a number of years) are in general available, allowing risk managers to model future price changes on the basis of frequency distributions of past price changes. For Credit-VaR, annual data of losses associated with credit quality and other relevant changes are rarely available over a sufficiently long time horizon for the construction of a PDF function. An appropriate pool of data has to be generated artificially.

14. The company KMV (for *K*ealhofer, *M*cQuon and *V*asicek; www.kmv.com) computes the expected default frequencies of companies, applying option pricing technologies to traded equity prices. This is an alternative to the ratings-based approach of credit risk migration.

15. Property and casualty insurance in broad terms coincides with the general insurance industry in Australia.

16. M. Barth, W. Beaver, and W. Landsman, 1998, for instance, regress companies' credit ratings on those variables that rating agencies emphasize in their ratings reports. They include companies' total assets, ROA, the ratio of debt to assets, and the probability

of dividend payment. The corresponding values of the variables of unrated firms are then plugged into the estimated equation. Provided the results are statistically acceptable and any parameter changes are appropriately captured through estimation updates, bankassurance companies are provided with a rich and objective source of ratings data. Alternatively, the KMV approach calculates expected default frequencies from share prices of publicly traded and nontraded private firms.

17. See, for example, Bansal and Dahlquist, 2000, for estimates of the so-called forward premium puzzle for developed and developing countries.

18. Examples abound. The almost vertical declines in the exchange rate of several Asian countries during 1997 blew up their foreign currency loans to Western banks, and the unexpected widening of yield spreads during the Russian crisis of 1998 almost brought the global financial system to its knees due to the recklessly leveraged hedge fund LTCM.

19. In terms of the nature of insurance products and services, the industry distinguishes generically between short-tail and long-tail business. Products involving claims related to loss or physical damage to property which can be settled relatively quickly are known as short-tail business. Long-tail business covers mainly liability products (public and product liability), professional indemnity, workers' compensation, and compulsory third-party car insurance.

20. By contrast, the unexpected loss data of Credit-VaR are based in a systematic fashion on the credit migration matrix, credit yield curves, forward rates, and other model features. The market value changes used in Market-VaR are derived from the stochastic path of prices and from portfolio theory. Approaches to model loss reserves distributions exist, of course (see McDonald, 1988). However, they are not as yet part of the regulatory arsenal (of Australia at least). For example, the Australian Prudential Regulatory Authority (1999) dealing with liability valuations standards of the P/C insurance and a position paper by Martin and Tsui (1999) published by the Institute of Actuaries of Australia both fail to deal with loss distributions as opposed to estimating their expected values.

21. Summary discussions of the NAIC's RBC and FAST approaches are given by Cummins, Grace, and Phillips, 1999.

REFERENCES

Australian Prudential Regulation Authority. (September 1999). *A Statutory Liability Valuation Standard for General Insurers.* Sydney.

Bansal, R., and M. Dahlquist. (2000). "The Forward Premium Puzzle: Different Tales from Developed and Emerging Economies." *Journal of International Economics,* 51, pp. 115–144.

Barth, M., W. Beaver, and W. Landsman. (February 1998). "Relative Valuation Roles of Equity Book Value and Net Income as a Function of Financial Health." *Journal of Accounting & Economics,* pp. 1–34.

Basel Committee on Banking Supervision. (April 1995). "An Internal Model-Based Approach to Market Risk Capital Requirements." Basel, Switzerland: Bank for International Settlements. www.bis.org.

Basel Committee on Banking Supervision. (April 1999). *Credit Risk Modelling: Current Practices and Applications.* Basel, Switzerland: Bank for International Settlements. www.bis.org.

Basel Committee on Banking Supervision. (June 1999). *A New Capital Adequacy Framework*. Basel, Switzerland: Bank for International Settlements. www.bis.org.

Boyd, J. H., G. A., Graham, and R. S. Hewitt. (1993). "Bank Holding Company Mergers with Nonbank Financial Firms: Effects on the Risk of Failure." *Journal of Banking and Finance*, 17, pp. 43–63.

Crouhy, M., D. Galai, and R. Mark. (2000). "A Comparative Analysis of Current Credit Risk Models." *Journal of Banking and Finance*, 24, pp. 59–117.

Cummins, J. D., M. F. Grace, and R. D., Phillips. (1999). "Regulatory Solvency Predictions in Property-Liability Insurance: Risk Based Capital Audit Ratios, and Cash Flow Simulations." *Journal of Risk and Insurance*, 66, no. 3, pp. 417–458.

Cummins, J. D., R. D. Phillips, and S. D. Smith. (1997). "Corporate Hedging in the Insurance Industry: The Use of Financial Derivatives by U.S. Insurers." *North American Actuarial Journal*, 1, no. 1, pp. 13–40.

Gupton, G., C. Finger, and M. Bhatia. (April 1997). *CreditMetrics™—Technical Document*. New York, JP Morgan. www.riskmetrics.com/research/techdocs/index.cgi.

Holzheu, T. (2000). "Solvency of Non-Life Insurers: Balancing Security and Profitability Expectations." *Sigma*, no 1.

Joint Forum on Financial Conglomerates. (February 1999). *Supervision of Financial Conglomerates*. Joint Forum on Financial Conglomerates.

Jorion, P. (1997). *Value at Risk, The New Benchmark for Controlling Market Risk*. Chicago: Irwin.

Kwan, S. H., and E. S. Laderman. (1999). "On the Portfolio Effects of Financial Convergence—A Review of the Literature." Federal Reserve Bank of San Francisco (FRBSF), *Economic Review*, no 2, pp. 18–31.

Laderman, E. S. (October 1999). "The Potential Diversification and Failure Reduction Benefits of Bank Expansion into Nonbanking Activities." Federal Reserve Bank of San Francisco (FRBSF) Working Paper.

Marcus, G. (2000). "Issues for Consideration in Mergers and Takeovers from a Regulatory Perspective." *BIS Review*, p. 2.

Martin, G., and D. Tsui. (1999). "Fair Value Liability Valuations, Discount Rates and Accounting Provisions." *Australian Actuarial Journal*, 5, pp. 351–455.

McDonald, J. (1988). "Some Statistical Distributions for Insured Damages." In *Managing the Insolvency Risk of Insurance Companies*, J. D. Cummins and R. A Derrig, eds. Boston: Kluwer, pp. 191–205.

McDonough, W. J. (April 2000). "Future Challenges for Bankers and Bank Supervisors." *BIS Review*, 32, pp. 1–8.

Panning, W. P. (1999), "The Strategic Use of Value at Risk: Long-Term Capital Management for Property/Casualty Insurers." *North American Actuarial Journal*, 4, pp. 86–105.

Santomero, A. M. (1996). "Discussions, Banking and Insurance." In *Universal Banking*, A. Saunders, and I. Walter, eds. Chicago: Irwin, pp. 413–417.

Whalen, G. (September 2000). "The Risks and Returns Associated with the Insurance Activities of Foreign Subsidiaries of U.S. Banking Organizations." Economics and Policy Analysis Working Paper, Comptroller of the Currency.

Chapter 10

Risks Associated with Mega Financial Institutions

Steven A. Seelig and Peter J. Elmer

INTRODUCTION

During the past several years, the banking and financial sectors have experienced a series of mergers on a magnitude not previously seen. This trend includes mergers between very large U.S. banks, very large international banks, and large investment banking, insurance, and merchant banking firms. For example, a recent sample of very large U.S. bank mergers includes the NationsBank Corporation acquisition of Bank of America, Banc One Corporation acquisition of First Chicago NBD, and the Chemical Bank purchase of Chase Manhattan Corporation. The Travelers Group Inc. purchase of Citicorp extended the trend across industries whereas the Deutsche Bank acquisition of Bankers Trust New York Corporation extended the trend across international boundaries. The result has been a growing trend toward giant or "mega" financial conglomerates at national and international levels.

Traditionally, bank regulators and supervisors were primarily concerned with issues of market concentration, public benefits, and safety and soundness of the resulting bank. However, the new global merger wave gives rise to additional policy concerns as well as new risks to the international financial system. Large financial conglomerates tend to depend on funding sources that are both more global and rate sensitive than traditional deposits. Thus, they may be more vulnerable to liquidity pressures than traditional large banking firms. In a competitive system, distressed banks should be allowed to exit the industry, with shareholders and creditors sharing the losses of the firm. Unfortunately, the creation of giant global financial institutions operating under many corporate structures and countries suggests a need for a structure to handle the insolvency of one of these institutions without international dislocations resulting from each country applying its own laws. In the absence of such a structure, the issue of whether giant financial firms are becoming "too-big-to-fail" simply because there are no international mechanisms to handle their insolvency may be a real one. Moreover, one must wonder whether the new wave of mega-international financial organizations either has, or will have, disproportionate economic and political power.

A prerequisite to understanding failure-related policy issues is the need to understand the special risks associated with mega-financial institutions. A tendency for larger institutions to place increased reliance on volatile and other nondeposit sources of funds increases their exposure to market runs and other liquidity risks. Management risks increase in response to limits on the ability of senior managers to oversee and control institutions engaged in a wide range of activities across the globe. Supervision issues arise as international banking operations extend beyond the sovereign authority of individual supervisory authorities and the complexity of worldwide operations overshadows the ability of examiners to analyze risks. In addition, as financial firms branch into an ever-growing range of financial activities, the number of supervisory entities increases as well, raising the specter of overlapping supervision.

Policymakers are beginning to express concern. In a statement issued after their recent meeting in Prague, the finance ministers and central bank governors of the Group of 10 countries noted that the wave of mergers in the financial sector is creating institutions that are larger and more complex, with a geographic reach, and a range of products that are much wider than in the past. The officials stated that this trend toward consolidation has implications for "financial risk, monetary policy, competition, and payments and settlements."[1]

This chapter seeks to make the reader aware of some of the risks associated with the recent growth of mega-financial institutions. To this end, we examine issues surrounding the creation of these institutions, with an eye toward raising policy issues and highlighting related risks. We do not attempt to provide an extended analysis of each issue. Rather, our hope is that by raising the issues, we will trigger further research and policy discussions. The following sections discuss the rising trend in financial megamergers, and the special types of risk associated with these mergers, as well as some of the policy issues raised by this trend.

RECENT TRENDS

Many countries, such as Canada, have banking systems dominated by a few large institutions. Others, such as the United States, have fragmented banking systems, with only a few very large depository institutions. With the recent merger boom, this trend is changing. In the early 1980s, the United States had about 15,000 banking organizations, but with the bank and thrift failures of the late 1980s and the mergers of the 1990s, the number has shrunk to about 8,000.[2] While large banks have been common for many years, the second half of the

1990s witnessed a remarkable jump in the size and concentration of the largest banking companies. These changes are especially noteworthy in the United States where geographic and antitrust restrictions inhibited U.S. bank expansion. Nevertheless, Figure 10.1 shows a dramatic increase in the size of the largest U.S. bank, which maintained a steady size on a relative basis until the mid-1990s and then doubled its assets to over $600 billion, primarily through mergers, in only a few years.[3] In sharp contrast, the assets of the smallest banks, represented by those with assets below $100 million, declined steadily through the 1990s. At the start of the 1990s, Figure 10.1 shows the assets of the largest bank equal to about 60% of the combined assets of all banks with assets of $100 million or less. However, by the late 1990s, these positions had reversed, as the largest bank grew to hold more than twice the combined assets of all banks with assets below $100 million.

The growth of the largest banks is not limited to U.S. banks. As shown in Figure 10.2, the assets of the largest bank in the world increased over 60%, from $533 billion to $843 billion, during the five-year period 1994–1999. The largest bank as of December 31, 1994, Deutsche Bank AG, moved from the number 10 position at year-end 1994, with $367 billion of assets, to the number 1 position in 1999, with $843 billion in assets. Much of this growth was accomplished through the acquisition of Bankers Trust Company and several investment banks. This movement also hints at a dramatic change in the international makeup of banks in the 1990s. In 1994, 9 of the 10 largest banking companies in the world were Japanese banks whose operations were heavily centered in Asia. However, by the end of calendar 1999 only 3 of the 10 largest banking companies were Japanese.

The trend toward growth through merger has continued, as evidenced by recent reports of results for fiscal years 1999 and 2000.[4] Internationally, the merger trend has created 12 financial institutions with assets greater than $500 billion. At year-end fiscal 1999, Deutsche Bank had total assets of $909 billion. In addition to the significant increase in size of these institutions, their global reach and complexity have grown as well. Rather than being oriented toward Asia, today's mega-institutions are more global in terms of their home countries and in the range of countries where they operate.

Risks

Liquidity Risk

Liquidity risk arises from the ability of creditors to disrupt business operations by withdrawing funds on relatively short notice. This risk is particularly relevant to larger banks and those with high-growth strategies because these institutions often utilize shorter term volatile liabilities that are easily accessed through the capital markets.

In fact, many of the largest banks have been shifting to more volatile sources

Figure 10.1
Assets of the Largest U.S. Bank versus Assets of All U.S. Banks < $100 Million

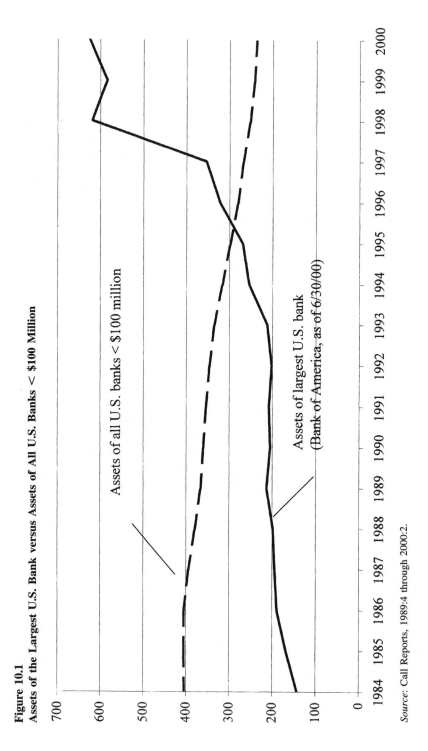

Source: Call Reports, 1989:4 through 2000:2.

Figure 10.2
10 Largest World Banking Companies, 1994 and 1999

	Name (1994)	Country	Assets ($ Billion)		Name (1999)	Country	Assets ($ Billion)
1	Sanwa Bank, Ltd.	Japan	522	1	Deutsche Bank AG	Germany	843
2	Dai-Ichi Kangyo Bank Ltd.	Japan	521	2	Citigroup	United States	716
3	Fuji Bank, Ltd	Japan	512	3	BNP Paribas	France	701
4	Sumitomo Bank Ltd.	Japan	507	4	Bank of Tokyo-Mitsubishi Ltd.	Japan	697
5	Sakura Bank, Ltd.	Japan	501	5	Bank of America Corp.	United States	632
6	Mitsubishi Bank Ltd	Japan	491	6	UBS AG (Group)	Switzerland	614
7	Sumitomo Trust	Japan	478	7	HSBC Holdings PLC	United Kingdom	569
8	Norinchukin Bank	Japan	444	8	Fuji Bank, Ltd.	Japan	552
9	Industrial Bank	Japan	388	9	Sumitomo Bank Ltd.	Japan	509
10	Deutsche Bank, AG	Germany	367	10	HypoVereinsbank AG	Germany	505

Source: American Banker, June 29, 1995 and September 20, 2000. The figures reported in *American Banker* are from financial statements dated 12/31/94 and 12/31/99, respectively.

of funds for some time. For example, the largest U.S. banks have been funding the bulk of their asset growth during the past five years with volatile liabilities, and uninsured deposits and other borrowings are the liabilities most responsible for the growth in volatile liabilities.[5] In contrast, insured deposits declined as a source of funds supporting the growth in assets. Large firm reliance on volatile funding should not be surprising, given that a key advantage that accrues to the largest firms is enhanced access to international capital markets. Thus, it is natural to expect mega-financial institutions to continue emphasizing volatile funding in the future.

Unfortunately, liquidity risk tends to rise as financial institutions place increased reliance on shorter-term and more volatile sources of funds. These sources of funds appeal to growing firms with good credit ratings because they are readily available and require almost no operating expenses to support. However, these characteristics can quickly turn into elements of risk that can cripple even the largest banking firms in the event of distress.

The largest bank failure in U.S. history, Continental Illinois, provides a classic example of liquidity-related problems in very large institutions.[6] Indeed, events surrounding this failure serve to illustrate the many problems that would likely develop for today's mega-institutions, if confronted with similar liquidity-based problems.

Reminiscent of today's mega-financial institutions, Continental Illinois chose a path of high growth over a relatively short period, although Continental's growth arose from lending, not merger. For example, Continental's loan portfolio approximately tripled, from $11.6 to $34 billion, between 1976 and 1982, making it the largest commercial lender and one of the 10 largest banks by assets in the United States. Profits were good, and credit ratings high (in the "AA" range), so the domestic capital markets were more than willing to extend credit. In the early 1980s, Continental Illinois CDs were among the most liquid in the secondary market, and the institution had developed extensive correspondent relationships with other banks.

In mid-1982, problems developed at another large U.S. bank, Penn Square. Penn Square's problems caused analysts to question Continental's health, and credit ratings dropped to the single "A" range. Although this financial slide was modest, it was sufficient to limit Continental's access to the highest quality funding markets, forcing it to turn to other funding sources that were more expensive and less stable.

While Continental Illinois continued to post a profit and its ratings remained in the investment grade range, rumors of problems persisted, eventually sparking a catastrophic bank run in the international financial markets. In less than one week, Continental Illinois was rendered insolvent by massive withdrawals of wholesale funds. Market discipline worked but not in the manner intended by modern theory. Instead of gradually pressuring Continental Illinois to change policies and reduce risk, market discipline effectively forced regulators to deal with a crisis, thus complicating the normal resolution process.

The case of Continental Illinois suggests that liquidity risk has many dimensions for the largest institutions. Clearly, even the largest institutions, including those with investment grades, can become engulfed by liquidity-related problems in a matter of days. The remarkable speed with which problems develop makes federal intervention almost inevitable. Resolving problems after they develop is more complicated for institutions of very large size because of the difficulties encountered in assessing the value of the institution's assets and the limited number of potential investors. These risks will likely become more important as large financial institutions continue to opt for rapid growth and reliance on shorter-term and volatile sources of funds.

Management Risk

In recent years, financial institutions and their supervisors have focused greater attention on risk management than in the past. Three years ago, the Group of Thirty, a group of major global banks, urged the world's major financial institutions to develop a global framework for comprehensive and effective management controls.[7] Much of the effort has gone into developing sophisticated models for estimating the credit risk faced by banks.[8] However, with the geographic and product expansion of financial institutions, the approaches to risk management have broadened as well. Firms are placing increased emphasis on consolidated risk management (sometimes called "integrated" or "enterprise-wide" risk management). This is a coordinated process focused on managing and measuring risk on a firm-wide basis. While this focus is healthy, it is not certain that it will be successful. As Cumming and Hirtle (2000) point out, "few if any financial firms have fully developed systems in place today."

With the enactment of the Gramm-Leach-Bliley Act in 1999, it is reasonable to assume that U.S.-based banks will expand into nonbank financial products, perhaps following the Citigroup model. This evolution poses tremendous challenges for management. A CEO sitting in Charlotte, New York City, or Frankfurt must be able not only to monitor the profits from various operations around the world, but also to control the risks being taken by the various business units. The increased size and complexity of financial institutions have made management more difficult. Excessive risk taking by traders, or inappropriate business practices by brokers, not only have a first-order impact on profits but potentially expose the institution to losses resulting from damage to the firm's reputation. Management's failure to adequately monitor risks taken by individual employees can be seen in the catastrophic actions of a rogue trader that led to the failure of Barings Bank in 1995. Similarly, Bankers Trust experienced legal and financial difficulties as a result of problems in their derivatives operation.[9]

As mega-institutions diversify their products and activities, they become increasingly vulnerable to increased operational risk. Financial institutions are now collecting insurance premiums, settling securities transactions, brokering insurance and securities, and engaging in payment processing and international funds transfer. The challenge is to assure that these are being done well and that systems are protected against intrusion and illegal transfers of information or funds. Moreover, as technology increases, so do customers' demands for privacy. These activities give rise to the business risks associated with poor performance as well as litigation risks associated with mishandling information and payment processing. Although comprehensive internal control and risk management systems should help mitigate these risks, Cumming and Hirtle (2000) show that there are significant costs and obstacles involved in the development of such systems. They find that both information and regulatory costs have affected the "trade-off between the value derived from consolidated risk management and the expense of constructing these complex risk management systems."

Oversight Risk

As noted earlier, the merger wave in banking is resulting in giant financial institutions that are international in scope and diversified as to lines of business. One can argue that these mergers reduce risk by increasing geographic and product diversification. Nevertheless, the heavy emphasis on cross-border financial activity raises issues for regulators responsible for supervising these institutions. The trend also raises significant issues regarding exit policies should one of these mega-banks fail.

The sheer size and complexity of financial institutions prompts us to ask whether bank supervisors adequately evaluate the riskiness of these firms. Although traditional examination methods have focused on ex-post evaluations of bank performance, there has been an increasing awareness of the risks these mega-banks pose to the system and the need to perform *ex ante* analysis with market-related information.[10] In response to academic work, economists in the Federal Reserve System have urged that large banks be required to issue publicly traded subordinated debt to provide regulators with the market's assessment of the bank's prospective financial condition as well as provide market discipline to the system. In addition, some researchers have suggested integrating stock market performance into early-warning systems, and some regulators are placing increasing reliance on banks' internal risk models.[11]

Banks and other financial service providers have operated across borders for many years. Large international banks, such as Chase and Citibank, have traditionally had branches or subsidiary banks in many countries. However, growth in international merger activity is creating banks with operations in foreign countries on a scope that may be larger than the lead bank's activities in its home country. This raises questions regarding the ability of home country supervisors to monitor and supervise the global operations of banking organizations headquartered in their countries.

In fairness, the globalization of banking has fostered greater international cooperation among financial sector regulators. For example, following the collapse of Long-Term Capital Management, the G-7 finance ministers and central bank governors commissioned the president of the Bundesbank to suggest ideas for enhancing international supervisory cooperation. His efforts gave rise to the creation of the Financial Stability Forum (FSF) in 1999.[12] This forum brings together ministries of finance, central banks, supervisory agencies, and other national authorities responsible for financial stability in significant financial centers. Countries represented include, in addition to the G-7, Australia, Hong Kong, Singapore, and the Netherlands. Also represented are the International Monetary Fund, World Bank, OECD, the regulatory organizations (IOSCO, the Basel Committee, and the IAIS), and two special committees of central bank experts. The stated objectives of the forum are to assess vulnerabilities affecting the international financial system, to identify and oversee actions necessary to address these vulnerabilities, and to improve coordination and information exchange among the various authorities responsible for financial stability.[13]

In addition to the FSF, the Basel Committee has provided a forum for improving international bank supervision standards and has served as a vehicle to facilitate communications between bank supervisors from different countries. This interaction has made it easier for supervisors to compare notes, share information, and otherwise coordinate supervisory actions across national borders.

Since many countries employ functional regulation, whereby banking, insurance, and/or securities regulation are separated, it is not clear that a single supervisor has the authority or responsibility for dealing with the organizational risks that cross product lines and geographic boundaries. Although the efforts of the Basel Committee have increased international communication and standards among bank regulators, this group typically excludes political decision makers that are represented at the FSF, and the support of these leaders is critical if large international institutions are to be supervised effectively. Indeed, it was this blending of central bankers, finance ministers, and regulators in the FSF that was supposed to overcome the perceived weakness of the Basel Committee. The FSF was designed to deal both with the increased vulnerability to the system arising from the creation of mega-institutions and with the macroeconomic consequences associated with financial sector instability.

Despite these efforts, some observers, such as Eatwell and Taylor (2000), argue that there is a need for a centralized international regulator, a "World Financial Authority." Eatwell suggests that the FSF has become a "think tank with nowhere to go," and so proposes that a World Financial Authority perform the functions of domestic regulators.[14] Such an authority would be responsible for chartering institutions, collecting information, and conducting surveillance. For this type of organization to work, it would have to have regulatory powers given to it by treaty. Otherwise it would be no different than the "soft law" approach of the Basel Committee, where international standards are developed but are left to each country for adaptation. While Eatwell and Taylor's proposal is interesting, it is uncertain that countries will be willing to surrender their regulatory sovereignty, absent a crisis precipitated by an international mega-financial institution.

Despite the efforts that have been made internationally to improve bank supervision and cooperation among supervisors, there is a need for greater effort.

With the growth of multinational financial conglomerates engaging in commercial banking, investment banking, insurance, and securities sales activities, there will be an increasing need for umbrella surveillance of these institutions and closer cooperation among banking and other functional supervisors.

Bankruptcy and Failure

Even with the best possible supervisory regime, in a competitive system the possibility always exists that some institution will fail. Hence, exit strategies should be in place that will allow a competitive market to function while mitigating systemic effects. However, in the case of large multinational institutions, the conflicting legal structures and rules will make this process difficult at best.

There are two basic regimes that deal with the insolvency of financial institutions—the single-entity regime and the separate-entity regime. In countries that follow the single-entity regime, such as England and Luxembourg, affiliated banks are resolved as one legal entity where all of the assets of a foreign bank are encompassed in the liquidation and creditors, regardless of where they are located, prove their claim in that proceeding. In countries that follow the separate-entity model, such as the United States, each legal entity is treated separately and liquidated as if it were a separate institution. All of the assets of the locally incorporated office and the parent bank in the host country are encompassed in the liquidation proceeding. Clearly, the single- and separate-entity models appear to be fundamentally different approaches to bankruptcy that are not easily reconciled.

To further compound matters, the bank subsidiary operating in the United States is not subject to the bankruptcy code but will be liquidated by the deposit insurer, the FDIC. The other subsidiaries and the parent holding company will come under the bankruptcy code. In each instance the shareholders, in the form of the parent company, will have a subordinated claim against the receivership estate.

The failure of the Bank of Credit and Commerce (BCCI) highlights many weaknesses in international supervision and bankruptcy resolution. BCCI was founded in 1972 by a Pakistani financier, though at the time of its closing it was 77% owned by the royal family of Abu Dhabi. The bank was registered in Luxembourg, had its headquarters in London, operated affiliates in 69 countries, and had a large retail network in Great Britain. In addition, BCCI used front men to purchase two banking organizations in the United States, First American Bankshares, which owned and operated banks in Washington, DC, and the Maryland and Virginia suburbs, and Independence Bank, located in California.

The resolution and liquidation of the various entities of BCCI were carried out under differing international models for bankruptcy, and depositors were treated differently depending on the deposit insurance rules in place in each country. Almost 10 years after the closing of BCCI, the liquidation process has not been completely resolved, and similarly situated creditors have been treated differently depending on where they did business with BCCI. The liquidator for the corporate entity in the United States recently completed the liquidation of the assets of First American Bankshares and was able to remit the balance (about $540 million), after satisfying all U.S. creditors, to the liquidation in Luxembourg. There it can be used to satisfy the remaining claims of depositors in other countries.[15]

Not only were the basic bankruptcy rules different between countries, but also depositors received differing degrees of protection based on the national deposit protection scheme. BCCI also highlighted differences in country practices regarding the right of offset, whereby mutual claims between parties, such as deposits and loans, are extinguished.

Overall, the BCCI case illustrates the need for a clear and consistent approach to handling the failure of a large multinational financial institution. The adoption of national depositor preference in the United States further disadvantages foreign depositors in the event a U.S.-based international bank fails. This disparity in the treatment of domestic versus foreign depositors is likely to further encourage ring fencing by national governments as they attempt to protect the interests of their citizens.[16] In addition to the legal structure issues surrounding the failure of a multinational bank, other problems may arise such as those associated with the netting of collateral on financial contracts. This risk in turn gives rise to temporal settlement risk if a bank is closed during its normal business hours.

Political and Economic Power

The recent trend in megamerger activity and the melding together of the financial sector is similar to other sectors of the economy in the past. The United States experienced two major merger waves in the post–World War II period, one in the 1950s and another in the 1960s. As these merger waves occurred, political concern about the concentration of resources and political power surfaced. At the time, observers referred to the experiences of Japan with its Zaibatsus (giant conglomerates combining banking and industry) and the economic and political clout that these firms were able use to get favorable treatment. The current trend toward the creation of giant financial conglomerates that are larger than the GDP of many countries also raises this issue.

Microeconomic theory and the industrial organization literature are replete with discussions of the market characteristics that affect the competitive behavior of businesses. Market power typically occurs when a single firm, or a small group of firms, can exercise significant discretion over market production, distribution, and pricing. Absent overt collusion, policymakers use measures of market concentration, such as the Hirschman-Herfindahl Index, as a proxy for market power. However, measures of concentration for a single product line or geographic market do not capture the "concentration of economic power" that may come with size.

In discussing the power that a firm gains from its absolute size, or aggregate concentration, Corwin Edwards wrote: "By virtue of its size, the large concern also has substantial advantages in activities that lie outside the process of production and sale. These advantages are particularly evident in litigation, politics, public relations, and finance."[17] In fact, as the largest financial firms grow through merger and *de novo* entry, they expand into additional markets and compete with each other. Traditional antitrust regulation deals with the market concentration effects of this activity. However, the sheer size of these financial conglomerates provides them with a comparative advantage in the areas described by Edwards such as significant political power.

Seelig (1979, p. 101) noted that despite the efforts of regulators, it would be very difficult to control the growth of bank holding companies and the increase in aggregate concentration that would accompany the expansion of the largest banking organizations. Subsequent developments have supported this view. Increased competition between regulators within the United States and liberalization of permissible activities have strengthened the political position of the largest financial conglomerates and, on the surface, weakened the overall regulatory structure.

Internationally, the expansion of large banks into other countries through significant acquisitions is creating international banks with a dominant presence in the financial sectors of several countries. (Besides the large institutions discussed above, the largest Spanish banks have acquired dominant positions in Mexico and other Latin American countries.) These banks are subject to different regulators with respect to both their various financial products and geographic boundaries. With immense resources and the ability to shift activities, resources, and legal structures to their advantage, financial mega-firms are clearly a match for the existing regulatory and political structures in many countries. This imbalance of political power, combined with the oversight risks discussed above, suggest a need to consider the development of strong umbrella regulators who would be responsible for monitoring and addressing the risks of each mega-financial institution.

CONCLUSION

The recent trend of mergers among very large banks and other financial service firms is creating mega-financial institutions that are dominant in a number of financial product lines, such as lending insurance and investment services. Some firms now exceed $1 trillion in total assets and control greater economic resources than exist in many countries. The creation of such mega-institutions raises public policy issues for the global financial system.

Although financial institutions have undoubtedly reduced risk through diversification, there is a tendency for these firms to fund themselves with more volatile liabilities, thereby increasing the risk of liquidity runs. The example of Continental Illinois, a bank that was buffeted by rumors in international money markets and faced a liquidity crisis so severe that the government had to intervene, illustrates that liquidity risk exists today.

Managing mega-institutions is a great challenge. Given the extensive nature of the risk taken by financial conglomerates, as well as the high degree of leverage used in banking and other financial activities, proper internal controls are critical. Although risk management has improved over the past decade, it is not clear that it has kept pace with the growth of the largest institutions. Nor is it clear that the control mechanisms have kept pace with the geographical reach of these institutions. The increased management risks associated with these mega-institutions should raise concerns for supervisors and require greater vigilance and attention to the adequacy of banks' internal control policies and mechanisms.

Although there has been international recognition that mega-institutions pose significant risks and that there is a need for greater cooperation among regulators, it is not clear to some observers, such as Eatwell and Taylor, that adequate steps have been taken. The creation of the FSF was a positive step, along with the increased dialogue between the Basel Committee and supervisors of the insurance and securities industries. However, given the scope and complexity of the new mega-institutions, the potential for miscommunication and "passing the buck" between regulators remains great. A large firm that operates banks in 10 countries, insurance activities in 5, and securities activities in 15 would potentially have 30 different regulators in at least 15 countries. While home country bank supervisors have lead responsibility for banking activities, they often do not have a lead position for nonbanking activities, such as insurance or investment banking. This overlap in supervisory jurisdictions, coupled with the economic and political power of these firms, suggests the need for a stronger supervisory structure.

The sheer size and scope of operations of modern mega-institutions raises the issue of aggregate concentration of resources. The largest institutions have the ability to capture significant market share in other products by using profits from one product line to gain market share in another. However, increasing economic and political power makes it difficult for many countries to exercise control over their activities. This raises the specter of having firms that can control political agendas, much as the Zaibatsus did in Japan.

NOTES

The views expressed here are those of the authors and do not reflect those of the Federal Deposit Insurance Corporation or International Monetary Fund or FDIC or IMF policy. The authors thank Kitty Chaney and Chau Nguyen for their assistance.

1. See Dow Jones, 2000.

2. Banking organizations include savings and loans (thrifts), unitary bank and thrift holding companies, and multibank and thrift holding companies. For a good discussion of the consolidation trend, see Holland, Inscoe, Waldrop, and Kuta, 1996.

3. This refers to the assets of the bank and not the combined assets of the bank holding company.

4. See "The World's 100 Largest Public Financial Firms," 2000.

5. "Volatile liabilities" are defined as the sum of large denomination time deposits, foreign office deposits, federal funds purchased, securities sold under agreements to repurchase, and other borrowings. "Uninsured deposits" include large-denomination time deposits and foreign office deposits, whereas "other borrowings" include federal funds purchased and securities sold under agreement to repurchase.

6. See Sprague, 1986, for a complete discussion of the liquidity and other problems that plagued Continental Illinois.

7. See Group of Thirty, 1997.

8. See, for example, Crouhy, Galai, and Mark, 2000, and Treacy and Carey, 2000.

9. For a more in-depth discussion of the derivatives problems at Bankers Trust, see "Bankers Trust," 1995 and Shirreff 1995.

10. See, for example, Seelig, 2000.

11. Elmer and Fissel, 2000, find that stock market variables significantly enhance the failure-predictive content of traditional or "ratio-based" early warning systems. Nuxoll, 1999, discusses problems associated with the use of value-at-risk models.

12. See Courtis, 2000.

13. For more details on the structure and activities of the Financial Stability Forum, see www.fsforum.org.

14. See Courtis, 2000, p. 25.

15. See *The Economist*, 2000 for more details.

16. See Marino and Bennett, 1999, for further discussion of the potential problems associated with the application of depositor preference in the United States.

17. Edwards, 1964, p. 345.

REFERENCES

"Bankers Trust: Shamed Again." (1995). *The Economist*, October 7, p. 87.

"BCCI Dead and Buried." (2000). *The Economist*, April 15, pp. 92–93.

Courtis, Neil. (2000). "Interview: Lord Eatwell." *The Financial Regulator*, 5, no. 2, pp. 23–27.

Crouhy, Michel, Dan Galai, and Robert Mark. (2000). "A Comparative Analysis of Current Credit Risk Models." *Journal of Banking and Finance*, 24, nos. 1–2, pp. 59–117.

Cumming, Christine M., and Beverly J. Hirtle. (2000). "The Challenge of Risk Management in Diversified Financial Companies." Paper presented at the Western Economics Association Meetings, Vancouver, Canada.

Dow Jones. (2000). "G10 Ministers Caution on Banking Sector Consolidation." Dow Jones International News Service, September 24.

Eatwell, John, and Lance Taylor. (2000). *Global Finance at Risk*. London: Polity Press/Blackwell Publishers.

Edwards, Corwin. (1964). *Maintaining Competition*. New York: McGraw-Hill.

Elmer, Peter J., and Gary Fissel. (2000). "Forecasting Bank Failure from Momentum Patterns in Stock Returns." Paper presented at the Financial Management Association Meetings, Seattle, Washington.

Group of Thirty. (1997). "Global Institutions, National Supervision and Systemic Risk." *A Study Group Report.* Washington, DC: Group of Thirty.

Holland, David, Donald Inscoe, Ross Waldrop, and William Kuta. (1996). "Interstate Banking—The Past, Present, and Future." *FDIC Banking Review*, 9, no. 1, pp. 1–20.

Marino, James A., and Rosalind Bennett. (1999). "The Consequences of National Depositor Preference." *FDIC Banking Review*, 12, no. 2, pp. 19–38.

Nuxoll, Daniel A. (1999). "Internal Risk-Management Models as a Basis for Capital Requirements." *FDIC Banking Review*, 12, no. 1, pp. 18–29.

Seelig, Steven A. (1979). "Aggregate Concentration and the Bank Holding Company Movement." *Acta Monetaria*, 3, pp. 89–103.

Seelig, Steven A. (2000). "Banking Trends and Deposit Insurance Risk Assessment in the 21st Century." In *The New Financial Architecture: Banking Regulation in the 21st Century*, Benton Gup, ed. Westport, CT: Quorum Books.

Shireff, David. (April 1995). "Can Anybody Fix Bankers Trust?" *Euromoney*, 34–36.

Sprague, Irvine H. (1986). *Bailout.* New York: Basic Books.

Treacy, William F., and Mark Carey. (2000). "Credit Risk Rating Systems at Large US Banks." *Journal of Banking and Finance*, 24, nos. 1–2, pp. 167–201.

"The World's 100 Largest Public Financial Firms." (2000). *Wall Street Journal*, September 25, p. R22.

Chapter 11

Addressing the Too-Big-to-Fail Problem

Ron Feldman and Gary H. Stern

INTRODUCTION

Governments have incentives to protect the creditors of large financial intermediaries from loss when these firms cannot repay their debts. These incentives
can sometimes extend to creditors of nonfinancial firms and even subnational
governments. Governments have acted upon such incentives by producing a
class of organizations deemed too-big-to-fail (TBTF). The problems associated
with a TBTF policy—which are normally implicit rather than codified in law—
include excessive firm risk taking, regressive income redistribution, and currency
crises. The potential costs of a TBTF policy are substantial.

To make matters more troubling, governments around the world may well
view more firms as TBTF in the future, and these firms will control an increasing
share of economic activity. Causes of the expanding TBTF problem include the
increasing size of financial intermediaries and the greater scope of their activities, the pressure on governments to meet policy objectives through off-budget
means, and the new technology of finance. Some observers view the TBTF
problem as intractable because of its current severity and potential for expansion.
Governments face enormous pressure to protect the creditors of these firms in
order to reduce the perceived and real costs associated with large-firm failure.
As a result, observers note, governments cannot make a credible commitment
to allow creditors of large firms to suffer losses upon firm insolvency.

We do not agree. It is true that a government cannot and should not commit
itself to forcing creditors of large financial firms, and other TBTF candidates,
to suffer complete loss after every failure. That said, governments can take steps
to limit the number of firms considered TBTF as well as the amount of protection that creditors of TBTF firms can expect to receive. In other words, gov-

ernments can implement credible or "time-consistent" policies for putting the creditors of these firms at risk of loss.

Indeed, a number of potential options are available for establishing a time-consistent policy. We categorize these policies into five groups based on the manner in which they address the incentives that policymakers face when deciding to bail out the creditors of TBTF firms. We then provide our views as to the likely effectiveness of the policies. Our goal is not to provide a comprehensive review of the commitment technologies available to policymakers. Rather, we hope our discussion makes clear that there are alternatives to the status quo. Options establishing credibility include the following:

1. Policymakers can prohibit bailouts or pass other simple legal restrictions. This strategy essentially requires regulators to ignore incentives to bail out creditors.
2. Policymakers can enact penalties or policies that increase the cost to regulators providing bailouts. This strategy intends that disincentives to bailouts should outweigh incentives.
3. Regulators can weaken the incentives that have led them to bail out creditors in the past. This strategy relies on changing the dynamics that created the time-consistency problem in the first place.
4. Elected officials can appoint regulators who have a predilection for resisting bailouts. This strategy focuses on the incentives internal to the decision maker.
5. Regulators can try to circumvent the need to provide bailouts by expressing concern about the TBTF problem but remaining ambiguous about the cases where they would provide a bailout (that is, follow a policy of "constructive ambiguity").

Not all of these suggestions are equally viable. The first two methods and the last-named, a policy of constructive ambiguity, are the least credible because they do not address the underlying factors that give policymakers incentives to bail out creditors at TBTF institutions. As a result, policymakers have significant cause to evade these reforms, making these strategies deficient. The third and fourth strategies have more potential because they try to alter underlying incentives, although they also raise implementation concerns. In any case, we hope this exercise encourages additional analysis of the options we have reviewed and new suggestions for establishing credibility.

DEFINING THE TBTF PROBLEM

Provision of insurance creates the well-known problem of moral hazard whereby the applicant for insurance coverage is more likely to suffer loss after becoming insured. Moral hazard arises because the insured has less reason to avoid actions that lead to financial loss if the insurer will absorb some of that loss. Provision of insurance and creation of moral hazard are two of the defining features of the TBTF problem. Specifically, the creditors of large financial firms and potentially those of other entities believe that the government will insure them against loss if the firm that owes them money cannot repay them fully or on time. This protection leads the creditors of firms to change their behavior in such a way that the government has a greater likelihood of having to bail them out. Because the manner in which governments provide protection for TBTF firms and the moral hazard and other problems it creates are not run-of-the-mill, we will provide more detail on each.

The Moral Hazard and Related Problems of a TBTF Policy

The prices that equity and debt holders charge a firm reflect, at least partly, the firm's risk taking. A firm taking on more risk has a higher chance of failure, all else being equal, and this probability of higher failure should force the firm to pay higher costs to issue equity or debt. These statements can hold true only if equity and debt holders think they will lose money upon the failure of the firm. In certain cases, the government has explicit programs in place to prevent such losses. Deposit insurance is a prominent example. Creditors of a failed bank that receive protection no longer have the incentive to fully price the bank's risk taking. Guaranteed and complete government protection effectively turns the insured obligations of financial institutions into securities issued by a country's national government. Consequently, the prices charged by creditors holding insured deposits will reflect the new, lower levels of default risk.

The actual risk taking by the insured financial institution and its probability of failure are likely to be higher than those of the government providing the insurance. As a result, the insured financial institution receives a price signal that is too low. Because insurance artificially represses the price, reducing the bank's cost of risk taking, the bank takes on more risk than it would otherwise. Excessive risk taking becomes a more serious problem when the insured entity becomes insolvent but remains open for business. The owners and managers can raise the value of their holdings only by taking on significant risk. Insurance not only distorts prices but also affects the quantity of funds the bank can raise. Without insurance, the bank might not be able to raise funds at all and would go out of business; with insurance, the funds continue to flow and support additional risk taking.

The issue of excessive risk taking is at the core of the TBTF problem.[1] Creditors of TBTF firms believe they have government insurance against loss. In some cases, governments have extended the protection to equity holders, debt holders, and the managers of TBTF firms. However, such extremely expansive protection is the exception. Generally, protection at TBTF firms is extended to cover only holders of fixed-income debt issued by the firm. Although more limited, this protection is particularly troublesome because fixed-income creditors normally have incentives to restrain excessive risk taking by the firm. Fixed-income creditors do not benefit from excessive firm risk taking because returns beyond those needed to repay principal and interest accrue to shareholders and managers. Indeed, excessive risk taking can reduce the chance that debt holders will receive full and timely repayment. The loss of potential market discipline from fixed-income creditors becomes especially damaging when the government providing the coverage for creditors of TBTF firms does not charge premiums that account for the insured's risk taking. Risk-based insurance premiums can help address the moral hazard problem by transferring the cost of risk taking back to the insured. When neither fixed-income creditors nor the government providing coverage for creditors of TBTF firms charges the correct price, the firms considered TBTF take on risk that they otherwise would not.

Ironically, a TBTF policy for large financial institutions can indirectly lead to excessive government support and risk taking at smaller institutions. During periods of uncertainty about banking conditions, a TBTF policy encourages creditors to shift funds from small institutions to large institutions. This naturally raises concerns about fairness and puts pressure on governments to provide similarly generous coverage for the uninsured creditors of smaller banks. Alternatively, the government could raise the deposit insurance limit for smaller banks. As a result, following a TBTF policy could eventually lead to excessive risk taking by all financial institutions, not just the largest.

Excessive risk taking by TBTF firms raises concerns about the misallocation of resources. The allocation problems result, for example, from excessive bank financing of certain projects or more than optimal investment in a given class of securities. The lavish but empty hotels and office buildings financed by thrifts in the United States during the 1980s epitomized this misallocation of resources. The provision of government support can also lead TBTF firms to be cost inefficient. Like a firm owned by the public sector, the private firm with a "soft budget" due to access to government support does not face full market competition and could potentially afford higher costs than a firm facing a hard budget.[2] Resources are thus diverted from their most efficient use.

Fairness or distribution concerns arise when governments effect transfer payments from taxpayers to creditors in order to reduce the losses that creditors would suffer. Such transfers could be regressive given the highly concentrated ownership of debt securities among the wealthy in many countries. Such transfers could have poor resource allocation implications as well, depending on how funds are raised. These transfers have been of enormous size, equaling 50% of some countries' economic output.[3]

Additional concerns arise if a TBTF policy makes currency crises more likely, as some analyses suggest.[4] A TBTF policy could require the government to finance massive payments in the future, and seigniorage represents a likely source of funding for the transfers. Such an inflationary policy can put a country's currency at risk for steep depreciation. The resulting currency crisis could trigger severe recessions with significant social costs. The restructuring of transfers and taxes likely to result from the recession also raises concerns about distribution. More broadly, currency crises have the potential to destabilize the entire social and governing structure of a country.

As we have indicated, TBTF policies are normally focused on the creditors of large financial firms, but they can be extended to commercial entities. However, the distinction between a policy of protecting creditors of TBTF commercial firms and protecting creditors of TBTF financial firms should not be drawn too sharply. In many cases, the protection of creditors of commercial firms had the ultimate intent of protecting the creditors of banking organizations. For example, the Korean government rescued Hanbo Steel to stop the failure of its creditor banks, and the Japanese government supported its real estate market in order to stop the failure of financial institutions holding real estate assets.[5] Moreover, the allocation and distribution concerns related to TBTF policies for creditors of large commercial firms are quite similar to those raised for TBTF policies for financial firm creditors. The allocation problems result from the government's oversupply of financial resources to commercial firms that private lenders would not finance as favorable. In these cases, the government effectively assumes the role of the TBTF lender willing to take on excessive risk. The fairness concerns are identical to those that result from the bailout of financial firms (for example, regressive transfers).

The problems associated with TBTF policies can extend beyond the environment of the firm to the intergovernmental realm. In this context, subnational governments believing they can extract *ex post* bailouts from the central government will take on financial liabilities that they cannot support. The central government will then transfer resources to make good on the obligations of the local government.[6] As in the case of TBTF protection for creditors of commercial firms, the central government takes on excessive risk by acting as the implicit guarantor, thus encouraging too many resources to flow to the subnational government. Concerns about regressive distributions are similar to the other TBTF situations described.

Providing TBTF Insurance

TBTF protection is implicit. Indeed, many countries have laws that specifically exclude these creditors from protection. For example, government deposit insurance programs normally cap their insurance coverage for depositors at an amount that is less than what is covered as part of a rescue of creditors of TBTF firms. Moreover, these insurance plans do not explicitly cover nondeposit liability holders (for example, bondholders). At the same time, we know that a TBTF policy can have a fairly substantial cost. Why then do creditors without any formal coverage believe they will be protected?

At the time that policymakers must force creditors of TBTF institutions to bear losses, they will face many incentives to renege on commitments to do so. First, policymakers will face the wrath of those who will lose money or that of their political supporters. The creditors of large financial and commercial institutions could have considerable political power, particularly in countries with highly concentrated ownership of large firms.

Second, and as a related point, in some countries there may not be a sharp distinction between policymakers and the creditors or others who will benefit from the TBTF bailout. The potential for self-dealing and looting gives a strong incentive to provide extralegal bailouts.

Third, policymakers may use banks as part of an industrial policy of allocating credit to favored industries or firms. Such policies could require banks to take on risks that creditors would not support absent the assumption of federal support. If the government wants to continue using the banking system to make loans to particular industries, it will have to step in to support creditors so that the creditors can continue to provide funds to banks.

Fourth, policymakers may believe that the failure of a large financial intermediary will lead to additional firm failures. These failures, in turn, could have significant costs for the real economy. Although policymakers do not normally articulate the mechanism by which such spillovers could occur, there are several candidates. For example, bank assets are opaque, and creditors could have difficulty after the failure of one institution in determining if other institutions have exposure to the failing institution or have characteristics similar to those that produced the original failure (for example, loans to certain types of firms). The uncertainty regarding bank exposure could lead creditors to take their funds out of other large banks. The sequential service constraint and the mismatch between banks' assets and liabilities could turn the desire to retrieve funds into a run and, potentially, a panic. To take another example, the failure of a large financial institution could lead to the insolvency of smaller respondent banks or other financial institutions owed funds by the failing bank (for example, through large interday credit exposures).

The failure of large financial institutions can pose a threat to the real economy through several means. Bank borrowers, particularly those that rely on banks rather than capital markets for funding, will face high costs to reestablish credit relationships. Very large banks also provide a number of services to commercial firms and capital markets, including payments processing, provision of hedging, and processing of security market transaction. The failure of a large bank could make it difficult, and perhaps even impossible, for various payment and transaction clearing systems to operate normally for an extended period of time. Such a disruption to the payments system could cause a significant decrease in commercial activity. The aggregate effect of financial market disruptions, moreover, could lessen consumer and business confidence. Ultimately, weaknesses in the financial sector could reduce output and employment in the real economy. By providing full protection against loss to uninsured creditors, policymakers may believe they have saved society from a potentially costly financial shutdown.

Fifth, and finally, policymakers may find the failure of commercial firms or subnational governments untenable, even though the systemic risks discussed here may be more hypothetical than real. The increase in unemployment from the failure of a large firm could present a political cost too exorbitant for policymakers. Alternatively, policymakers may argue that the potential failure and liquidation of certain firms, such as those manufacturing items deemed critical for national defense, could threaten national security or national pride. Central governments may not allow a subnational government to go bankrupt because of perceived political costs or disruptions to the provision of public services.

Because of these reasons, it is not time consistent for regulators and policymakers to simply say that they will not bail out creditors. Creditors will recognize the incentives that policymakers have to ignore their own policies, and, therefore, they will behave as if they have nothing to lose. This fact underscores the importance of making a credible commitment to putting creditors at risk of loss. Without this commitment, significant costs associated with TBTF policies are inevitable.

One might question why policymakers do not make such a commitment given that the high costs associated with a TBTF policy are so well known. In other words, isn't the potential downside that we have described a large enough disincentive to outweigh the incentives to bail out creditors? One answer is that policymakers might think they will act differently the next time decisions on bailouts must be made. Moral hazard will not occur, policymakers might think, because creditors will recognize that the current bailout is a one-time event. Creditors, on the contrary, recognize that policymakers will encounter the same incentives for a bailout each time a potential failure forces them to make a decision. Alternatively, because the costs of moral hazard are realized in the future whereas the benefits of a bailout are received today, policymakers may conclude that the incentives to bail out creditors are greater than the disincentives.

It might also be claimed that research suggesting that the ripple effect of failure has been exaggerated is sufficient justification for policymakers not to address the TBTF problem. In other words, if a significant incentive for bailouts of TBTF firms is the fear that a failure will spread, then the potential that the fear is groundless should remove the incentive. Some economists have argued that creditors' losses from bank failures in the past were not so large as to produce significant spillovers. Others have argued that bank creditors exhibit rational behavior even during panics (for example, depositors differentiate between financially sound and unsound banks during panics).[7] Policymakers, having seen this evidence, will have little reason to bail out creditors of large banks in the current period (so the reasoning goes).

However, we do not believe these findings will persuade policymakers to change their decision making. At a minimum, there is disagreement as to the conclusions one should draw from research on banking "contagion."[8] Moreover, policymakers may not find the findings relevant to the particular bank failure that they will face in the future. Policymakers are likely to believe that there is some chance that making decisions on the basis of past experience will be wrong. The costs of an inappropriate decision (that is, not providing government support in the rare case when it may be needed) will likely appear so high to policymakers as to swamp the rationale for not taking action. As former FDIC chairman William Seidman put it, "Nobody really knows what might happen if a major bank were allowed to default, and the opportunity to find out is not one likely to be appealing to those in authority or to the public."[9]

It is clear to us, therefore, that credibility will have to be explicitly and deliberately established through commitments that put creditors at risk of loss. We cannot count on addressing moral hazard by jawboning or having creditors spontaneously changing their minds and pricing risk accurately. This recognition is particularly important because the TBTF problem is getting worse.

WHY THE TBTF PROBLEM IS GETTING WORSE BUT IS STILL TRACTABLE

Several trends will likely intensify the TBTF problem. First, significant consolidation in the financial services industries has led to more and larger institutions considered TBTF.[10] In the United States, for example, the percentage of total banking assets held by the largest banking organizations has increased almost twofold during the 1990s (from 25% to 44%). This growth has come almost entirely from mergers and acquisitions.[11] Some analysts argue that increasing the potential for TBTF support helps explain the rise in megamergers because economies of scale do not justify them.[12] Consolidation has also occurred in the nonfinancial sector leading to the possibility of additional TBTF firms.[13]

Second, financial institutions have been and are likely to continue increasing their scope. In particular, there has been an increase in merger activity among financial institutions, including banks, securities firms, and insurance firms. This consolidation raises TBTF concerns. Combining firms whose history of government protection is meager or even nonexistent with banks that have a more clearly established TBTF tradition may lead creditors of the less protected firms to believe that they will now benefit from TBTF protection. For example, governments might protect the creditors of the insurance firm affiliated with a TBTF bank so that the failure of the insurance firm does not spill over and imperil the bank. Rather than benefiting from diversification, the universal bank approach can produce combined entities with a greater chance of receiving government support.[14]

Third, the rapid advances in financial, computing, and communication technology could make TBTF rescues more likely to occur. As the activities of financial intermediaries become more complex, regulators have a harder time effectively limiting their risk taking. Moreover, complex transactions mean that governments will find it more difficult to resolve the failing financial institutions without significant fear of disrupting the financial and real economies. Indeed, regulators find themselves at a severe disadvantage relative to market participants in understanding how the failure of a large financial intermediary or commercial firm will affect the market liquidity and solvency of other participants in complex securities markets (for example, many derivative markets). As a result, regulators may have to rely on the opinion of those who will benefit from the bailout when assessing the need for government support.[15]

Advances in technology have also increased the ability of financial managers to take on financial exposure outside their country of residence and to shift funds internationally. International exposure of financial institutions makes it more difficult for regulators and private creditors to resolve failed institutions in an expeditious manner. Rather than face significant legal and financial uncertainty, policymakers may find it more feasible to bail out creditors. Moreover, the rapid movements in funds, particularly those with a short-term maturity, have been associated with banking and currency crises, leading to protection for firm creditors in many countries.[16]

Fourth, countries face growing internal and external pressure to reduce fiscal deficits. As a result, countries have reason to achieve social and economic objectives through means not recorded in their national budgets or financial accounts. Countries may encourage banks to support certain industries partly to take such lending off the books of the national government. Similarly, governments can create off-budget, pseudogovernmental entities that benefit from implicit TBTF government support, called government-sponsored enterprises in the United States, in order to evade budget discipline. Such incentives help explain the growth of contingent liabilities in both the developed and developing world.[17]

Finally, the precedent that governments have set by providing bailouts encourages creditors to believe that they will continue to benefit from TBTF protection. In the United States, for example, the first cases in which regulators officially sanctioned government support for bank creditors beyond legal requirements involved very small banks with African American ownership. Policymakers provided such protection in the hopes of preventing racially focused violence. What appeared as isolated incidents created the venue for bailouts on a much larger scale.[18] Each successive government action having even the patina of a bailout makes it harder to convince creditors that they will suffer losses. Some analysts fear that the International Monetary Fund in supporting countries suffering currency and banking crises set new precedents in the 1990s.[19] In addition, the transition of many firms from public control in planned economies to private control in a more market-oriented economy could lead governments to increase their implied support. In these countries, there is a natural presumption that the government will continue to support firms previously under government control.

The tone of this discussion so far has been bleak. Governments have strong incentives to bail out creditors of large firms, and these incentives have become stronger despite widespread recognition that these policies have a very high potential cost. Indeed, this view has led some to conclude that the TBTF problem is intractable. Certainly, the TBTF problem will not go away on its own.

But the problem of time consistency is not unique to the TBTF problem, having first been analyzed in the context of setting monetary policy. The proven ability of central banks to establish credible low-inflation policies suggests that policymakers can commit to policies that produce short-term economic and political pain in order to achieve long-term benefits.[20] To address the TBTF problem, policymakers must enact commitment strategies that give the creditors of most financial firms, commercial firms, and subnational governments reason to believe that they will suffer full loss; creditors of the few exceptional institutions must believe that they might suffer at least some loss. Consequently, it is useful to review and categorize strategies that can conceivably be used to establish credibility in addressing the TBTF problem. We will also provide some general discussion as to which of these strategies are likely to be effective.

IDENTIFYING AND ASSESSING METHODS FOR ACHIEVING CREDIBILITY

To be somewhat systematic about our discussion, we will group strategies by how they affect the incentives to bail out creditors. Strategies include (1) rules or laws that prohibit bailouts of uninsured creditors and thus require policymakers to ignore incentives, (2) policies that penalize policymakers for bailouts or otherwise increase the explicit disincentives to provide protection, (3) reforms that try to eliminate high losses and potential spillovers from the failure of large financial institutions or otherwise mitigate against the very incentives policymakers have for bailing out creditors, (4) appointment of policymakers with a natural disinclination to bail out creditors, and (5) constructive ambiguity policies that try to obscure how policymakers might respond to incentives. (Though listed separately, many reform plans use multiple commitment strategies.)

After describing the types of proposals that fall under each category, we will provide some initial thoughts on the likelihood that these proposals will be time consistent. That is, will they be credible and alter incentives enough to make creditors believe they are at risk of loss? These comments are aimed at generating additional discussion and suggestions rather than at presenting an all-encompassing review.

Bailout Prohibitions and Other Rules That Force Policymakers to Ignore Incentives

A direct response to the time-consistency problem is to forbid policymakers from acting on incentives when deciding to bail out creditors. This would be most simply accomplished by forbidding in law the coverage of all creditors of a certain type (for example, coverage allowed only for those with bank deposits under $100,000). This approach has been associated with some radical plans to address the TBTF problem. For example, plans that eliminate public deposit insurance and replace it with a private insurance system or with nothing at all essentially rule out government protection.[21] Similarly, the collateralized deposit system created by narrow banking plans creates a group of "wide banks" whose creditors would not be eligible for legal insurance coverage.

Establishing an explicit cap on coverage has also been linked with shifting from a policy regime where TBTF coverage was provided to one where such coverage is discouraged. The staff of the International Monetary Fund, among others, has recommended that countries establish guaranteed deposit insurance programs with clear caps on coverage.[22] Countries without a clear limit are assumed more likely to provide excessive support to creditors. Setting a limit on coverage acts as a signal about the new policy of not routinely providing protection to creditors of TBTF firms.

A somewhat similar approach focuses on the organizational structure of firms. For example, a government could decide to increase the powers available to banking organizations but allow only legal entities distinct from the bank to exercise such powers. These policies assume that policymakers will be less likely to bail out creditors, and creditors will be less likely to expect a bailout, when they have a financial relationship with an entity legally distinct from the bank. In other words, these creditors are simply not legally entitled to *ex post* protection.

Policymakers can take a number of additional steps as part of their organizational design to convince creditors that they will not receive support in the future. Banking legislation in the United States, for example, calls for functional regulation where bank regulators do not have primary responsibility for monitoring insurance or securities affiliates of the banking organization. Instead, that task falls to securities and insurance regulators. This arrangement also relies on the legal status of the nonbanking creditors. If bank regulators do not have legal responsibility for the firm, the thinking goes, they will have less reason and opportunity to effectuate bailouts.

The rule-based approach is quite easy to implement, and it offers a simple and direct way to convey the sentiments of policymakers to creditors. But is it credible? That is, will it change the decision that policymakers make when a TBTF bank is failing? Although these rules might be better than none, we do not think they have a high degree of credibility. A credible rule must be difficult to evade. Moreover, to be credible, policymakers must have little desire to evade the rule. We think the rule-based approach fails both tests.

First, rules of this sort do not change any of the incentives to provide bailouts. Policymakers will still fear the economic and political costs associated with large firm failure and will have a strong rationale for evading the rule. Second, a fair number of options are available to policymakers for circumventing prohibitions, including emergency legislation, lending from the central banks, and resolution techniques that accomplish the economic substance of a bailout without violating the legal restriction.[23] We don't think a complete contract that addressees all the methods that policymakers can use to effect bailouts can be written. As such, we think it unreasonable to believe that policymakers will shackle themselves when the incentives to extend the protection appear, as they surely will some day.

Penalties and Other Disincentives to Providing Bailouts

A variety of commitment strategies attempt to increase the costs to policy-makers of engaging in bailouts without relying on prohibitions per se. The Federal Deposit Insurance Corporation Improvement Act of 1991 (FDICIA) in the United States has reforms of this nature. In particular, FDICIA requires poli-cymakers to take a series of votes that will be reported to the public before bailouts occur. FDICIA increases costs as a result of the extra publicity and voting procedures that accompany an attempt to bail out creditors. FDICIA combines this approach with a legal rule that requires resolution of a failed institution on a least-cost basis. This rule requires the FDIC to quantify the cost of protecting uninsured creditors (as well as creating an explicit *ex post* levy on banks to pay for bailouts). Resolutions are then subject to review by government auditors.

Are such disincentives examples of commitment strategies that establish cred-ibility? It does appear that the voting mechanism, along with the least-cost test, is materially reducing implicit coverage at smaller institutions. However, in pre-vious comments we have noted that the new process that FDICIA created for approving bailouts appears quite similar to the old, informal process that regu-lators used prior to FDICIA when they protected creditors of Continental Illi-nois.[24] While FDICIA may have increased the disincentives to initiate bailouts, we join others who are not convinced that the disincentives currently exceed the incentives for providing coverage.[25]

Another commitment strategy that relies on disincentives and has received attention in the literature on credible monetary policy involves explicit contracts. For example, a contract could penalize policymakers monetarily for actions that make implicit coverage more likely or for the coverage itself. (Professor Carl Walsh has recommended contracts for central bankers to meet inflation tar-gets.)[26] A second approach would require an issuance of debt, which pays hold-ers a lump sum if a bailout occurs and nothing if a bailout is not necessary.[27] This option raises the explicit costs of bailouts and puts the burden on the taxpayer. Not only could the costs associated with these bonds discourage such bailouts, but the manner in which markets price the debt instruments would offer an assessment of the likelihood of bailouts. (A higher yield would signal a low chance of bailout.)

Again, these explicit means of convincing creditors of TBTF firms that they are at risk of loss are better than doing nothing. Moreover, these strategies are not as extreme as general prohibitions and thus cannot be dismissed as easily. But their lack of political viability aside, these contracts may not prove a useful means to alter future decisions of policymakers. The problem here is one of implementation. It appears difficult to write the contracts so that all contingencies and actions by policymakers are covered. Thus, the same types of evasion that are possible under the rules-based reforms could occur here as well. While the rationale for evasion remains as strong for prohibition, it is still a concern.

Reducing the Incentives to Provide Bailouts

Whereas the previous section reviewed more moderate plans that focused on penalties, this section discusses commitment strategies that try to achieve credibility by reducing incentives to bail out creditors. Methods to minimize these incentives include reducing the likelihood of large firm losses and spillover failures and redefining who is at risk of loss.

Reducing Large Firm Losses

The deep insolvency of a large firm or subnational government deemed TBTF represents the immediate cause of bailouts. Policymakers can make TBTF bailouts less likely by reducing losses from insolvency and reducing the probability that entities will get so large that they qualify for TBTF status. Even if such steps do not fully accomplish their goals, they could have some value in signaling that policymakers' attitudes have changed. Enacting such reforms could make policymakers appear "tough," prepared to take action against firms assuming excessive risk. Propagating such a reputation raises uncertainty for creditors about the probability of a bailout. Moreover, a sufficiently large policy shift away from the generous treatment of creditors of large firms can reduce policymakers' ability to bail out creditors later, especially when policymakers stake their own credibility and outside economic assistance on the change.[28]

Analysts have offered several methods for reducing the severity of firm insolvency. One general approach would require regulators to shut down firms when they still have positive net worth.[29] An early closure policy would prevent firms from taking on more risk and building up huge embedded losses, as they have incentive to do upon insolvency. A properly constructed early resolution method has particular attraction in times of economic deregulation. In many cases, regulations, such as those preventing free entry, artificially increase the value of firms, and the elimination of the regulations can quickly reduce the firms' net worth. To be successful, however, regulators must measure firm capital on a marked-to-market basis and this is not, at least right now, an easy task. In contrast, book value accounting, which is still the most common type of measure that regulators use, can show firms with positive net worth even when they are deeply insolvent.

A second approach to reduce the severity of firm insolvency involves enhancing banking supervision. This step has the greater chance of reducing existing excessive risk taking in countries where firms assume risk through straightforward methods, where relatively little if any constructive supervision occurs, and where the scope of the regulation (for example, the number of firms reviewed) is small. Indeed, even in the most favorable cases, regulation may be too crude to effectively reduce risk taking. Instead, the largest returns from regulation could come from signaling a reduced likelihood that policymakers will support after-the-fact bailouts.

A third effort focuses on improved pricing of government guarantee programs (both explicit and implicit). As noted, effective insurance pricing can reduce excessive risk. A fourth and related method of reducing losses would require that firms receiving government support disclose meaningful information about their financial condition to market participants. In turn, regulators would use the market signals set by participants, which could include creditors or private insurers, both to price government insurance and set the level of regulation and powers that a firm faces. These efforts are unlikely to reduce risk taking, for the prices set by participants will not accurately assess risk without there first being steps to build credibility. The very act of monitoring and incorporating the prices in regulations will not by itself make the imposition of losses credible.

Finally, the government should develop and publicize effective means for resolving most failed institutions. Establishing a resolution process ahead of time rather than trying to create one when a large firm fails reduces the chances for the massive disruption and confusion that could culminate in government bailouts. To minimize the special circumstances surrounding the failure of large firms, governments should consider applying their standard bankruptcy procedure in all cases of firm failure. Using a standard process as a starting point for resolution would minimize ad hoc government intervention and the potential for special government treatment.

As part of the resolution process, the government could create policies to manage the central bank when it acts as the lender-of-last-resort (LOLR). The availability of a LOLR may encourage policymakers to impose losses on creditors of insolvent firms because it provides a tool to protect solvent firms when they suffer a liquidity crisis. Governments can use the LOLR to conduct bailouts as well, and standard LOLR procedures, such as the taking of collateral, do not prevent central banks from lending to insolvent firms.[30]

To reduce massive losses of large firms, governments can also enforce polices that restrict undesirable firm growth (for example, growth that reduces social welfare). For example, a country could enforce an antitrust policy to limit the exercise of monopoly power. In addition, countries should take care to avoid the creation of government-owned or -sponsored corporations and take steps to reduce their likelihood of being considered TBTF upon their privatization (for example, where consistent with efficiency, split large firms before sale). The elimination of regulations that artificially increase the value of firms, such as geographic restrictions on the provision of service, could also represent a helpful step in reducing the size of firms. As with most of the attempts to limit the severity of insolvency, these basic policies benefit a limited number of countries (for example, countries with relatively current legal and market infrastructure that are transitioning to market economies).

Spillovers

A major incentive for providing coverage is the management of systemic risk and the prevention of spillover failures and contagion. If a plan could eliminate these events, then policymakers would have less incentive to offer such coverage. A few reform efforts of this nature focus on the payments system. (Proponents of this type of plan include Tom Hoenig, president of the Federal Reserve Bank of Kansas City, and Professor Mark Flannery.)[31] Proponents argue that spillovers from the failure of a large financial institution are transmitted through the payments system. The plans include methods for limiting or better managing the amount of risk transferred by means of the payments system, making it less likely, in theory at least, that the failure of one institution will lead to failures of or problems with other institutions. Reforms of this type were also enacted in FDICIA which, for example, required regulators to issue rules limiting interbank credit exposure.[32]

A second type of spillover reduction plan focuses on the amount of loss borne by uninsured creditors. Proponents of these types of plans do not try to prohibit bailouts, viewing that option as inherently not credible and potentially undesirable. Instead, the goal is to limit the loss borne by uninsured creditors to a large enough amount to motivate them to monitor financial institutions with which they have relationships but not so large that it leads to their own insolvency. As a result, the failure of one bank would not lead to the failure of other creditor banks. We have proposed a plan that implements this idea through the application of a co-insurance "haircut" for uninsured creditors at TBTF banks.

Professor Frederic Mishkin has suggested a novel rule to address policymakers' concerns about spillovers.[33] Specifically, creditors of the first large institution that fails cannot be bailed out, but creditors of institutions that subsequently fail could receive bailouts. This proposal could assuage policymakers' fears of spillover failures. At the same time, the plan increases creditors' incentives to price risk correctly so that they are compensated in the event that their bank is the first to fail.

Risk of Loss

A different commitment approach relies on policymakers' disinclination to assist certain types of creditors. Subordinated debt plans exemplify this approach. Holders of this debt are sophisticated and well aware that the low priority of their claims in a bankruptcy means they should not expect significant proceeds after a bank fails. There is some evidence that holders of a banking organization's subordinated debt already believe they are at risk of loss.[34] A few subordinated debt plans have taken this notion one step further, explicitly requiring particular groups to hold the debt. One plan would restrict the ownership of subordinated debt to foreign banks. Others fear that these restrictions may not be enough to prevent the bailout of subordinated debt holders. As such, these skeptical analysts call for something akin to the co-insurance plan described above. For example, the subordinated debt contract could require that the holder of the debt suffer at least some loss if the government provides funds to protect creditors of the failed bank.[35]

In total, these plans cover a wide range, and it is difficult to evaluate their credibility concisely. A few of them seem unlikely to alter incentives and put creditors at risk of loss. For example, although distribution matters likely play some role, bailouts are not largely driven by these issues. Instead, we think policymakers, rightly or wrongly, genuinely fear systemic risk. We have already expressed some skepticism about the plans that would supposedly reduce the severity of loss or the size of firms. They would probably benefit some countries, but governments do not have the ability to reduce the risk taking of TBTF firms prior to establishing a credible policy of imposing losses.

The rest of these plans to reduce the underlying incentives for bailouts present quite complex and difficult issues to evaluate. Developing a resolution process for large firms, as noted, is by its nature a very challenging task. Some have also questioned, for example, the ability of policymakers to devise the co-insurance loss rate that would prevent spillovers. Perhaps the focus on payment systems would not adequately limit exposures between financial institutions. We certainly don't intend to review all of these questions, and we are not sure that all of them are amenable to clear answers, given available evidence. But valid reservations notwithstanding, it can be argued that several of these proposals are credible; that is, they alter the underlying incentives that policymakers face. It will be extremely difficult to reduce the likelihood of bailouts without reducing the incentives that policymakers have to make them. In contrast, reforms that focus on prohibitions and disincentives seem likely to fail precisely because they do not reduce the incentives that lead to bailouts in the first place.

Appointment of Regulators with a Disinclination to Provide Bailouts

Another method for addressing the underlying incentives for bailouts is to appoint regulators who put a high value on moral hazard. These regulators could be said to have a low discount rate, which means that they will place a high value in the present on future moral hazard costs. When these regulators come to decide on bailouts, they will find that the disincentives, namely, the future costs of their actions in terms of moral hazard, could very well outweigh the incentives to provide bailouts. As such, their commitment to avoid bailouts will be relatively credible. This is especially true if conservative regulators operate in an independent environment in which they can demonstrate their toughness prior to the failure of a large firm (for example, in supporting penalties for firms that take on excessive risk or refusing to use monetary policy to inflate asset values).

This suggestion derives from the work of Professor Kenneth Rogoff, which shows that the appointment of a central banker who is more "conservative" than the general population could lead to a credible commitment by the central bank to not follow an inflationary monetary policy.[36] This idea has both theoretical and practical appeal, and the reasons that make the Rogoff suggestion welcome for monetary policy would seem to apply here as well.

Is the appointment of conservative regulators sufficient? Indeed, some may argue—based on insight gained as a regulator or from close contact with them— that we have overstated the desire of regulators to provide protection. That is, we could already have fairly conservative policymakers. Even if this were the case, society would be better off if steps were taken to establish a credible no-bailout regime.[37] Creditors base current decisions on expectations of the future. Policymaker ambivalence about the future of bailouts might lead to an under-pricing of risk that could only be corrected by forcing creditors to absorb losses. Regulators can address this costly learning process by getting creditors to believe in the real potential for future losses and the need to more accurately price risk. Better pricing should lead to a reduction in excessive risk taking. This process could result in fewer potential bank failures, obviating the need for regulators to impose losses in the first place. As a result, accompanying the appointment of conservative regulators with other commitment strategies would appear a more judicious method of effecting change.

Constructive Ambiguity

A final method for addressing the TBTF policy involves so-called constructive ambiguity. This policy involves general government statements that the government will not routinely provide bailouts to large firm creditors without explicitly detailing the conditions under which a bailout will occur. However, a policy of constructive ambiguity does not directly address policymakers' incentives to provide bailouts. Instead, this policy tries indirectly to limit the need for bailouts by getting creditors to believe that the lack of a clear policy puts them at risk of loss. We believe constructive ambiguity is unnecessarily costly if policymakers oppose bailouts. The absence of an overt strategy to communicate the no-bailout position to creditors creates more doubt than is justified given the likely actions of the regulator. In contrast, one could argue that ambiguity is better than an explicit extension of the safety net in that it will produce more market discipline, at least initially.[38] But this honeymoon period will come to an end, or at least be greatly attenuated, after a bailout occurs. Assuming that regulators will not act randomly, the delivery of a bailout will lead market participants to construct rules from the pattern of regulators' actions for when the government will provide support.

CONCLUSION

The TBTF problem is serious because of the high costs it can impose, the breadth of its application, and the trends that could make it more severe going forward. However, governments can adopt a number of methods that will let them credibly put some creditors at risk of loss who currently think they have TBTF protection. All of these methods are not equally effective, and we would not recommend several well-known reforms. Among the reforms discussed here are some that could mitigate the damage that ignoring or minimizing the TBTF problem will create.

NOTES

Some of the analysis in this chapter first appeared in Gary Stern, "Thoughts on Designing Credible Policies after Financial Modernization," Federal Reserve Bank of Minneapolis, *Region* (September 2000), pp. 3–5, 24–29.

1. For evidence on the existence of Too-Big-to-Fail policies, see Maureen O'Hara and Wayne Shaw, "Deposit Insurance and Wealth Effects: The Value of Being Too Big to Fail," *The Journal of Finance*, 45 (1990), pp. 1587–1600; Harold Black, Cary Collins, Breck Robinson, and Robert Schweitzer, "Changes in Market Perceptions of Riskiness: The Case of Too-Big-to-Fail," *The Journal of Financial Services Research*, 20 (1997), pp. 389–406; and Steve Johnson and James Lindley, "The Reaction of Financial Markets to Changes in FDIC Policies on Bank Failures," *Journal of Economics and Finance*, 17 (1993), pp. 43–58.

2. Ann Bartel and Ann Harrison, "Ownership Versus Environment: Why Are Public Sector Firms Inefficient," National Bureau of Economic Research Working Paper 7043 (March 1999) discuss the soft budget and the efficiency of public and private firms.

3. Edward Frydl, "The Length and Cost of Banking Crises," International Monetary Fund Working Paper 99/30 (1999).

4. Craig Burnside, Martin Eichenbaum, and Sergio Rebelo, "Understanding the Korean and Thai Currency Crisis," Federal Reserve Bank of Chicago, *Economic Perspectives* (Third Quarter 2000), pp. 45–60.

5. Benton Gup, "Too-Big-to-Fail: An International Perspective" (mimeo, 1997), p. 8.

6. David Wildasin, "Externalities and Bailouts: Hard and Soft Budget Constraints in Intergovernmental Fiscal Relations," World Bank Policy Research Papers 1843 (November 1997).

7. For a summary of this work, see George Benston and George Kaufman, "Is the Banking and Payments System Fragile?" *Journal of Financial Services Research*, 9, nos. 3–4 (1995), pp. 15–46.

8. Stuart Greenbaum, "Comment," *Journal of Financial Services Research*, 9, nos. 3–4 (1995), pp. 105–108.

9. As quoted in Benton Gup, "Too-Big-to-Fail: An International Perspective" (mimeo, 1997), p. 3.

10. Ron Feldman and Arthur Rolnick, "Fixing FDICIA: A Plan to Address the Too-Big-to-Fail Problem," Federal Reserve Bank of Minneapolis, *Annual Report* (March 1998), p. 10.

11. Kevin Stiroh and Jennifer Poole, "Explaining the Rising Concentration of Banking Assets in the 1990s," Federal Reserve Bank of New York, *Current Issues in Economics and Finance*, August 2000.

12. For a recent discussion of this issue, see Edward Kane, "Incentives for Banking

Megamergers: What Motives Might Regulators Infer from Event-Study Evidence?" *Journal of Money, Credit and Banking*, 32 (August 2000), Part 2, pp. 671–701.

13. For a recent discussion on the increase in mergers across many industries, see Organization for Economic Cooperation and Development, *Financial Market Trends*, 74 (2000), pp. 30–32.

14. This point is made in Anthony Santomero and David Eckles, "The Determinants of Success in the New Financial Services Environment," Federal Reserve Bank of New York, *Economic Policy Review*, October 2000, p. 5.

15. A similar concern was raised with regards to the rescue of Long-Term Capital Management. See Martin Mayer, "Is Everything Too Big to Fail," *The International Economy* (January/February 2000), pp. 24–27.

16. For a brief discussion on the issues, see Mark Spiegel, "Short-Term International Borrowing and Financial Fragility," Federal Reserve Bank of San Francisco, *Economic Letter*, 2000-26, September 2000.

17. Hana Polackova, "Government Contingent Liabilities: A Hidden Risk to Fiscal Stability," World Bank Policy Research Working Paper 1989, 1999.

18. Robert Hetzel, "Too Big to Fail: Origins, Consequences, and Outlook," Federal Reserve Bank of Richmond, *Economic Review*, 77, no. 6 (1991), p. 8.

19. For a discussion of the recent role of the International Monetary Fund, see *The Report of the International Financial Institution Advisory Commission*, March 2000 at http://phantom-x.gsia.cmu.edu/IFIAC/USMRPTDV.html.

20. Marvin Goodfriend and Jeffrey Lacker, "Limited Commitment and Central Bank Lending." Federal Reserve Bank of Richmond, *Economic Quarterly* 85, no. 4 (1999), pp. 1–27.

21. For examples, see Bank Administration Institute, *Building Better Banks: The Case for Performance-Based Regulation* (Chicago: Bank Administration Institute, 1996), pp. 63–70; Richard Kovacevich, "Deposit Insurance: It's Time to Cage the Monster," Federal Reserve Bank of Minneapolis, *Fedgazette* (April 1996), pp. 14–15; Bankers Roundtable, *Deposit Insurance Reform in the Public Interest* (Washington, DC: Bankers Roundtable, 1997).

22. Gillian Garcia, "Deposit Insurance: Actual and Best Practices," International Monetary Fund Working Paper 99/54 (April 1999).

23. President Alfred Broaddus of the Federal Reserve Bank of Richmond recently expressed concern that discount window lending could offer a way to support failing institutions. See Remarks by J. Alfred Broaddus, Jr., "Market Discipline and Fed Lending" for the Federal Reserve Bank of Chicago's Bank Structure Conference, May 5, 2000.

24. Feldman and Rolnick, "Fixing FDICIA," p. 8.

25. Santomero and Eckles, "The Determinants of Success," p. 8.

26. Carl E. Walsh, "Optimal Contracts for Central Bankers," *American Economic Review*, 85 (March 1995), pp. 150–167.

27. Wall has suggested a similar type of instrument called capital notes, which would measure the health of the deposit insurance system. Larry Wall, "Taking Note of the Deposit Insurance Fund: A Plan for the FDIC to Issue Capital Notes," Federal Reserve Bank of Atlanta, *Economic Review*, 82 (1997), pp. 14–31. Insurance firms have issued so-called catastrophic bonds that make payouts if a disaster occurs but pay nothing if it does not. In addition, several financial institutions issued so-called goodwill certificates

that paid investors some portion of payments the firms would receive if they won a series of legal decisions from the federal governments.

28. Guillermo Calvo and Jacob Frenkel, "Credit Markets, Credibility, and Economic Transformation," *Journal of Economic Perspectives*, 5, no. 4 (1991), pp. 139–148, discusses these and other methods for building credibility.

29. A discussion of this policy is found in George J. Benston and George G. Kaufman, "Deposit Insurance Reform in the FDIC Improvement Act: The Experience to Date," Federal Reserve Bank Chicago, *Economic Perspectives* (Second Quarter 1998), pp. 2–20.

30. Goodfriend and Lacker, "Limited Commitment and Central Bank Lending."

31. Thomas Hoenig, "Rethinking Financial Regulation," *Economic Review*, 81, no. 2 (1996), pp. 5–13, and Mark Flannery, "Modernizing Financial Regulation: The Relation Between Interbank Transactions and Supervisory Reform," forthcoming in the *Journal of Financial Services Research*.

32. These and other reforms are discussed in Larry Wall, "Too-Big-to-Fail after FDICIA," Federal Reserve Bank of Atlanta, *Economic Review* (January/February 1993), pp. 1–14.

33. Frederic Mishkin, "Moral Hazard and Reform of the Government Safety Net," paper presented at "Lessons from Recent Global Financial Crises" sponsored by the Federal Reserve Bank of Chicago, October 1, 1999; and Frederic Mishkin and Philip Strahan, "What Will Technology Do to Financial Structure," Brookings-Wharton Papers on Financial Services, 1999.

34. Mark Flannery and Sorin Sorescu, "Evidence of Bank Market Discipline in Subordinated Debenture Yields: 1983–1991," *Journal of Finance*, 51, no. 4 (1996), pp. 1347–1377.

35. William Lang and Douglas Robertson, "Analysis of Proposals for a Minimum Subordinated Debt Requirement," Office of the Comptroller of the Currency Economic and Policy Analysis Working Paper, 2000–4, March 2000.

36. Kenneth Rogoff, "The Optimal Degree of Commitment to an Intermediate Monetary Target," *Quarterly Journal of Economics*, 100 (November 1985), pp. 1169–1190.

37. Richard Clarida, Jordi Gali, and Mark Gertler, "The Science of Monetary Policy: A New Keynesian Perspective," *Journal of Economic Literature*, 37 (December 1999), p. 1680.

38. Douglas Cook and Lewis Spellman, "Taxpayer Resistance, Guarantee Uncertainty, and Housing Finance Subsidies," *Journal of Real Estate Finance and Economics*, 5, pp. 181–195.

Chapter 12

How Some Mergers Go Wrong

Benton E. Gup

"How Mergers Go Wrong" was the headline on the cover of *The Economist* magazine in July 2000. The article that followed stated that mergers are like second marriages, a triumph of hope over experience. The analogy between mergers and marriages is widespread. One article in the *Financial Times* about mergers was titled "Marrying in Haste" (Skapinker, 2000). The cover of *Business Week* (June 7, 1999) showed the pictures of John S. Reed and Sanford I. Weill, co-CEOs of Citigroup, and it asked, "Is This Marriage Working?" While there is some similarity between mergers and marriages, mergers have a higher failure rate than marriages. Up to 36% of all marriages in the United States end in divorce.[1] A study 700 international mergers by KMPG ("Unlocking Shareholder Value," 1999) and one by Barrett et al. (1999) both reported that more than half of the mergers destroyed shareholder value. The KPMG study indicated that cross-border mergers had a worse track record. Mergers between U.S. and European firms were 11% less likely than average to be successful. The previously cited *Economist* article "How Mergers Go Wrong" went on to say that "above all, personal chemistry matters every bit as much in mergers as it does in marriage. It matters most at the top of the organization. No company can have two bosses."

Building on that theme, this chapter examines how corporate culture may cause a merger to go wrong. Corporate culture, including hubris, are the most visible factors associated with failed large mergers because of the notoriety that arises when former CEOs and other executives leave their posts under duress. Other factors, such as bad strategy, and bad execution, are no doubt the root cause of many failures, but they are not examined here.

ONE CULTURE

One does not have to look far to find examples of merged companies in which only one culture survived. Usually, it's the firm with the strongest culture that is exemplified by the top officer's personality, ego, and hubris. For example, Jürgen E. Schremp's culture could be described as "teutonic." That appellation should not be surprising because he was chairman of Daimler-Benz, the German automobile manufacturer when it acquired Chrysler in 1998. The German corporate culture is built on loyalty and trust (Sanchanta, 2000). Trust me and you will do it my way—and be loyal—or pay the consequences.

When Daimler-Benz acquired Chrysler to form DaimlerChrysler AG, Chrysler was a very profitable U.S. automobile manufacturer. Schremp said the combined firm would "have the size, the profitability and the reach to take on everyone. . . . (and be) the most profitable automobile company in the world" (Ball and Miller, 2000a, p. 22). Unfortunately, it didn't work out that way.

Many outside observers called the Daimler-Benz and Chrysler merger in 1998 a "merger of equals." However, Schremp did not view it that way. He is quoted as saying "If I had gone and said Chrysler would be a division, everybody on their side would have said, There is no way we'll do the deal. . . . But It's precisely what I wanted to do" (Howes, 2000). Accordingly, "The Daimler-Chrysler marriage has been rocky from the start. Cultural differences between the Germans and Americans proved difficult to overcome" (Tierney et. al., 2000).

Part of the problem with this merger involved reorganizing overlapping businesses in order to cut costs. This was not easily accomplished. However, the Germans wanted it done their way, not Chrysler's way. The result was that Chrysler's CEO and other key officers left the organization (Muller, Kerwin, and Ewing, 2000). Within two years, a profitable U.S. auto company was sustaining losses and floundering. The following newspaper headlines tell us that this merger has not worked out:

"DaimlerChrysler's Wrong Turns," *Wall Street Journal* (5/26/00).

"For Two Car Giants, A Megamerger Isn't the Road to Riches," *Wall Street Journal* (Ball, White, and Miller, 10/27/00).

"Daimler Drives Chrysler into a Ditch," *Wall Street Journal* (Yates, 11/8/00).

"Chrysler Will Miss Profit Target for 2000 and Likely Post Loss for Fourth Quarter," *Wall Street Journal* (Miller and Ball, 11/17/00).

"New Chief of Chrysler Unit Begins Job with Pink Slips for Three Top Executives," *Wall Street Journal* (Ball and Miller, 11/21/00).

The story does not end here because Daimler also acquired stakes in Japan's Mitsubishi Motors and Korea's Hyundai Motor Company. Subsequently, Daimler increased its stake in troubled Mitsubishi, where it will have three of the 10 board of directors positions. Only time will tell how these cultures will blend or bend. However, it is already certain that these are not marriages made in heaven.

ONE BOSS

Many large mergers are called "mergers of equals" because the firms are of similar size. However, because of egos, hubris, and other factors associated with corporate culture, it does not work out that way. One of those factors is who is going to be in charge. A simple analogy is that there can be only one king in each kingdom; co-kings are not a viable option for most kingdoms or most firms for that matter. The merger of Citibank and Travelers (insurance) illustrates part of the point. This merger did add to shareholder value, but the co-bosses didn't work out. The giant bank and insurance companies merged to form CitiGroup.

Travelers Sanford I. Weill and Citibank's John Reed were co-chairs of the newly organized Citigroup. Soon enough it became clear that the two did not have the same visions about the future and that one of them would have to go. Sanford Weill dominated the new organization, and John Reed retired shortly after the merger. Weill's vision of the future was to expand beyond commercial banking in the traditional sense of the word and investment banking. Subsequently, Citigroup acquired Associates First Capital Corp. for $31 billion. Associates First deals primarily in high-yielding consumer finance that targets lower-middle economic classes where interest rates and fees tend to be higher than those charged by banks (Milligan, 2000). Associates First will be merged with CitiFinancial and will have more than 2,300 offices.

Next let's consider the case of Hugh L. McColl, Jr., the chairman and chief executive officer (CEO) of NationsBank Corp. McColl built a relatively small Charlotte-based North Carolina National Bank (NCNB) into a megabank by acquiring other banks. During this process, NCNB became NationsBank simply because people in other states may not want to deal with a bank named for another state. Subsequently, NationsBank acquired Bank of America, which in turn changed its name to BankAmerica.

David A. Coulter, the former CEO of BankAmerica, became the merged bank's president and heir-apparent to Hugh McColl ("Outsting of Coulter," 2000). However, he was dismissed shortly after the merger was completed, albeit with a large golden parachute severance package—about $29 million. The former BankAmerica had sustained large losses that were carried over into the newly merged bank, and the losses were blamed for Coulter's fall. It is not clear if the losses were an "excuse" for getting rid of Coulter or if they were the "real" reason behind his departure.

It is interesting that the "due diligence" that preceded this megamerger was not adequate. In any case, McColl survived and reigned over the new organization.

WALKING AWAY FROM THE ALTAR

Firms sometimes recognize in advance that their union will not work out, and after preliminary negotiations they decide not to merge. One reason for abandoning the merger is that one of the two allegedly equal partners does not want to be dominated. The failed merger of Deutsche Bank and Dresdner Bank in April 2000 illustrates this point. The proposed merger was billed as one that would transform Germany's financial landscape, and it would have created the largest bank in the world with $1.4 trillion in assets ("German Banks to Merge?" 2000; Sanchanta, 2000). Part of the change was that Deutsche Bank's investment banking group wanted to sell Dresdner Bank's Kleinwort Benson investment banking group and the Dresdner group did not want to be sold. Deutsche Bank only wanted Dresdner's investment banking client base, not the investment group per se. Equally important, Deutsche Bank managers saw themselves as the dominant partner, and Dresdner Bank managers did not want to be dominated (Skapinker, 2000). As a result, the deal fell apart.

CONCLUSION

Every corporation has a unique culture. Sometimes the cultures of prospective merger partners are like oil and water, and they don't mix. Other times they blend well. The degree to which they mix depends largely on the personality of the CEOs. The companies discussed in this chapter have CEOs who tend to have dominating personalities and hubris. The problems of blending cultures are exacerbated when cross-border mergers are involved. Thus, although some mergers may seem logical in a strategic or financial sense, they may not work out because of the personalities involved.

NOTE

1. Divorce rates for women in 1990, the latest data available, range from 12.5% for 20–24 year olds to 35.8% for 40–44 year olds. Data are from U.S. Department of Commerce, *Statistical Abstract of the United States*, 1999, Table 161, Marriage Experience for Women, by Age and Race: 1980 and 1990.

REFERENCES

Ball, Jeffrey, and Scott Miller. (2000a). "DaimlerChrysler's Wrong Turns." *Wall Street Journal*, May 26, p. A18.

Ball, Jeffrey, and Scott Miller. (2000b). "New Chief of Chrysler Unit Begins Job with Pink Slips for Three Top Executives." *Wall Street Journal*, November 21, p. A3.

Ball, Jeffrey, Joseph B. White, and Scott Miller. (2000), "For Two Car Giants, a Megamerger Isn't the Road to Riches." *Wall Street Journal*, October 28, pp. A1, A8.

Barrett, Amy, Ellen Licking, John Carey, and Kerry Capell. (1999). "Addicted to Mergers." *Business Week*, December 6, pp. 84–90.

"DaimlerChrysler's Wrong Turns." (2000). *Wall Street Journal*, May 26, p. A18.

"German Banks to Merge?" (2000). CNNfn (http://cnnfn.com), March 7 (visited 3/7/00).

"How Mergers Go Wrong." (2000). *The Economist*, July 22–28, p. 19.

Howes, Daniel. (2000). "Schremp Has Painted Himself into Corner with U.S. Employees." *Detroit News* (www.detnews.com), November 7.

Miller, Scott, and Jeffrey Ball. (2000). "Chrysler Will Miss Profit Target for 2000 and Likely Post Loss for Fourth Quarter." *Wall Street Journal*, November 17, p. A3.

Milligan, Jack. (October 2000). "Sandy Strikes Again." *U.S. Banker*, pp. 44–55.

Muller, Joann, Kathleen Kerwin, and Jack Ewing. (1999). "Man with a Plan." *Business Week*, October 4, pp. 34–36.

"Ousting of Coulter Isn't the Only Fracture at New BankAmerica." (2000). *Wall Street Journal*, October 23, pp. A1, A10.

Sanchanta, Mariko. (2000). "Merger Foiled by Culture of Trust." *Financial Times*, April 8, 9, p. xxvii.

Skapinker, Michael. (1999). "Marrying in Haste." *Financial Times*, April 12, p. 14.

Tierney, Christine, Matt Karnitschnig, Joann Muller, Rafael Mrowczlynski, Ken Belson, and Moon Ihwan. (2000). "Defiant Daimler." *Business Week*, August 7, pp. 91–94.

"Unlocking Shareholder Value: The Keys to Success." (November 1999). KPMG Mergers and Acquisitions, Global Research Report.

Yates, Brock. (2000). "Daimler Drives Chrysler into a Ditch." *Wall Street Journal*, November 8, p. A26.

Selected Bibliography

Amihud, Yakov, and Geoffrey Miller, eds. (1998). *Bank Mergers & Acquisitions*. Boston: Kluwer Academic Publishers.

Browne, Lynn E., and Eric S. Rosengran, eds. (1987). *The Merger Boom*. Boston: Federal Reserve Bank.

Cooke, Terence E. (1986). *Mergers and Acquistions*. New York: Basil Blackwell.

Davidson, Kenneth M. (1985). *Megamergers: Corporate America's Billion-Dollar Takeovers*. Cambridge, MA: Ballinger Publishing Co.

Dymski, Gary Al. (1999). *The Bank Merger Wave: The Causes and Social Consequences of Financial Consideration*. Armonk, NY: M. E. Sharpe.

Galpin, Timothy J., and Mark Herndon. (1999). *The Complete Guide to Mergers and Acquisitions: Process Tool to Support M&A Integration at Every Level*. San Francisco: Jossey-Bass.

Gaughan, Patrick A. (1991). *Mergers and Acquistions*. New York: HarperCollins.

Gup, Benton E. (1989). *Bank Mergers: Current Issues and Perspectives*. Boston: Kluwer Academic Publishers.

Marks, Mitchell L., and Philip H. Mervis. (1998). *Joining Forces: Making One Plus One Equal Three in Mergers, Acquistions, and Alliances*. San Francisco: Jossey-Bass.

Nelson, Ralph. (1959). *Merger Movement in American Industry: 1895–1956*. Princeton, NJ: Princeton University Press.

Post, Alexandra. (1994). *Anatomy of a Merger: The Causes and Effects of Mergers and Acquistions*. Englewood Cliffs, NJ: Prentice-Hall.

Ravenscraft, David J., and F. M. Scherer. (1987). *Mergers, Sell-Offs, and Economic Efficiency*. Washington, DC: The Brookings Institution.

Reed, Stanley Foster, and Alexandra Reed. (1998). *The Art of M&A: A Merger Acquistion Buyout Guide*. New York: McGraw-Hill Professional Publishing.

Shull, Bernard, and Gerald A. Henweck. (2001). *Bank Mergers in a Deregulated Environment: Promises and Peril*. Westport, CT: Quorum Books.

Steindl, Josef. (1965). *Random Process and the Growth of Firms: A Study of the Pareto Law*. New York: Hafner Publishing Co.

Weston, J. Fred, Kwang S. Chung, and Susan H. Hoag. (1990). *Mergers, Restructuring, and Corporate Control*. Englewood Cliffs, NJ: Prentice Hall.

Index

Achleitner, P., 91
Adelman, Irma, 3
Agrawal, Anup, 124
Agrrawal, Pankaj, 9
Alchain, Armen, 3
Alliances, 140
Anderson, Christopher, 121
Ansoff, H., 87
Ariff, Mohamed, 8
Asian financial crises, 114
Asquith, P., 26
Australia, 103

Bailouts, 198, 199
Ball, Deborah, 140
Ball, Jeffrey, 208
Bank of Tokyo, 115
Banking laws, 68
Bankruptcy, 180
Banks, 32, 108, 164
Barrett, Amy, 207
Belson, Ken, 208
Berger, Allen, 72, 73, 75, 97
Bernet, B., 87, 97
Bhatia, M., 158, 159
Black, Joseph, 8
Bliss, Richard, 125
Bolger, Andrew, 143

Borg, Rody, 22
Boyd, J., 152
Bradley, M., 59
Bühner, R., 96
Burns, Tom, 139

Cameron, Doug, 126, 143
Campbell, Terry, 121
Capell, Kerry, 207
Cary, John, 207
Cha, Ariana, 141
Chatterjee, A., 86
Clayton Antitrust Act, 22, 24
Catalysts for mergers, 6, 67, 86, 138
Characteristics of mergers, 29, 35, 46, 55
Chung, Kwang, 9
Coenenberg, A., 86
Competition, 87
Concentration. See Consolidation
Consolidation, 1, 10, 11, 114, 128, 143, 172
Continental Illinois Bank, 176
Cooke, Terence, 25
Corporate control, 3
Corporate culture, 125, 126, 208
Corporate values, 121
Coy, Peter, 8
Credit ratings, 158, 159

Credit-value-at-risk. *See* Value-at-risk
Cross-border mergers, 135, 139
Cumming, Christine, 177, 178
Cummins, J., 164

Dai-Ichi Kangyo Bank, 7, 115
Darwin, Charles, 2
Davidson, Kenneth, 20, 21, 24, 26, 30
Demsetz, Rebecca, 72
Demutualization, 105, 143
Desai, A., 59
DeYoung, Robert, 12
Diversification, 71, 89, 151
Dodd, P., 26
Double, Mary Beth, 137, 139, 140
Dvorak, Phred, 120, 128
Dymski, Gary, 33

Eastern culture, 121
Eatwell, John, 179
Economic disturbance theory, 91
Eisenbeis, Robert, 124
Energy industry mergers, 30, 35
Eun, C., 89
European Community, 138
Ewing, Jack, 208

Failure, 180, 207
Fairlamb, David, 135, 136
Federal Trade Commission Act, 22
Felsted, Aredea, 143
Fifth wave of mergers, 34
Financial Institutions Modernization Act
    of 1999. *See* Gramm-Leach-Bliley
    Act
Financial sector mergers, 36
Finger, C., 158, 159
First wave of mergers, 4, 19, 94
Flannery, Mark, 201
Fourth wave of mergers, 27
Free cash flow, 4
Freedman, Milton, 112
Frey, Eric, 136
Fritch, Peter, 142
Fulford, Benjamin, 116

Garai, G., 87
Gaskins, Darious, 75

Gaugin, Patrick, 1
George, Henry, 1
Germany, 94
Gibrat, Robert, 3, 9
Globalization, 124
Goffee, Rob, 126
Goodman, Peter, 8
Gort, M., 91
Government support in Japan, 113
Grace, M., 164
Graham, G., 152
Gramm-Leach-Bliley Act, 6, 65, 68, 149,
    177
Griffin, Ralph, 137, 140
Gup, Benton, 2, 3, 5, 9, 112, 114
Gupton, G., 158, 159

Hall, Maximilian, 114
Halpern, P., 26
Hannan, Timothy, 75
Hargreaves, Deborah, 143
Harris, Clay, 128
Harris, Nichole, 142
Health care industry mergers, 39
Hewitt, R., 152
Hirschleifer, D., 90
Hirschman-Herfindahl Index (HHI), 12,
    66, 69
Hirtle, Beverly, 177, 178
Hoag, Susan, 9
Hoenig, Thomas, 123, 201
Holl, P., 87
Holzheu, T., 163
Horvitz, Paul, 75
Hoshi, T., 112, 113, 114
Houston, Joel, 124
Howes, Daniel, 208
Hubris theory, 90
Hummler, K., 88, 99
Humphrey, D., 97
Hutchison, M., 113
Hyatt, Joel, 121

Ibison, David, 128
Ihwan, Moon, 208
Information technology, 126
Information theory, 88

Insurance connection, 126
Iskander, Samer, 128

Jaffe, Jeffrey, 124
James, Christopher, 124
Japan, 111; economy in, 123
Jensen, Michael, 4, 9
Johnson, Brian, 35
Jones, C., 10
Jones, Gareth, 125
Joumard, Isabelle, 137

Kaden, W., 97, 98
Kane, Edward, 4, 123
Karnitschnig, Matt, 208
Kashiwagi, Akiko, 114, 120, 122
Kashyap, A., 113, 114
Kerler, P., 86, 96
Kerwin, Kathleen, 208
Khalid, Ahmed, 8
Kim, E., 59
Kindleberger, Charles, 112
Kohn, Robert, 137, 140
Kolodny, R., 89
Kover, Amy, 124
Kraus, James, 124
Kremmerer, Donald, 10
Kwan, Simon, 124, 151

Laderman, E., 151, 152
Landers, Peter, 122
Lang, H., 89
Langetieg, T., 26
Latin America, 142
Leeth, John, 22
Leveraged buyouts (LBOs), 5, 28
Leyden, Peter, 121
Licking, Ellen, 207
Life cycle, 9
Liquidity risk, 164, 173
Livermore, Shaw, 21
Lowry, Alex, 10
Lumpkin, Stephen, 135

Mackintosh, James, 128
Macroeconomic conditions, 67
Major, Tony, 136, 143
Management, 88, 90, 125, 177

Mandelker, G., 26
Mansingka, Surenda, 26
Market power, 87
Market-value-at-risk. *See* Value-at-risk
Markham, Jesse, 19, 20, 21, 22, 26
Marris, Robin, 3
Marshall, Alfred, 2
Matlack, Carol, 138
McReynolds, Rebecca, 7
Media mergers, 33, 38
Miller, Scott, 208
Mishkin, Frederic, 201
Mitsubishi Bank, 115
Mizuho Financial Group, 7, 116
Moral hazard, 189
Motives for mergers, 5, 67, 70, 72, 86, 91, 104, 106, 151
Moules, Jonathan, 120
Mrowczlynski, Rafael, 208
Mueller, Dennis, 3, 90
Müller-Stewens, G., 90
Muller, Emma, 128
Muller, Joann, 208

Nakamae, Naoko, 114, 122
Nelson, Ralph, 4
Nelson, Richard, 3
Neugebauer, G., 85
Number of acquisitions, 51, 65

Oversight risk, 178

Panning, W., 161
P/E (price/earnings) ratios, 9, 14, 25, 57, 143
Penrose, E., 87
Pfeiffer, Eric, 10
Phillips, R., 164
Pilloff, Steven, 77
Pooling of interest, 5, 8, 27
Porter, M., 86
Pound, John, 47
Power, Carol, 142
Pravda, S., 87
Premiums, 56
Process theory, 90

Property/casualty insurance companies,
    149
Pursche, W., 86

Ramaswami, K., 87
Ravenscraft, David, 2, 5, 24, 26
Real estate, 112
Reed, Stanley, 138
Rhoades, Stephen, 73, 77
Rogoff, Kenneth, 202
Roll, Richard, 90
Rose, Lawrence, 8
Rosen, Richard, 125
Rumelt, Richard, 26
Ryngaert, Michael, 124

Saigol, Lina, 143
Salami, A., 87
Salter, Malcolm, 20, 23, 24, 26
Samson, William, 5
Sanchanta, Mariko, 208
Sandler, G., 86
Santomero, Anthony, 151
Sanwa-Tokai-Toyo Trust, 120
Sautter, M., 86
Scharlemann, U., 88
Scheraga, C., 89
Scherer, F., 2, 3, 20, 22, 23
Schumpeter, Joseph, 10, 13, 90
Schwartz, Peter, 121
Second wave of mergers, 5, 22
Seelig, Steven, 182
Sellers, Patricia, 125
Sherman Antitrust Act, 20
Shleifer, A., 88
Shull, Bernard, 75
Siegwart, H., 85
Sirower, M., 87
Siu, Juan, 35
Six pillars policy (Australia), 103–104
Skapinker, Michael, 207, 210
Slembeck, T., 98
Spain, 135
Spiegel, M., 113
Steindl, Josef, 3
Steiner, Peter, 21, 24, 26
Stigler, George, 20, 23
Strahan, Philip, 72, 73

Streitfield, David, 141
Strom, Stephanie, 122
Stulz, R., 89
Sumitomo-Sakura Bank, 119
Sundarsanam, S., 86, 87
Suter, R., 88, 90
Switzerland, 94
Synergy theories, 87
Szep, Jason, 120

Tapscott, Don, 10
Taxes, 88
Taylor, Andrew, 139
Taylor, Lance, 179
Technology, 10, 140
Telecommunications mergers, 31, 37
Tett, Gillian, 112, 114, 122, 127
Third wave of mergers, 5, 23
Ticoll, David, 10
Tierney, Christine, 208
Toffler, Alvin, 10
Too-big-to-fail (TBTF) policy, 71–72, 76,
    123, 187–204
Tricks, Henry, 142

Value, 52, 53, 54, 135, 136
Value-at-risk (VaR), 150, 154–157, 160–
    162
Varaiya, N., 90
Varian, Hal, 9
Vishny, R., 88
Vitzhum, Carlta, 139, 142
Volkart, R., 88, 92

Walker, Mark, 13
Wall, Larry, 2
Wallis Inquiry, 104, 108, 109
Wasserstein, Bruce, 20, 21, 25, 26, 27,
    28, 30, 32, 33, 35, 36, 37, 38, 39
Weinhold, Wolf, 20, 23, 24, 26
Wessel, David, 136
Weston, Fred, 9, 26, 35
Whalen, G., 152
William, John, 137, 143, 144
Williams Act, 25, 26
Williamson, O., 90
Winter, Sandy, 3

About the Contributors

CAROLYN A. CARROLL is an Associate Professor of Finance at the University of Alabama, where she teaches a course on corporate mergers. Her research interests involve merger and stock market issues. She has published extensively in academic journals.

PETER J. ELMER is a Senior Economist with the Federal Deposit Insurance Corporation. His work has focused on financial and risk analysis of distressed financial institutions, including extensive involvement with the Resolution Trust Corporation. He has published more than two dozen articles in both academic and professional journals.

RON FELDMAN is an Assistant Vice President at the Federal Reserve Bank of Minneapolis with responsibility for Applications, Surveillance, and Special Studies. His areas of research include government-sponsored enterprises, deposit insurance, federal budgeting, trends affecting financial institutions, and banking supervision. He has previously worked for the Congressional Budget Office.

BENTON E. GUP holds the Robert Hunt Cochrane–Alabama Bankers Association Chair of Banking at the University of Alabama. Dr. Gup is the author of 20 books and more than 90 articles concerning banking and financial topics. He has served as a consultant to government and industry. In addition, he teaches a course at the University of Melbourne, Australia.

GERALD A. HANWECK is a Professor of Finance at George Mason University. He was a visiting scholar at the Federal Deposit Insurance Corporation's Division of Research and Statistics. Before joining George Mason, he was an economist with the Division of Research and Statistics at the Board of Governors of the Federal Reserve System. His research interests include public policy regarding financial institutions and their market performance.

IAN R. HARPER is a Professorial Fellow at the Melbourne Business School at the University of Melbourne, Australia, where he teaches economics, banking, and international finance. He has a consulting firm, is a Director of the Australian Derivatives Exchange Limited, and works with other major consulting firms. He was formerly a member of the Wallis Inquiry, which led to financial reforms in Australia.

D. JOHANNES JÜTTNER is a Professor of International Finance at Macquarie University, Sydney, Australia. He is the author of 12 books and more than 90 articles in academic and professional publications. He has held visiting professorships in the United States and Europe, and he has acted as a consultant to the Organization for Economic Cooperation and Development (Paris), the German Council of Economic Experts, the Australian Financial System Inquiry, and private sector firms.

JONATHAN M. KARPOFF is the Visiting Alumni Professor of Finance at the Goizueta Business School at Emory University. He came to Emory from the University of Washington, where he was the Norman J. Metcalfe Professor of Finance. His research interests range from natural resources management and regulation to corporate governance issues.

STEVEN A. SEELIG is a Financial Sector Advisor at the International Monetary Fund. Previously, he was the Deputy Director of Research and Statistics at the Federal Deposit Insurance Corporation (FDIC), as well as editor of *The Banking Review*. He also served as Director of the Division of Liquidation and was the Chief Financial Officer for the FDIC. He has taught at George Washington University and Fordham University.

BERNARD SHULL is a Professor of Economics at Hunter College of the City University of New York and a Special Consultant, National Economic Research Associates. He specializes in banking, financial institutions, competition, and regulation, and he has published widely in scholarly journals, as well as monographs and other books. Prior to his current affiliation, he held various positions in the Board of Governors of the Federal Reserve System and the Office of the Comptroller of the Currency.

GARY H. STERN became President and Chief Executive Officer of the Federal Reserve Bank of Minneapolis in 1985, after serving as the bank's Senior Vice President and Director of Research. Before joining the Minneapolis Fed, he was a partner in a New York–based economic consulting firm. His prior experience includes seven years with the Federal Reserve Bank of New York.

RUDOLF VOLKART is a Professor of Corporate Finance and Banking and the Director of the Swiss Banking Institute at the University of Zurich, Switzerland. Besides his academic activities, he is active in consulting and in the educational programs of firms. He serves on several boards, and he has published a series of books in the field of corporate finance.

DAVID WESSELS is an Assistant Professor of Finance at the Goizueta Business School at Emory University. His research focuses on empirical corporate finance, with an emphasis on organizational structure, agency theory, and capital budgeting. He formerly worked in a venture capital firm and was a management consultant.